IRISH FAMILY NAMES

irish

family names

arms, origins, and locations

brian de breffny

COLOUR PHOTOGRAPHS BY GEORGE MOTT

W. W. Norton & Company

NEW YORK   LONDON

SOUTH SAN FRANCIS PU

This book was designed and produced by
Strawberry Hill Press Ltd, 24 Walpole Road
Twickenham, Middlesex, TW2 5SN

First published in 1982 by W. W. Norton & Company, Inc.
500 Fifth Avenue, New York
NY 10110, USA

0-393-01612-9

Printed in Great Britain

title page picture: Landscape in the west of Co. Kerry (Courtesy Bord Failte)

Contents

Preface   6

The Hundred Most Numerous Surnames in Ireland   7

1 The Counties of Ireland   9

2 Map of Ireland – showing Locations of Family Names   52

3 One Thousand Irish Family Names – in alphabetical order   57

4 Index of Additional Names mentioned – in the alphabetical text   188

Glossary of Terms   191

Further Reading   191

Acknowledgments   192

It was decided, in planning this book, that it could not reasonably be confined to treat exclusively those families which, because of their ancient native Irish origins, might be classified as '*Irish* families' as opposed to others, established in Ireland but originally coming from England, Wales, Scotland, Normandy, or some other place in continental Europe. Such an arbitrary decision would have meant excluding the Fitzgeralds, Butlers, and Burkes, for instance, who came to Ireland with the Anglo-Norman conquistadors, but are now so very much identified as being truly 'Irish'. And then what of the next wave of settlers, Plunketts, Cusacks, Dillons? What of the numerous families named Walsh, now the fourth commonest surname in Ireland but also of immigrant origin?

The only reasonable criterion for inclusion had to be the numerical strength of the surname in Ireland. I have included, therefore, all of the two hundred most common surnames and then several hundred more of the most representative surnames. The armorial coats of families are shown, the selection here being based on a choice of the older leading septs and prominent families. Many of the families for whom a coat of arms is not shown, have, however, at some time been recipient of a grant of arms.

Just as restrictions of space did not allow for the illustration of all coats of arms, nor could the places of origin of all the hundreds of families be illustrated. Here again, the reader is offered a broad selection, and in the portrait illustration, just a tantalizing sampling of Irish faces from the rich iconographical sources which are available.

The four maps on pages 52–55 show the distribution of surnames, most of which are mentioned also in the text.

Migration into Ireland over the last eight centuries has resulted in a greater intermingling than is readily accepted. Of the ten commonest surnames in England and Wales, however, only two, Smith and Brown, are among the one hundred commonest in Ireland. The heavy settlement of immigrants from Scotland in Ulster in the 17th century has resulted, on the other hand, in eight out of the ten commonest surnames in Scotland being among Ireland's one hundred commonest. This list of the hundred most numerous surnames in Ireland contains several surnames which came at the end of the twelfth century with the Anglo-Norman invaders, such as Walsh, Lynch, Fitzgerald and Power.

A steady trickle of immigrants, settlers, traders and mercenaries from Britain in the 13th, 14th and 15th centuries increased in the latter years of the 16th century with the plantation schemes in Leix, Offaly and Munster, and much more in the 17th century with the settlement of thousands of Scottish immigrants in Ulster and of Cromwellians in all the provinces as well as, in lesser numbers, the arrival of Huguenot refugees from France. The last significant group immigration was the settlement of the German Palatine refugees in Ireland early in the 18th century.

The often fanciful anglicization of an Irish surname has not infrequently all but obscured its native origin. By the same means some imported surnames have been gaelicized or hibernicized so that they appear to be native Irish names. This volume aims to indicate the origin of the surnames and the locality of origin or principal association.

6

THE HUNDRED MOST NUMEROUS SURNAMES
IN IRELAND

Murphy	Hughes	Burns
Kelly	Farrell	Flanagan
Sullivan	Fitzgerald	Mullan
Walsh	Brown	Barry
Smith	Martin	Kane
O'Brien	Maguire	Robinson
Byrne	Nolan	Cunningham
Ryan	Flynn	Griffin
Connor	Thompson	Kenny
O'Neill	Callaghan	Sheehan
Reilly	O'Donnell	Ward
Doyle	Duffy	Whelan
McCarthy	Mahony	Lyons
Gallagher	Boyle	Reid
Doherty	Healy	Graham
Kennedy	Shea	Higgins
Lynch	White	Cullen
Murray	Sweeney	Keane
Quinn	Hayes	King
Moore	Kavanagh	Maher
McLoughlin	Power	McKenna
Carroll	McGrath	Bell
Connolly	Moran	Scott
Daly	Brady	Hogan
Connell	Stewart	Keeffe
Wilson	Casey	Magee
Dunne	Foley	McNamara
Brennan	Fitzpatrick	McDonald
Burke	Leary	McDermott
Collins	McDonnell	Moloney
Campbell	McMahon	Rourke
Clarke	Donnelly	Buckley
Johnston	Regan	Dwyer
	Donovan	

1 The Counties of Ireland

COUNTY ANTRIM

IT is not known at exactly what date a region in north-eastern Ulster was erected into the county of Antrim but by 1584 the Lord Deputy, who was then attempting to subdue Ulster and subject it to English government, divided the county into baronies. Co. Antrim contains most of Lough Neagh, the largest lake in Great Britain and Ireland, about 80 miles in circumference and covering about 154 square miles. The most striking land feature of the county, however, must be the mountains stretching from north to south which attain their greatest height near the coast where, in places, they rise in rugged grandeur above the sea and then gradually descend inland. On the northern coast cliffs of perpendicular basalt columns stretch for miles providing strikingly magnificent scenery, particularly at the Giants' Causeway. Rathlin Island stands off the northern coast of the county.

The chief town is the port-city of Belfast. Due to the growth of industry in the Lagan valley since the 19th century there has been a heavy movement of population into the city and the surrounding area. The next most prominent urban centres are Lisburn, Carrickfergus and Larne. There are numerous thriving market-towns in the county, Antrim, Ballycastle, Ballymena, Ballymoney, Broughshane, Glenarm, Portrush and Randalstown.

Following the subjugation of the Irish chieftains in Ulster, Scottish and English settlers were induced to establish themselves in Co. Antrim as in the other counties of the province and many of

ANTRIM *Dunluce Castle, once the stronghold of the warlike McDonnells*

these settlers were encouraged by the government to engage in the cultivation of flax both for linen manufacture in the county and for export as yarn. Further encouragement was given to this industry at the end of the 17th and early in the 18th centuries when Huguenot refugees received grants to enable them to share their experience of textile manufacture and instruct those engaged in branches of the industry in Co. Antrim to improve their methods of flax cultivation and linen manufacture, particularly in and around Lisburn, so that by the latter decades of the 18th century Co. Antrim produced almost one half of the total Irish exports of brown linens. There were numerous bleach-greens throughout the county, some of which, it was reported in 1837, could finish 80,000 pieces of linen each annually. The cotton trade was first introduced in 1777 at Belfast and by 1784 there was one mill functioning near the city for spinning twist by water. Only a few years later, by 1800, about 27,000 persons were employed in and around Belfast in various branches of the cotton industry and 10 years later it had grown so much that 22,000 were employed in spinning, 25,000 in weaving, and a further 5000 in auxiliary trades. Meanwhile, the population growth of the immigrant Scots-Irish settlers was such that, especially among the tenant-farmer and labourer class many of whom found themselves landless, there was continual emigration to the New World.

Because of the numerous settlers who established themselves in Co. Antrim the five commonest names in the county, Smith, Johnston, Stewart, Wilson and Thompson are all of

Scots or English origin. O'Neill, the name of the ancient overlords of the area comes sixth in numerical order, followed by mostly settler names, Campbell, Moore, Bell, Robinson, Miller, Brown, Boyd, Scott, Graham, Reid, Martin, Kerr and Hamilton.

COUNTY ARMAGH

ARMAGH is an inland county of Ulster bounded on the north by Lough Neagh, on the east by Co. Down, on the south-east by the Leinster county of Louth, on the south-west by Co. Monaghan and on the north-west by Co. Tyrone. Co. Armagh once formed part of the ancient territory called Oriel; its existence as a county dates from 1586 about which time the power of its ancient leading families, the O'Neills, the O'Hanlons and the McCahans, came to an end and the ascendancy of new incoming landlords like the Achesons and the Brownlows began. The plantation scheme for the county in the reign of James I arranged for the re-assignment of over one fifth of the total acreage of the county, comprising the good arable and pasture land, divided into lots of 2000, 1500 and 1000 acres. The scheme which called for the settlement of English and Scottish undertakers and servitors and the banishment to Connacht or Munster of the Irish swordsmen of the county was only partially successful.

The main city of the county is Armagh, the ancient ecclesiastical capital of Ireland and consequently the residence of both the Roman Catholic and the Protestant primates. Part of Newry is in Co. Armagh; the other market towns of the county are Crossmaglen, Lurgan, Market-hill, Middleton, Newton Hamilton, Portadown and Tanderagee, of which Lurgan is the largest and the most important. The soil in the county is generally fertile but because of the density of its population the farms have tended to be small in size. Extensive grazing has been mostly in the Fews Mountains. The once flourishing woollen trade of the county dwindled after the end of the 17th century but linen manufacture took its place; bleaching was pursued particularly on the River Callan at Keady. Many of the population were engaged in both linen manufacture and agriculture, the nature of the linen industry being such that they could be engaged in it at home without having to congregate around a factory.

This secondary occupation is said to have provided the farming population with a better standard of living than that enjoyed by those in other counties generally. The collapse of the linen industry consequently brought unexpected distress to the population.

Because of the partial failure of the plantation in Co. Armagh, native Irish surnames figure in about equal numbers now with settler surnames. Murphy, the commonest surname in Ireland, is also the commonest in Co. Armagh. It is followed there numerically by three settler names, Hughes, Wilson and Campbell, then comes the Irish name O'Hare, followed by the ubiquitous Smith and then two more Irish families McCann and Donnelly. Next in order come alternately settler and Irish names, Watson, Quinn, Johnston, Kelly, Thompson.

COUNTY CARLOW

CARLOW is an inland county of Leinster bounded on the north and east by Co. Wicklow, on the south and east by Co. Wexford, on the north by Co. Kildare, and on the west by Co. Leix and Co. Kilkenny. The region fell to the Anglo-Normans soon after their invasion of the country and to help hold it they erected castles at Carlow on the banks of the River Barrow, at Tullow and at Leighlin but the English tenure long remained frail and the real power was vested in the Kavanagh family which claimed descent from the McMurroughs, the ancient rulers of the region and their allies the O'Nolans. The last Kavanagh McMurrough chieftain was forced to surrender his jurisdiction in the middle of the 16th century and even after that the family frequently rose in rebellion and the people of Carlow were prone to take up arms against the government whenever an opportunity arose.

The chief town of the county is Carlow; the market-towns are Bagenalstown (now Mhuine Beag), Hacketstown, Leighlinbridge and Tullow. The broad valleys of the Barrow and the Slaney which flow through the county are both beautiful

and very fertile. Along the Wexford border to the south-east of the county is the peak of Mount Leinster and the rugged Blackstairs Mountains. Both arable and dairy farming have proved profitable in Co. Carlow where, at least since the 18th century, the standard of agricultural improvement has been high.

The commonest surname in Co. Carlow is Ireland's commonest also, Murphy. Next in

CARLOW *Prehistoric Dolmen at Browne's Hill, near the town of Carlow*

numerical order come Byrne, Doyle, Nolan, Neill, Brennan, Kelly, McDonald, Kavanagh, Whelan, and Ryan. From this list it may be seen that the old prominent Irish families of the region are still present there in considerable numerical strength.

COUNTY CAVAN

CAVAN is an inland county of Ulster, one of the three of the nine counties of the province which became part of the independent Irish state when the island was divided and the other six kept under British jurisdiction as Northern Ireland. Co. Cavan is bounded on the north by the Ulster county of Fermanagh, on the west by the Connacht county of Leitrim, on the south by the Leinster counties of Longford, Westmeath and Meath, and on the east by the Ulster county

of Monaghan. Almost all of the county anciently formed part of the Kingdom of Breffny, being the eastern part, known as Breffny O'Reilly because the O'Reillys were its overlords. It was made into a county by the Lord Deputy in 1584 but because of the wild nature of much of the terrain, woods, lakes, hills and bogs, the native inhabitants were not easily dislodged. In order to better secure the region, therefore, the county was divided into seven baronies and each was

granted to an individual landlord in order to reduce the power of the O'Reilly chieftain. He was assigned only two of the baronies; three others were assigned to other members of the ruling O'Reilly family and the remaining two baronies, mostly mountainous country, were left to the septs who had been seated there, the McKernans and the McGaurans. This measure failed, however, in its intention of bringing the county under English law and to a state of submission and obedience. In the reign of James I it was deemed that most of the land in the county had been escheated to the Crown by the outlawry and rebellion of the native landlords and so the county could be included in a plantation scheme for resettlement by English and Scottish planters. The scheme for Cavan was a detailed one providing also for the division of the plantation area into 26 parishes in each of which a Protestant church was to be erected, and also the building of a new town, which was Virginia. The scheme was not fully implemented but by 1619, 386 British families who could muster over 700 adult armed men had been settled in the county.

Cavan is the chief town of the county; the market-towns are Arvagh, Bailichorough, Ballinagh, Ballyconnell, Ballyhaise, Ballyjamesduff, Belturbet, Cootehill, Killeshandra, Kingscourt, Shercock, Stradone, and Virginia. The lakeland area of the county is extensive; the larger lakes cover hundreds of acres and there are numerous small ones with a network of streams flowing into Lough Erne and Lough Ramor. The west and north-west part of the county is mountainous. The soil for the most part is not particularly fertile, save where it has been improved by drainage and liming, but dairy farming was successful on the clay of the vales. Until the latter years of the last century agricultural improvement in the county was slow. Antiquated farming methods persisted particularly in the mountainous parts of the county which remained remarkably isolated with few roads and where the Irish language and ancient customs long survived. Small farmers frequently also engaged in weaving at home to supplement their income.

CAVAN *Hiberno-Romanesque doorway, Kilmore Cathedral*

Linen manufacture, before its decline, was an important industry in the county which had twelve bleaching establishments in 1800 mostly in the neighbourhood of Cootehill and Bailieborough.

The family name of the ancient ruling sept is the commonest surname in the county, O'Reilly and Reilly, followed by Smith which, in this instance, is largely in use as a translation of McGowan and O'Gowan. Next in numerical order come Brady, Lynch, McCabe, Clarke, Farrelly, Maguire and McGuire, Sheridan, Galligan, Fitzpatrick, Dolan, McGovern and Magauran, Donohoe, Martin and McMahon.

COUNTY CLARE

THE maritime county of Clare on Ireland's western seaboard is bounded on the west by the Atlantic Ocean, on the north-west by Galway Bay and on the east and south by the River Shannon and the Shannon estuary which separate Clare from the rest of Munster.

Clare was the Kingdom of Thomond. The O'Briens, whose stronghold was Kincora near Killaloe, held sway over about one half of the present county; others who ruled in the county were the O'Loghlens and the McNamaras. The O'Briens contrived to retain their sovercignty into the 16th century when the chief, whose seat was then at Bunratty Castle, was created Earl of Thomond under the British crown. Thomond was erected into a county of Connacht in 1565 and renamed Clare. In 1602 it was detached from Connacht and attached to Munster. The chief town of Co. Clare is Ennis and there are three other market-towns in the county, Corofin, Ennistymon, and Kilrush.

On the west coast the Cliffs of Moher rise magnificently and precipitously above the sea to a height of about 1000 feet. The northern extremity of the county, the barony of Burren, is very rocky; its unusual limestone landscape is beautified in the late springtime by the flowering of rock plants, especially Blue Gentian. In the west of the county there is much waste bogland

CLARE *The Cliffs of Moher, Co. Clare*

and the richest land in the county, both arable and pasture, is in the south, in the southern part of the barony of Bunratty, where formerly beans were extensively grown as a crop, and also around Kilfenora. The powerful Atlantic winds sweeping across from the west buffet the west of the county, especially a belt stretching for fifty miles or so from the coast, and have blown in sand which has formed large sandhills. Boisterous gales are fairly frequent.

In the past centuries some of the people made coarse diaper cloth for their own use but there was no textile industry in the county. At Corofin and Ennistymon strong coarse woollen stockings were knitted. Baskets were made at home from sallow trees but not commercially. Few cottages were without sallow trees from which the cottagers made kishes and baskets. Most cottages had a potato patch.

Despite the numerous creeks, bays and harbours the fishing was little exploited. This was largely due to the unsuitability of the craft available – small wickerwork vessels covered with hides or canvas, excellent for riding the waves but not adapted for fishing. Herring, turbot, bass, mullet, mackerel and whiting abound off the Clare coast. There were famous oyster beds off the Burren coast and others in the Shannon estuary. Crabs and lobsters are found particularly off the northern shores of the county in Galway Bay. Salmon have abounded in the Shannon which runs along the eastern boundary of Co. Clare and then sweeps westwards by Killaloe to its sixty-mile long estuary which broadens out until it is nine miles in width where it opens into the Atlantic Ocean.

County Clare boasts many castles, many of them in ruins. Of about one hundred and twenty listed castles as many as sixty are reputed to have been strongholds of the once powerful MacNamaras. McMahon is now the most numerous surname in the county followed by McNamara, Moloney and O'Brien in that order, all names that have become famous in the history of Clare.

The next commonest names in descending numerical order are McInerney, Kelly, Keane, Murphy, Griffin, Halloran and O'Halloran, Ryan, Lynch, and Clancy.

COUNTY CORK

THE maritime county of Cork, in Munster, is bounded by the sea on the south-west, the south, and the south-east. To the east it has land boundaries with the counties of Waterford and Tipperary, to the north with Limerick, and to the west with Kerry. Anciently the county formed part of the kingdom of Desmond. After the Anglo-Norman invasion the whole of the present county, save the city of Cork (which had been founded by Vikings) and its surroundings, was granted in 1177 by Henry II to Anglo-Norman knights who brought over their followers and established a military colony. The erection of the region into a county dates from the reign of King John. Eventually the Fitzgerald Earls of Desmond acquired control of most of the county as part of their vast palatinate but were obliged to surrender all in 1582 thus providing an opportunity for a plantation or settlement scheme which aimed to re-people the county with English residents loyal to the Crown. Although this scheme was not a success a number of descendants of the English settlers of the Elizabethan plantation in Co. Cork can still be found in the county. More English settlers came in the Cromwellian period.

The populous and flourishing sea-port city of Cork is the chief town of the county. There are ten market-towns in the county, Bandon (founded by the Elizabethan adventurer, Richard Boyle, 1st Earl of Cork), Bantry, Cobh (formerly Queenstown), Dunmanaway, Fermoy, Kinsale, Macroom, Mallow (which also enjoyed a reputation as a spa), Skibbereen and Youghal. There are in addition a number of other sizeable small towns with their own commercial life such as Midleton, Clonakilty, Mitchelstown and Charleville (Rathluirc), to name but a few.

For the most part West Cork is rocky and mountainous while the north and east of the county are remarkable for rich, fertile gently undulating land. The county is noted also for the mildness of its climate which is due to the Gulf Stream and so lush vegetation flourishes.

Apart from agricultural employment was provided by numerous slate quarries along the southern coast of the county, some collieries in the Blackwater valley, copper mining, particularly in the Bere peninsula, until that important industry was ruined by the opening of the Rhodesian copper mines in the last century, some manganese mining, wool-combing, the manufacture on a small scale of flannel and frieze, the manufacture of woollen cloth, stuff and calico, also of paper, fishing, and the many commercial activities of Cork city. Nevertheless, the living conditions of the labouring poor in the county were appallingly wretched in, the last century; many inhabited one-room mud-built cabins with an unglazed window aperture and a smoke-hole instead of a chimney. Their diet was equally miserable, often almost only potatoes.

Despite the considerable intermixture of English ancestry in the county through alliances with centuries of English settlers, many of whose names survive, the principal surnames of the county now are still those of the old Irish

CORK *The prehistoric stone circle at Drombeg, Co. Cork*

DERRY *The Sperrin Mountains, Co. Derry*

families long associated with it. O'Sullivan and Sullivan is the commonest, followed quite closely by Murphy. Next comes McCarthy but with less than three quarters of the numerical strength of the O'Sullivans and Sullivans. Fourth, after another considerable drop in numbers, comes O'Mahony and Mahony, fifth O'Donovan and Donovan, sixth Walsh, seventh O'Brien, eighth O'Callaghan and Callaghan, ninth O'Leary and Leary and tenth Crowley. After these, in descending numerical strength, come Collins, O'Driscoll and Driscoll, O'Connell and Connell, Barry, Cronin, Buckley, Daly, Sheehy, O'Riordan and Riordan, Kelleher, O'Connor, Hurley, Regan, O'Keefe, Harrington and Fitzgerald.

COUNTY DERRY

THE Ulster county of Derry is a maritime county bounded on the north by the Atlantic and on the north-west by Lough Foyle. The eastern boundary of the county is with Co. Antrim, the western with Co. Donegal, the southern and south-western with Co. Tyrone. Officially Londonderry, the county is still popularly called Derry. It was renamed, with the prefix 'London' added to its old name, in the reign of King James I, when the former county of Coleraine, the towns of Coleraine and Derry and attached lands were made part of an ambitious plantation scheme in which most of the county was granted to City of London Companies for resettlement and development. The principal companies engaged in the scheme were the Clothworkers who got part of the borough of Coleraine, the Drapers in the region of Moneymore, the Fishmongers obtained Ballykelly, the Goldsmiths a portion of the liverties of Derry, the

Grocers, Muff and its environs; the Haber-
dashers got an estate around Aghanloo and
Bovevagh, the Ironmongers got Aghadowey, the
Mercers were allotted Kilrea and its environs,
the Merchant Tailors, Macosquin, the Salters,
Magherafelt, the Skinners, Dungiven, and the
Vintners, Bellaghy. Subsequently some of the
companies disposed of their estates to private
individuals. Each company improved its allot-
ment, building houses and introducing Scottish
and English Protestant colonists loyal to the
Crown. Thus, most of the Irish inhabitants, of
whom the O'Donnells, O'Conors and O'Cahans
were the most important, were displaced,
although the O'Cahans managed to remain as
native freeholders in the first reorganization but
lost their lands later in the century.

CORK *Parliament Bridge and Holy Trinity
Church, Cork city*

Despite this scheme and because the resettlement was not as successful as it was in eastern
Ulster east of the River Bann, it is still the names
of native Irish families which prevail today.
Among the dozen commonest surnames now in
Co. Derry, only four, Bradley, Campbell, Smith
and Brown, may be of alien immigrant origin,
although the first three of these surnames were
also assumed by native Irish families, Ó Brollacháin, Mac Cathmhaoil and Mac Gabhann or
Ó Gabhann.

The most numerous surname now in Co.
Derry is O'Doherty and Doherty, a family which
originated west of the Foyle in Co. Donegal as
did the family whose name is the next commonest,

McLaughlin or McLoughlin, originally from the Inishowen peninsula. Next in numerical order come Kelly and O'Kelly, Bradley (which in many cases was adopted instead of O'Brallaghan or O'Brollaghan by descendants of the Donegal sept Ó Brollacháin) Brown, Mc Closkey (the name of a branch of the O'Cahans), Campbell, Mullan, Smith, O'Neill, Kane, Moore, and Gallagher, this last also the name of one of the principal Donegal septs.

Besides the city of Londonderry (Derry) the county had two other boroughs which were market-towns, Coleraine and Newtownlimavady, and other market-towns: Castledawson, Dungiven, Draperstown, Moneymore, Garvagh, Maghera, and Magherafelt. During the Williamite wars, in 1689, the city of Londonderry became an asylum for Protestant refugees. About 30,000 fled there for safety from other parts of Ulster. The defence of the city under siege by the Jacobite forces at that time is still commemorated in Ulster today.

The fertile and profitable lands in Co. Derry are the vales of the Faughan, the Foyle, the Moyola and the Roe, the shoreland of Lough Neagh, the north-western coastland and the flats of Lough Foyle. Along the twelve mile stretch of Atlantic coast in the north the scenery is varied, with many creeks between Portrush and the mouth of the Bann at Port Stewart, and then a range of steep cliffs rising from the sea upon which the eccentric 18th century Earl-Bishop, Earl of Bristol and Bishop of Derry, built his extravagant mansion, Downhill and the Mussenden Temple. Most of the good woil was tilled by the farmers, many of whom were smallholders, the average farm-holding in the county in the first quarter of the 19th century being eight acres. Barley was then the principal crop, the others being, in the main, flax, oats and potatoes, with some wheat, beans, turnips, mangelwurzels and rye. It was an old dictum of the farmers that the flax crop paid the winter's rent and the barley crop the summer's. Lime was used for a fertilizer and, in the coastal regions, oyster, mussel, and cockle shells. Most farmers and cottagers kept a pig which was home-slaughtered and then the meat sent to market for sale. Linen was the principal manufacture of Co. Derry, the farmers themselves becoming spinners and weavers in the months when they were not occupied by agricultural work. Coleraine was reputed to make the finest fabric of the region. The county also provided some employment in breweries and distilleries and, mainly in the city of Derry, in artisan trades first introduced by the London Companies, such as hat-making, locksmithing, tanning, tallowchandling and farrying.

COUNTY DONEGAL

THE maritime Ulster county of Donegal in the extreme north-west of Ireland is bounded on the west and north by the Atlantic ocean, to the south by Donegal Bay and an extending extremity of Co. Leitrim on the east by Lough Foyle which separates it from Co. Derry and to the south-east by land boundaries with Co. Tyrone and Co. Fermanagh. The ancient name of the region was Tyrconnell or Tirconnell and its chief families were the ruling O'Donnells and the O'Dohertys, and the more important septs subordinate to the O'Donnells, the McSweeneys and the O'Boyles. The county was erected by the Lord Deputy in 1584 and after the forefeiture to the Crown of the O'Donnell estates on the attainder of the O'Donnell, Earl of Tyrconnell in 1612, the lands of the county were included in the ambitious Ulster plantation scheme. About four-fifths of the cultivable land in the county was allotted for settlement in 62 portions, 47 for English and

Scottish undertakers and servitors and 15 for the native Irish. The rest of the good land was assigned to the established church for its support, to Trinity College, Dublin, for the support of schools in Derry and Donegal and to five corporate towns.

Besides Donegal town, there are ten other market-towns in the county, Ballyshannon, Buncrana, Carn, Killybegs, Letterkenny, Lifford, Moville, Raphoe, Ramelton and Stranorlar.

Much of the county is mountainous, but there is some fertile land in the valleys. The area known as Gweedore in the west of the county is particularly desolate and its inhabitants, in the last century, were the most wretched in Ireland, many not even possessing any clothing or

DONEGAL *Harbour at Greencastle, Co. Donegal, at the mouth of Lough Foyle*

furniture but covering themselves with rags and living in the most miserable primitive hovels. Drainage schemes in the county in the early 19th century achieved some improvement but the poor quality of so much of the land and the humidity of the climate resulted in much poverty and distress even before the famine. Apart from some whiskey distilleries in the county practically the only alternative employment to fishing and agriculture was linen manufacture from home-grown flax, cotton and velveteen weaving at home, and in one area woollen stocking knitting was carried on.

O'Gallagher and Gallagher is the commonest name in the county, outstripping O'Doherty and Doherty and Boyle, the two next in numerical order. The O'Donnells in fourth place are only about half as numerous as the O'Gallaghers and Gallaghers. In fifth place comes McLoughlin followed by McSweeney and Sweeney, Ward, Kelly, McGinley, McFadden, McGowan, O'Duffy and Duffy and Campbell.

COUNTY DOWN

THE south-eastern Ulster county of Down is bounded on the east and south by the Irish Sea, on the north by Co. Antrim and Belfast Lough (which is, in fact, a deep bay into which the River Lagan flows) and on the west by Co. Armagh. To the south-west another deep bay, Carlingford Lough, narrowly separates Co. Down and Leinster county of Louth.

Anciently, Down formed the greater part of the kingdom which gave its name to the whole province of Ulster; its principal families, whose descendants are still found in the county, were the O'Neills, the Mc Guinnesses and the Mc Cartans, as well as two hibernicized immigrant families which came to Co. Down centuries before the 17th century plantations, the Savages in the Ards peninsula, and the Whites in the barony of Dufferin. Due, however, to massive immigration in the 17th century, mostly from Scotland, the commonest names in Co. Down today are of Scottish and English origin. Thompson and Smith are the most numerous surnames in the county, fairly closely followed by the Scottish Campbell and Patterson. None of the old Irish families now rank among the top fifteen in numerical strength because they were reduced in numbers and dispersed west of the Bann or into Leinster when Ulster was resettled. The next commonest surnames in Co. Down after the four cited above, and in descending order, are Martin, Wilson, Graham, Johnston, Murray, Brown, Robinson, Hamilton, Bell, Scott and Boyd. It is significant that of these fifteen commonest surnames in the county, all but two figure among the fifty commonest surnames in Scotland. Thompson and Smith, the two most numerous in Co. Down, are respectively fourth and first in numerical strength in Scotland and Smith is also the commonest surname in England.

The county had fifteen market-towns, Downpatrick (which is also of ancient ecclesiastical importance, claiming to be the burial place of St. Patrick), Newry, Bangor, Newtownards, Hillsborough, Killyleagh, Portaferry, Donaghadee, Banbridge, Saintfield, Kirkcubbin, Rath-

DOWN *Windmill in Lecale*

friland, Castlewellan, Dromore, and Ballinahinch. Six of these market-towns, Bangor, Downpatrick, Hillsborough, Killyleagh, Newry, and Newtownards, were also boroughs, each of which sent two members to the Irish parliament prior to the Union in addition to the two elected for the county at large. The gaol and courthouse for the county were at Downpatrick where the assizes were held as well as at Newry.

The mountainous region of the county in the barony of Mourne including the peak of Slieve Donard rising to nearly 2800 feet, is famous for the beauty of its landscape while Strangford Lough with its numerous islets is remarkable for its wild life. The agricultural land in Co. Down has been brought to a high stage of development largely due to the industry of the settler families who persevered in tilling and particularly in sowing oats and barley and in cultivating flax for the textile industry. Since the end of the 17th century, when its growth was stimulated by the advice and activity of skilled French Protestant refugees, the linen industry was of primary importance in the county; the production included fine linen, damask, cambric, drill and common household linens. Dromore was the most important linen market, handling the finer quality linens. Other commercial activities of note in the county were tanning, spade and scythe making, and fishery.

COUNTY DUBLIN

THE maritime county of Dublin, with its thirty miles of coastline on Ireland's eastern seaboard, is bounded on the east by the Irish Sea which separates Ireland from the land mass of Great Britain, on the north and west by Co. Meath, on the west and south-west by Co. Kildare and on the south by Co. Wicklow.

As the county contains the capital city it is the most heavily populated county in the country. The city of Dublin which began with Viking settlers (whose dwellings have been excavated on Wood Quay) became the centre of the English administration of Ireland after the Anglo-Norman invasion. It was the seat of the Irish parliament until the Act of Union. The city and its hinterland were, therefore, particularly subject to English influence and to an influx of immigrant settlers, administrators, merchants and artisans. Today, Dublin is a busy capital and not without beauty, although many Dubliners deplore the disappearance of many of its elegant 18th and early 19th century buildings which are being demolished by developers and speculators. The greatest amenities of the city today are probably its proximity to the sea and harbours and to the magnificent hill country to the south.

In the 18th century the city of Dublin enjoyed its heyday and boasted a flourishing commercial and cultural life. As well as the Royal Exchange and the Bank of Ireland which was established by Act of Parliament, there were three other large banks and several private ones. Dublin Castle, dating from the reign of King John, was the seat of the Vice Regal government. Trinity College, founded in the reign of Queen Elizabeth I, was, for centuries, Ireland's only university and housed the most important library in the country. Another important library was established in Dublin by Archbishop Narcissus Marsh. The Royal Dublin Society stimulated progress in the fields of art and science. The Royal Irish Academy promoted political, literary, scientific and antiquarian studies. Dublin boasted some fine hospitals. The Lying-in Hospital, subsequently known as the Rotunda, Steevens Hospital and Mercer's Hospital all date from the 18th century. Medical and surgical students attended the Royal College of Surgeons in the city, while its College of Physicians was empowered to examine all medical practitioners in the country and to inspect the premises of apothecaries and others connected with preparing and dispensing medicines. The genius of the architect Gandon gave Dublin its elegant neo-classical Four Courts and its splendid Custom House overlooking the River Liffey. At the time that those edifices were built, Dublin counted a number of theatres, clubs, music halls, dancing academies and places of entertainment.

Trading ships plied between the port of Dublin and Liverpool, where many goods bound for Ireland, such as tobacco from North America, were trans-shipped. Other Dublin ships traded directly with the Levant carrying imported figs and raisins, with Portugal and Spain, bringing wines, raisins and citrus fruits, with France, bringing table wines, brandy and other goods, with Italy, bringing marble, brimstone, and oil, and with the Low Countries, from which Ireland

DUBLIN *The Four Courts, Dublin, elegant neo-classical architecture, 1786*

bought spices, flax and tobacco pipes. West India trading ships brought sugar and mahogany into the bustling port of Dublin; ships travelled also to and from the Baltic ports with cargoes of timber, tallow, hemp, tar, linseed, and other commodities. Before the upsurgence of Belfast much of the Irish linen was exported through the port of Dublin. Between Dublin and the interior of the country many goods were transported by boat along the canals.

Outside Dublin (which had its principal wholesale market in Smithfield and commodity markets in Kevin Street, Petticoat Lane, Boot Lane, Halton Street and Little Green, as well as ten retail markets for meat, poultry, vegetables and fish) there was only one other market-town in the county, at Ballymore Eustace. There were, however, a number of post-towns, fishing-ports and thriving villages, some of which are agglom-

erated in the sprawling suburbs of Dublin. Swords and Newcastle, which have lost their political significance, were once boroughs and corporate towns, each sending two members to the Irish parliament.

Due to widespread migration into the capital from all parts of Ireland, especially over the last hundred years, today almost every Irish surname can be found in Co. Dublin. Nevertheless some of the old names of central Leinster still predominate, with Byrne in the first place, as it is also in Co. Louth to the north and Co. Wicklow to the south. Next after Byrne, but in far lesser numbers, comes the ubiquitous Kelly, followed by Doyle, Murphy, Smith, O'Brien, and Kavanagh, in that order. Most of the remainder of names of considerable numerical strength are generally common surnames, Dunne, O'Neill, Reilly and O'Reilly, Nolan, Connor and O'Connor, Walsh, Farrell, Carroll, Ryan, and Moore.

COUNTY FERMANAGH

ALTHOUGH the Ulster county of Fermanagh is an inland county it is well watered by Lough Erne, its most distinguishing natural feature, in reality

two connecting lakes which stretch across the county for forty miles from north-west to south-east. The lower lake is seven and a half miles across at its broadest, the upper lake four and a half miles in breadth. These lakes, embayed by mountains and studded with two hundred islets, are celebrated for their natural beauty.

Enniskillen, once the stronghold of the powerful Maguires, Chiefs of Fermanagh, is the county town. The other market-towns of the county were Irvinestown (previously called Lowtherstown) and Brookeborough, both named after settler families in the region, Lisnaskea and Maguiresbridge. The county was one of those escheated to the Crown and resettled with immigrants from Scotland and England. Many of the names of the principal settlers listed in a report of 1619 are still found in the county, Cole, Hume, Hamilton, Archdall, Dunbar, Lowther, Davis, Harrison, Atkinson. Despite the displacement and reduction of the native families, however, Maguire is the commonest name in Co. Fermanagh today and only five settler surnames, Johnston, Wilson, Thompson, Elliott and Irvine, now rank among the top fifteen in numerical order in the county. The second commonest surname in Co. Fermanagh, following Maguire but far less numerous, is McManus, followed in numerical order by Dolan and Mc Govern. The other native surnames among the top fifteen are McHugh, Cassidy, McLoughlin, Gallagher, Murphy, Reilly and O'Reilly, Fitzpatrick, and Flanagan.

The people of Fermanagh were reputed to be the tallest and the most robust in Ulster but nevertheless they also enjoyed the reputation of being lethargic. Samuel Lewis remarked in 1837 that the Fermanagh countrymen habitually rose late and often did not milk their cows until noon. Most families owned a spinning-wheel and reel and sold their home-spun flax in the market-towns. However, as agriculture was the principal means of support of the people those in the mountainous country lived in wretched conditions in mud cabins with doors made of wattles. At Belleek there was a salmon fishery on Lough Erne but the name of the town is widely known for the factory founded there in the late 1850's which first produced domestic pottery and stoneware and, a decade later, high quality porcelain.

COUNTY GALWAY

COUNTY Galway acquired a separate identity from the rest of Connacht when that province was divided and shired in 1585. The county is bounded on the west by the Atlantic Ocean and on the south by the waters of Galway Bay and a land boundary with Co. Clare. To the north lie the counties of Mayo and Roscommon; the latter also flanks Co. Galway to the east. To the east also Co. Galway is separated from Co. Offaly and Co. Tipperary by the River Shannon and Lough Derg.

Prior to the Anglo-Norman infiltration of Connacht the chief families were the O'Kellys and O'Dalys, the O'Hallorans, and the O'Flahertys. Subsequently their importance was eclipsed by families, mostly of Anglo-Norman origin who acquired lands in the county and prospered also in mercantile pursuits in the city of Galway. These families, known as 'The Tribes of Galway' were Burke, Blake, Lynch, Martin, French, Morris, Skerret, Browne, Darcy, Athy, Kirwan, Joyce and Bodkin. Another Anglo-Norman family of importance in the county, but not counted among the so-called tribes, were the Berminghams, co-founders of the town of Athenry. Today Kelly and O'Kelly is the commonest surname in Co. Galway. Burke is the second commonest and is the only one of the 'Tribes' save Joyce to appear on the list of the twenty commonest surnames in the county in modern times; Joyce is fourth in numerical order of strength. The other names on the list, in descending numbers, are Conneely, McDonagh, Walsh, Fahy, Mannion, Flaherty, and O'Flaherty, Murphy, Connolly, Keane, King, Forde, Connor and O'Connor, Lyons, Mullan, Egan, Kenny, and Toole or O'Toole.

The walled city of Galway, which contained about one-tenth of the population of the county before the famine of the 1840's, was of prime importance in the county with a flourishing commercial port and the handsome dwellings of the merchants. The borough of Galway sent two members to the Irish parliament prior to the Act of Union, as did each of the two other corporate towns in the county, Athenry and Tuam. Those three boroughs were also market-towns and there were five other market-towns in the county, Ballinasloe, Eyrecourt, Gort, Headford, and Loughrea.

The county is roughly divided into an eastern and a western part by Lough Corrib which covers about 30,000 acres and is fed by streams in Joyces Country. The smaller western portion, the baronies of Moycullen, Ross and Ballinahinch, is mostly rugged and mountainous, beautiful but barren, with scant arable land. The larger eastern part of the county comprises more level fertile land in several baronies. In Connemara, where much of the land is barren moor and bog, the inhabitants helped to eke out their existence by knitting woollen stockings which were famed for their softness and elasticity. Other textiles manufactured in the county were not of high quality, mostly coarse linen, frieze and rough woollen blankets. Home-made frieze was used for the men's clothing; the women usually wore blue or dark red flannel petticoats and jackets. In the coastal regions kelp was manufactured by burning seaweed and, at one time, exported in considerable quantities. The city of Galway had a few light industries by the beginning of the 19th century, the manufacture of paper, of black marble chimney-pieces, and coarse pottery, but a greater source of employment were the several flour mills, oatmeal mills, and malt mills. The abundance of fish on the coast was not efficiently exploited as an industry until the present century and formerly the catch barely supplied the local demand. In the herring season, however, in early spring, one boat might expect to bring in as many as five thousand herring on an average night's fishing. A large percentage of the male population of the villages around Galway participated, temporarily abandoning their usual trade or occupation for the season.

Co. Galway long remained an Irish speaking region and the language has survived as a first language in the remoter parts and in the Aran

GALWAY *Dun Guaire Castle dating from the 16th century on the site of a prehistoric fort*

Islands off the coast of Galway Bay. Old customs too, such as the wake, and keening at funerals, died out slowly in this area.

Lobsters were so abundant in the last century that travellers in Connemara complained of the quantity they were served in place of other fare. Oysters now being a prized and somewhat costly delicacy, the Co. Galway oyster beds have been developed and are carefully tended. In the past the fine oysters from Connemara, abundant on the coast, were a food eaten by the poor.

COUNTY KERRY

THE maritime Munster county of Kerry juts out into the Atlantic on its western side. To the north the county is bounded by the broad estuary of the Shannon which separates it from the southern coast of Clare. The southern boundary of Co. Kerry is the Atlantic, the estuary of the Kenmare River, and a land boundary with Co. Cork which extends to form, with the border of Co. Limerick, the eastern confines of the county of Kerry. Although Co. Kerry surpasses many other Irish counties in fertility, nevertheless about one half of the

territory in the county is bog or mountain. The McGillycuddy's Reeks are the highest mountains in Ireland. While much of the territory is uncultivated land, the county is justly famed for the magnificence of its scenery. The rugged Dingle peninsula and the celebrated lakes of Killarney are the principal scenic attractions, but there are many other beautiful bays, passes and islands in the county. The climate, although moist, is mild. Trees and plants from warmer places, like the arbutus, have found a happy lodgment in Co. Kerry and flourish there.

KERRY *The Gap of Dunloe*

For centuries agriculture remained in a backward state in Co. Kerry but progress in recent times, especially in dairy farming on the rich grasslands, has now made Kerry internationally famous for its production of butter and since early in the last century improved breeds of cattle have been introduced. In the Dingle peninsula, where flax was grown on potato soil, coarse linen used to be manufactured in exceptional lengths by the inhabitants and it enjoyed a good reputation abroad on account of the careful preparation of the yarn. In some mountainous regions the tenants used to pay their rent to the landlord, not in cash or farm produce, but in home-manufactured flannel which was then sent for sale in the market at Tralee or Dingle.

Tralee is the chief town of the county and was a borough; the only other market-towns were Dingle, Cahirciveen, and Killarney. Tralee and Dingle sent two members each to the Irish parliament prior to the Act of Union, two others were sent from the ancient incorporated town of Ardfert, and two from the county.

Before the Anglo-Norman invasion of Ireland the principal families in Co. Kerry were the O'Connors, O'Sullivan, O'Moriartys, O'Mahonys, and O'Donoghues. Soon after the invasion, as the newcomers pushed into western Munster, the McCarthys retreated into Kerry. The Geraldine FitzMaurices and FitzGeralds gained a foothold in the county by the 13th century and eventually extended their power there at the expense of the earlier overlords. With the Elizabethan plantation of the sequestered estates of the Fitzgeralds of Desmond, new settlers came. The leading families of adventurers were Herbert, Browne, Denny, Blennerhassett, Conway, Rice, Gunn and Spring. All these names are still found in the county borne by persons in many walks of life. O'Sullivan and Sullivan is, however, the commonest surname by far in the county and about twice as numerous as the next commonest, O'Connor and Connor. Next in numerical order come O'Shea and Shea, Murphy, McCarthy, Moriarty, Fitzgerald, Griffin, O'Connell and Connell, Brosnan, Foley, O'Leary and Leary, Clifford, Walsh, Lynch, O'Mahony and Mahony, and Daly. Of the leading ancient chiefs, only the name of O'Donoghue does not rank today among the twenty commonest in the county.

COUNTY KILDARE

KILDARE is an inland county of Leinster, much of which, since the Anglo-Norman invasion, formed part of the Pale, the area of English influence in Ireland where the authority of the Crown and the royal writ were observed. On the east Co. Kildare is bounded by the counties of Dublin and Wicklow, on the south by Co. Carlow, on the west by Offaly and Leix and on the north by Co. Meath. More than four-fifths of the land in the county is cultivated, the general surface being fairly level. Wheat was a commercially viable crop as were barley and oats. The other principal crops in the county were potatoes, mangelwurzels, turnips and rape. The largest area of uncultivated land has been the extensive Bog of Allen in the north and north-west part of the county. In the 18th century cotton mills were built at Clane and at Leixlip but were not successful and had to be abandoned; subsequently a more successful mill operated near Ballytore.

KILDARE *The 9th century High Cross that stands at Moone*

The canals, which formerly carried much traffic, brought considerable activity to Co. Kildare. The Grand Canal traverses the county from east to west with a branch reaching Naas, another branched off at Robertstown to communicate with Athy and the south-east of Ireland through the River Barrow, and another branch communicated with Portarlington and Mountmellick in Co. Leix. The Royal Canal enters the county from Dublin and provided communication with Co. Meath to the north.

Co. Kildare contains the remains of many castles, some from the Anglo-Norman period, and some of them restored and inhabited, also the ruins of a number of monastic and ecclesiastical foundations and many fine mansions of later date, the most impressive of which are the splendid Castletown built by Speaker Conolly at Celbridge and the grandiose Carton at Maynooth, the seat of the Fitzgeralds, Earls of Kildare and Dukes of Leinster.

The surname Kelly is the commonest in Co. Kildare, closely followed by Murphy, Dunne and Byrne, all names which are generally common in Leinster. Next in numerical order of strength come Nolan, Connor and O'Connor, Smith, Farrell and O'Farrell, Ryan, Moore, Carroll and O'Carroll, O'Neill and Neil, Bolger, and Doyle, none of which are peculiar to Co. Kildare and all of which rank among the commonest surnames in at least one other Leinster county.

COUNTY KILKENNY

THE inland Leinster county of Kilkenny is bounded on the north by Co. Leix, on the east by the counties of Carlow and Wexford, on the south by Co. Waterford and on the west by Co. Tipperary. The city of Kilkenny with its splendid Gothic cathedral on the hill built of Kilkenny limestone, and its great castle of the Butlers overlooking the River Nore, is the chief town of the county and, of the towns of Leinster, second only to Dublin. In the 14th century King Edward III convened a parliament at Kilkenny and in the 17th century the city briefly enjoyed political importance when the Catholic Confederation met there in 1642. The county had besides five other market-towns, Callan, Thomastown, Gowran, Castlecomer, and Graiguenamanagh.

The county was heavily colonized by the Anglo-Normans and while a few Irish families of the region like the O'Brennans and the O'Sheas managed to retain some influence for several centuries, it was the descendants of the immigrant families, albeit often hibernicized, who figured largely in the history of the county – Butler, Power, Walsh, Purcell, Archer, Cantwell, Comerford, Tobin, Shortal, Rothe, Grace and Archdeacon, and later arrivals such as the Wandesfordes from Yorkshire who came to the county in the 17th century, as did the Blundens of Castle Blunden and the Ponsonbys from Cumberland, later Viscounts Duncannon and Earls of Bessborough. Today the commonest surname in the county is that of one of the old Irish families who were in the region before the Anglo-Norman invasion, Brennan and O'Brennan, but it is closely followed in numerical order by the immigrant surname Walsh. Three other surnames which came with the Anglo-Normans, Butler, Power and Purcell, rank now among the fourteen commonest names in Co. Kilkenny. After Brennan and Walsh the list runs in descending order of numerical strength, Murphy, Ryan, O'Carroll and Carroll, Byrne and O'Byrne, Butler, Maher, Dunne, Phelan, Kelly, Neill and O'Neill, Power, Purcell, O'Brien and Brien, O'Shea, Shea and Shee, Delany, and Dowling.

There is plenty of good agricultural land in the county both for tillage and grazing and because good stone was available most of the farmhouses were built of stone although they were usually cemented with clay rather than mortar. Stone quarried in Co. Kilkenny was exported, the fine grain stone from Drumdowney being particularly prized for mill-stones; near the city of Kilkenny fine black marble was quarried. Early in the 18th century coal was discovered by men raising iron ore in the north of the county and a field extending over about thirty square miles was mined and exploited subsequently, giving employment to 1000 men in the Castlecomer area at its zenith. The coal was of excellent quality, having a very high carbon content. Samuel Lewis reported, however, in 1837, that although the coalminers' pay was relatively higher than that of other workmen their living standards were lower because, according to Lewis, they were addicted to spirits. These miners lived in miserable hovels built of sods, some of them without a chimney or window.

In the first half of the 16th century the 8th Earl of Ormonde and his countess brought Flemish master-weavers to Kilkenny to introduce the manufacture of tapestry, carpets and fine diaper. In the 17th century, the Duke of Ormonde established woollen and linen manufacture, the latter principally just outside the county, but employing families in Co. Kilkenny in the region of Carrick-on-Suir where the industry flourished in the 18th century. Other industries in the county were woolcombing and flour-milling, with over twenty mills on the River Nore between Durrow and Inistiogue, others on its tributaries, and on the stretch of the River Barrow in Co. Kilkenny.

COUNTY LEITRIM

THE Connacht county of Leitrim is all but landlocked, having a coastal outlet to the Atlantic only two miles in length on Donegal Bay between the boundaries of Co. Sligo and Co. Donegal. Co. Leitrim is otherwise bounded to the west by Co. Sligo and Co. Roscommon, to the south by Co. Roscommon and Co. Longford, to the east by Co. Cavan and Co. Fermanagh, and to the north by Co. Donegal. Co. Leitrim, therefore, has boundaries with both Ulster and Leinster. Leitrim, once the county town, has the remains of a castle and some other ancient buildings, but has lost its former importance and dwindled to a village. Carrick-on-Shannon became the chief town of the county, which had one other borough, Jamestown, built for settlers in the 17th century, and three other market-towns, Manorhamilton (which derives its name from its 17th century settler founder, Sir Frederick Hamilton), Ballinamore, and Mohill.

Anciently the county formed part of the kingdom of Breffny whose overlords, the O'Rourkes, retained some power until the confiscations of the 16th and 17th centuries;

LEITRIM *Parke's Castle, built in the 16th century by Lough Gill. This stronghold of the O'Rourkes became the seat of a settler family called Parker*

Dromahaire had, by that time, become their principal seat. After the sequestration of the O'Rourke chieftain's territory, it was erected into the county of Leitrim in 1565. Prior to that time and the subsequent arrival of settlers the principal families besides the O'Rourkes were the subordinate septs, McGlanchy or McClancy, McGoldrick, McRannall (which has frequently become Reynolds), McGovern or Magauran, McLoughlin, McMorrow, and McTernan. By 1879 not one O'Rourke held land in the county according to a list of landowners of upwards of one acre. The commonest surnames today in the county are the ubiquitous Kelly or O'Kelly and the indigenous Reynolds in about equal numbers, followed, after a considerable gap in numbers, by Flynn and O'Flynn, McLoughlin, McHugh, Rooney and O'Rooney, McMorrow, and McTernan, all in about equal numbers, and then, in descending numerical order, Keany, McGowan, Moran, Reilly and O'Reilly, Dolan, Maguire, Beirne and O'Beirne, Gallagher, McDermott, McGovern, McSharry, Mulvey.

The county, which is thinly populated, is hilly, ranging from shaggy brown hills to lofty mountains, and with deep valleys. There are several beautiful lakes of which the best known are Lough Gill, Lough Allen, Lough Garadice, Lough Glenade, Lough Rynn, and Lough Melvin whose western shore is in the county of Leitrim and the eastern in the county of Fermanagh; many of the smaller lakes are also picturesque. The county, in the medieval period, was thickly forested and five great forests endured into the 17th century but they have disappeared leaving bleak tracts of country. The soil of Co. Leitrim is exceptionally retentive of water which accounts, with its many lakes, for a standard joke that land in the county is sold by the gallon rather than by the acre. Despite the cold and damp climate agriculture has improved over the last century when the principal crops were potatoes, flax and oats. However, even in poorer times in the past, almost every Leitrim family kept at least one cow. A great quantity of butter was made in the county and sent in firkins to the markets whence it was exported to England. There were also large farms in the county where cattle were fattened for the Dublin and English markets. There was but little commercial activity in Co. Leitrim and scant manufacture, but coal mines were opened up in the 19th century to the east of Lough Allen and where a vein was discovered in the Munterkenny Mountains. Sandstone, quarried in the Glanfarn region, was worked into ornamental objects. In the mid-18th century, working of the county's rich deposits of iron ore was abandoned due to lack of timber to fuel the furnaces. A few years later one O'Reilly family started an iron works designed to smelt the iron with coal but this was a financial failure due largely to lack of foresight and uneconomical experiments in trying to produce malleable iron instead of cast-iron.

COUNTY LEIX

In the reign of Queen Mary I, two districts, Glenmaliere and Leix, were reduced to shire ground and given the name of the Queen's County with an assize town named after the Queen, Maryborough. Since Irish independence in 1922 the county was renamed, Leix, and Maryborough became Portlaoise. Until Tudor times the O'Mores, who had risen to power in the 13th century, held sway over the territory that became the Queen's County. Settler families were introduced to the county by the Tudor plantation schemes, the most prominent of whom came to be known, in imitation of the Seven Septs of Leix, the previously powerful Irish families, as the Seven Tribes of Leix, the families of Barrington, Bowen, Cosby, Hartpole, Hetherington, Hovenden or Ovington, and Ruish. Of these, one family, Cosby, is still seated on the lands acquired by their ancestor at Stradbally in the 16th century. The Hovendens were still on their ancestral estate at the beginning of this century, and descendants of the Barringtons, Bowens, and Hetheringtons are still in Ireland today although they are no longer in possession of the estates of their settler forebears in Co. Leix.

Of other Tudor settlers in the county, a few, such as the Pigott family and the Vicars family, were until recent years in possession of the lands of their 16th century settler ancestors, but have since gone away. The Cootes from Norfolk came to Leix in the 17th century, and the Dawsons, later Earls of Portarlington, and the Veseys, later Viscounts De Vesci, came still later. In the 17th century a number of Quaker families of English origin settled in the county, particularly around

Mountmellick and Mountrath, and towards the end of that century Huguenots, French Protestant refugees, settled in and around Portarlington.

Many of the old Irish families of the region have, however, survived there although the O'Mores, many of whom became Moore, were driven away and their name is no longer one of the commonest in the county. The commonest surname in Co. Leix today is, in fact, Dunne, followed by Delany, Conroy, Lalor or O'Lalor (sometimes now Lawlor) one of the Seven Septs of Leix, Phelan, Fitzpatrick, Ryan, O'Carroll and Carroll, Whelan, O'Byrne and Byrne, Kavanagh, Kennedy and O'Kennedy, Brennan, Kelly, and Murphy.

The county had three boroughs, Portarlington, Ballinakill and Maryborough (Portlaoise) which were also market-towns, and four other market-towns, Abbeyleix, Mountmellick, Mountrath and Stradbally. Each of the three boroughs sent two members to the Irish parliament prior to the Act of Union and two more were elected for the county at large. Wheat, which was grown extensively, barley, turnips, rape, and potatoes were the principal crops grown in Co. Leix where in some parts the stiff clay soil was found to be particularly adapted to growing wheat, which was grown even in the mountain districts. The rich lowland pastures provided excellent grazing land for fattening bullocks. Throughout the county there are patches of bog, some of which yields turf of good quality for fuel. Most farmers in the county used to keep both pigs and goats. Coal was mined in the county, the field of about six square miles at one time had seven collieries; it is an extension of the Co. Kilkenny coalfield. In the mid-19th century five collieries were operating with sixty-four pits employing seven hundred men. Sandstone and slate were quarried in the county. Broadcloth was woven at Maryborough (Portlaoise) and Mountmellick. The cotton factories at Abbeyleix, Cullinagh and Mountrath supplanted the manufacture of serge in the 19th century but were not commercially successful. At Mountmellick there were breweries, tanneries, a distillery and an iron foundry. At Donoughmore starch was manufactured, and there was a flour-mill there as well as at Mountmellick, Rathdowney, Stradbally and several other places.

COUNTY LIMERICK

THE Munster county of Limerick is bounded on the north by the River Shannon and its estuary which separates the county from its northern neighbour, Co. Clare, on the west by Co. Kerry, on the south by Co. Cork and on the east and north-east by Co. Tipperary. The cathedral city of Limerick is the chief town of the county which had two other corporate towns, Kilmallock, once famed for the elegance of its tall stone houses, and Askeaton, where the Earls of Desmond built a fine castle above the River Deel. As well as the markets in those three places there were seven other market-towns in the county, Ballingarry, Bruff, Glin, Kilfinane, Newcastle, Pallaskenry and Rathkeale.

Prior to the Anglo-Norman penetration into Munster at the end of the 12th century the principal Irish families in the county were O'Brien, O'Collins (Cullane), O'Hallinan, O'Kerwick, O'Sheehan, O'Hurley, O'Kinneally, O'Scanlan, and Mc Eniry; O'Donovans from Co. Cork and O'Gradys from Co. Clare also established themselves in Co. Limerick at an early date. With the Anglo-Norman incursion came the Fitzgeralds, followed by families of Anglo-Norman origin who became prominent in the county and the city of Limerick, de Lacy, Bourke, Woulfe, Fanning, and others as well as families like Stritch, of English origin, who arrived before the Reformation, and the Mc Sheehys or Sheehys, who came as mercenaries in the service of the Fitzgeralds. With the sequestration of the estates of the Earls of Desmond and the resettlement of their Palatinate at the end of the 16th century, new names appeared such as Berkeley and Courtenay, the major undertakers of the plantation. Many of the lesser settlers of the Elizabethan plantation returned, discouraged, to England but others like the Odell, Bourchier or Bouchier, Hart, and Conyers families remained, put down roots and spawned a numerous descent in the county. Early in the 17th century came other settlers like the Maunsells and the Southwells, names which became well-known in Co. Limerick as did those of such settler families who established themselves in the county later in the 17th century, Cox, Lloyd, Upton, Langford, Rose, Massy, Pery, Gubbins, Gabbett, Hunt, Oliver, Waller and Westropp, to name some of the most

LIMERICK *View of the town of Bruree*

prolific. In the early 18th century German Protestant refugees came to Co. Limerick bringing a new crop of surnames to the county, among them Switzer, Delmege, Ruttle, Boven hizer, Doupe, Ledger and Sparling.

In 1876 the resident landowners in the county (excluding the city of Limerick) with 100 acres or more were Ahern, Alleyn, Ambrose, Apjohn, Atkinson, Barry, Bayly, Beary, Bennett, Bevan, Blackhall, Blennerhassett, Bouchier, Bourke, Bredin, Brown, Browne, Browning, Butler, Cahill, Cantillon, Caulfield, Cleary, Coll, Condon, Considine, Conyers, Coote, Copley, Cosgrove, Cox, Croker, Curtin, Cussen, D'Arcy, de Burgho, de Gernon, Delmege, De Vere, Dickson, Donovan, Dove, Drew, Duggan, Dwyer, Ellard, Evans, Ferguson, Finch, Fitzgerald, Fitzgibbon, Fitzpatrick, Fosbery, Franks, Frend, Frewen, Furlong, Furnell, Gabbett, Gavin, Geale, Gibbings, Gleeson, Gloster, Goggins, Goold, Grady, Graham, Greene, Gubbins, Harnett, Harris, Hartigan, Hayes, Hewson, Hogan, Howley, Hunt, Ivers, Kearney, Keating, Kieran, Laggan, Langford, Ledger, Lehan,

LIMERICK *View of the town of Bruree*

Lloyd, Lowe, Lucas, Lyons, Lysaght, McCarthy, Macdonald, McMahon, McMurray, McNamara, Madigan, Magner, Mason, Massy, Maunsell, Deane-Morgan, Morgan, Moroney (Odell), Mulqueen, Murphy, Murray, Noonan, O'Brien, O'Connor, O'Donnell, O'Grady, O'Leary, O'Regan, O'Shaughnessy, Patterson, Pery, Pitts, Plummer, Powell, Power, Wyndham-Quin, Richardson, Rice, Roche, Rose, Rowan, Royce, Russell, Ryan, Scanlan, Sexton, Shannon, Sheehy, Shelton, Smith, Spillane, Staunton, Studdert, Sullivan, Synan, Taylor, Touchstone, Tracy, Trench, Tuthill, Tyrell, Unthank, Upton, Vandeleur, Vincent, Wallace, Waller, Walsh, Watson, Webb, Westropp, White, Wilkinson, Yielding. This shows that the majority of the larger holdings belonged to the descendants of English settlers.

The list of resident landowners at the same date with holdings of ten acres or less in the county, on the other hand, show that the majority in this category were of native Irish descent:

Baggott, Bennett, Biggane, Boyle, Bridgeman, Broderick, Burns, Cagney, Callaghan, Carmody, Carroll, Carter, Casey, Clifford, Collins, Conway, Corkerry, Daly, Donohue, Doran, Dore, Dunworth, Fennell, FitzGerald, Fox, Gillard, Gleeson, Green, Greene, Griffin, Guinan, Hall, Hannon, Hanrahan, Hartigan, Hayes, Hedderman, Heffernan, Hogan, Horgan, Hynes, Keating, Kelly, Keough, Kirby, Latchford, Leahy, Long, Lynch, McCarthy, McDonagh, McDonnell, Molony, Moylan, Mulcahy, Noonan, O'Brien, O'Connor, O'Dell, O'Donovan, O'Grady, O'Halloran, O'Keeffe, O'Neill, O'Sullivan, Powell, Quaid, Rafferty, Reilly, Riordan, Roche, Russell, Ruttle, Ryan, Scully, Sheehy, Sullivan, White and Wren.

Today the commonest surname in Co. Limerick is Ryan which, not surprisingly, appears in the list of both small holders and larger proprietors in the last century and which was prevalent in the county before the arrival of the Anglo-Norman invaders.

The next most numerous surnames in descending numerical order are O'Brien, Fitzgerald, Sullivan, and Hayes, which all also figure on both lists of landowners above. These surnames are followed in descending numerical order by Walsh, Collins, O'Connell, Moloney, O'Connor, Lynch, McNamara, O'Donnell and Ahern, all of which except O'Connell appear on one or other of the lists of the two categories of landowners, and some on both.

COUNTY LONGFORD

THE county of Longford in the province of Leinster is an inland county bounded on its western and north-western side by the Connacht counties of Leitrim and Roscommon, on the north-east by the Ulster county of Cavan and on the south-east by Co. Westmeath. The River Shannon, which flows along the western boundary of Co. Longford into Lough Ree at the southern extremity of the county, separates it from Co. Roscommon. Longford is, and was, the chief town. There were three other market-towns which were also boroughs, as were Longford, Granard, Lanesborough, and St. Johnstown (Ballinalee) which has dwindled in size to become no more than a village. Two other market-towns in the county, Edgeworthstown (now called Mostrim), and Ballymahon, were not boroughs. St. Johnstown, whose population shrank to less than three hundred, continued to send two members to the Irish parliament prior to the Act of Union as did each of the other three boroughs, while two more represented the county at large.

Before the Anglo-Norman invasion the most powerful Irish family in the area which became Co. Longford was the O'Farrell sept whose principality was named Annaly. Next in importance, but with a much smaller territory, was an O'Quin sept. Both those surnames rank today among the ten most numerous in the county, demonstrating that many of the descendants of those septs have not moved far from their ancestral homeland over the last thousand years. The surname O'Reilly and Reilly from

eastern Breffny is now, however, the commonest surname by far in Co. Longford; Farrell and O'Farrell in second place has less than half the number bearing the name. After these two, in descending numerical order come Kiernan, Kelly and O'Kelly, Donohoe or O'Donoghue, Murphy, Brady, Quinn, and Smith, usually a translation of Ó Gabhann or Mac Gabhann.

The principal immigrant newcomers who acquired estates in the county were the families of Bond, from Yorkshire (who settled first in Co. Derry and subsequently in Co. Longford), Edgeworth (who came to Ireland in the reign of Queen Elizabeth I and gave their name to Edgeworthstown), Forbes, from Scotland, ennobled as Earls of Granard, Fetherstonhaugh, who shortened their surname to Fetherston, and Tuite, a family which came to Ireland with the Anglo-Normans at the end of the 12th century, obtained estates in Co. Westmeath and then, after the Williamite wars, in Co. Longford.

Scenically the county of Longford is dull, being, for the most part, flat, with large stretches of bog, save in the north, where the Clonhugh Mountains rise near the Co. Leitrim border. However, even they are bleak and barren in appearance. Only in the south of the county is the landscape somewhat more attractive near Ballymahon and the shore of Lough Ree with its many islets. In the south of the county the soil is richer, suitable for all kinds of grain and green crops which were raised there. Much of the land in the county was given over to pasturage but, as it was not efficiently drained, it was

for its tranquil beauty. Commanding a magnificent view of this bay, rises the lofty, conical peak of Croagh Patrick, also called 'The Reek', a place of pilgrimage, famed as the spot from which, according to the long-told story, St. Patrick banished the snakes from Ireland. Higher than Croagh Patrick by just over one hundred feet is Nephin, which rises grandly to a height of 2640 feet in the south of the barony of Tirawley, its peak often shrouded in clouds. The northern part of Lough Corrib lies in Co. Mayo with the village of Cong at its northern extremity. Connected to Lough Corrib by subterranean courses is Lough Mask; Lough Carra, studded with wooded islets, Lough Conn, which has ruined castles and churches on its islands, Lough Cullen, and Lough Dan near Castlebar, are the other principal lakes of the county. There are many smaller lakes too but the county has no rivers of importance. Of the islands in the Atlantic belonging to the county some, like Clare Island, Innisturk, and Innisboffin, are inhabited. In the winter-time they can be inaccessible by boat when the seas are rough.

Castlebar is the chief town of the county which has ten other market-towns, Ballina, Ballinrobe, Ballaghdireen, Claremorris, Crossmolina, Foxford, Killala, Newport, Swinford and Westport. Killala and Westport were also sea-ports and there was a smaller sea-port in the extreme north-west of the county at Belmullet. Only four members were sent from Co. Mayo to the Irish parliament before the Act of Union, two from the borough of Castlebar and two from the county at large. After the Union the parliamentary representation of Mayo was reduced to two members for the entire county.

In the southern part of the county wheat was grown, in the higher areas, potatoes, oats, barley and flax, but much of the more elevated land was devoted to pasture, the grass being of good enough quality for feeding calves but not rich enough for fattening cattle generally; rearing young cattle prevailed over dairy-farming. Because, habitually, pigs were not kept in Co. Mayo, when the famine struck it was particularly severe in this part of the country with its high proportion of poor land. Near Westport, a town whose elegance is due to its planning in the 18th century by the Marquess of Sligo, there was a brewery established in 1800, a whiskey distillery established in 1826, a second brewery, a tannery, corn-stores, salt-works, oat-mills and flour mills, and, in the neighbourhood, slate quarries, a linen

MAYO *Sheep graze on the slopes below Croaghpatrick*

factory and two cotton factories. There was another textile manufactory at Ballyclare but these enterprises were mostly in one area and all together provided but scant employment for a population which was around a quarter of a million in the early 19th century and grew rapidly and alarmingly despite the wretched living conditions of the majority.

Several of the surnames which were prominent in Co. Mayo before the 17th century upheavals, such as Burke and O'Malley, still number among the commonest surnames in the county today, although others, once prominent, like Costello and Jordan, are not among the top twenty in numbers today. One of the surnames which came to Ireland in the wake of the Anglo-Norman conquest is the commonest surname now in Co. Mayo, but, it is not one readily associated with Connacht. The surname Walsh is widespread but more usually remembered for its association with south-eastern Leinster. Other surnames which came with, or soon after, the Anglo-Normans to Connacht, and which now rank among the twenty commonest in Co. Mayo are Gibbons (a branch of the Burkes), eighth in numerical order, Joyce (which originated in Wales) comes ninth. Burke comes but in fourteenth place because many branches of the Burkes adopted other surnames. The other surnames on the list following Walsh, the most numerous by far, are Gallagher, Kelly and O'Kelly, O'Malley, Moran, Duffy, Mc Hale, O'Connor and Connor, Conway, O'Higgins and Higgins, Murphy, O'Reilly and Reilly, Durkan, O'Doherty and Doherty, Mc Hugh, Sweeney and Mc Sweeney, and Lyons. The principal immigrant newcomers to the county who obtained estates were the Gores who held over 50,000 acres, the various branches of the Knox family who held over 50,000 acres, the Palmers who held over 80,000 acres, the Brownes, who with the head of the family the Marquess of Sligo, held around 120,000 acres, and Viscount Dillon who held over 80,000 acres.

COUNTY MEATH

THE Leinster county of Meath is bounded on the east by Co. Dublin and by a coastal stretch on the Irish Sea, on the south by the counties of Dublin, Kildare and Offaly, on the west by Co. Westmeath and on the north by the counties of Cavan, Monaghan and Louth. This county thus has boundaries with seven other counties of Ireland's thirty-two. In fact, the name of Meath derives from the Irish Midhe, meaning middle; it was so named because of the central situation of the ancient kingdom of Meath. The ancient kingdom was granted in its entirety by King Henry II to the Anglo-Norman adventurer Hugh de Lacy, to be held by the service of fifty knights. De Lacy divided a part of his grant among his henchmen, Gilbert Nangle (de Angulo), Jocelyn FitzGilbert, Adam Pheipo, Robert Misset, and Gilbert Fitz Thomas. Other Anglo-Normans were settled in the territory, among them the

MEATH *Inn being thatched near King William's Glen*

ancestor of the Flemings of Slane, the de Cussacs who became Cusack, and the Plunkets of Dunsany, families still found in the county today. In the reign of Henry VIII Meath was divided into two counties, the present county of Meath and the adjacent county of Westmeath (q.v.). Due to the dissolution of the monasteries and the sequestration of church property in that reign and to the incursion of the O'Neills from Ulster, who pillaged and burned along their path, the county was reduced by the latter years of the 16th century, from its former prosperity to a state of wretchedness with many of its churches in ruins.

The county boasted six boroughs, Trim, Kells, Navan, Athboy, Ratoath and Duleek, of which the first four named were also market-towns. All six sent two members each to the Irish parliament prior to the Act of Union; two other members represented the county at large. There were a number of other small towns and populous villages in the county, but Slane was the only other market-town, making five in all in Co. Meath.

Apart from the hills of Loughcrew in the western part of the county its surface is mostly level, the most pleasant scenery being along the banks of the rivers, the Blackwater, the Nanny, and the Boyne which enters the county at Clonard and flows across it to empty into the sea at Drogheda where its estuary forms the harbour. The city of Drogheda itself, however, is in Co. Louth. Until the present century, industrial enterprise in Co. Meath was scarce, although in recent years it has considerably changed the aspect of the town of Navan. Farming the excellent land of the county was previously the principal activity, with farms varying in size from small holdings of one or two

acres to vast estates of several thousand acres. Lord Dunsany seated at Dunsany Castle owned just under 4000 acres in the county in the last century. His neighbour and kinsman, another scion of the Plunket family, the Earl of Fingall, seated at Killeen Castle, held over 9000 acres in the county. The Marquess Conyngham at Slane Castle held 7000, Lord Athlumney at Somerville, a little over 10,000 acres, Viscount Gormanstown at Gormanstown Castle, over 9000 acres, and his kinsman, Mr. Preston at Bellinter, over 7000. The Marquess of Headfort at Headfort House near Kells held over 7000 acres. Mr. Naper at Loughcrew, over 18,000 acres. The largest landowner in the county at the end of the 19th century was the Earl of Darnley who kept a residence near Athboy, where his ancestors named Bligh, from Devonshire, had settled; he held almost 22,000 acres in Co. Meath.

Today the commonest surname in Co. Meath by far is O'Reilly and Reilly, borne by descendants of the East Breffny sept who spread south-eastward into the county from Co. Cavan. The second most populous surname in the county is Smith, borne by descendants of English settlers, but for the greater part by descendants of the Breffny sept, Mac Gabhann, who also migrated into Co. Meath from Co. Cavan. Next in descending numerical order but all in far lesser numbers come Lynch, Brady, O'Farrell and Farrell, Farrelly, Kelly and O'Kelly, O'Brien and Brien, Daly, and Maguire, then Duffy (the name of a family which spread into Co. Meath from Co. Monaghan), Dunne, Byrne and O'Byrne, O'Connor and Connor, McMahon and Mahon, Clarke, Martin, and Mathews. The notice for Co. Louth explains the probable origins of Clarke, Lynch and Mathews in this part of Ireland.

COUNTY MONAGHAN

THE inland county of Monaghan, in the south of Ulster province, is bounded on the south by the Leinster county of Meath, on the east by Co. Armagh and the Leinster county of Louth, on the north by Co. Tyrone, and on the west by the counties of Fermanagh and Cavan. Anciently, with parts of Co. Armagh and Co. Louth the county of Monaghan formed part of the territory called Oriel. The MacMahons were the most powerful sept in this region, next in importance being the McKennas and the O'Connollys.

Today Duffy is the commonest name in Co. Monaghan, that sept having evidently been very prolific but it is followed very closely by Connolly and O'Connolly, McMahon and McKenna, indicating that in this county the principal families have remained in their ancestral home-land for a thousand years or more. Fifth in numerical strength in the county comes the surname Hughes, normally an English and Welsh patronymic but here probably also widely in use by descendants of an Ó hAodha sept. Following

Hughes on the list comes the ubiquitous Murphy, then McCabe, the name of a galloglass family who were once mercenaries in Breffny whence they spread eastwards into Co. Monaghan. Martin is next in numerical strength followed by Smith, Kelly and O'Kelly, Quinn, Maguire, Murray, and Woods. Of the three once most important families there was not one landowner named McMahon in the county in 1879, the large population of that name all being tenants, only two landowners named McKenna, one with thirty-five acres and one with only thirteen and only one landowner named Connolly, with ninety-three acres. There were only three persons with the commonest surname, Duffy, owning land in the county, none with more than twenty-three acres. The ownership of the land had changed radically since the end of the 16th century. The principal immigrant families who settled in the county and acquired estates were the family of Shirley from Warwickshire who were granted lands at Lough Fea in the 16th century, and others who came in the 17th century, Ancketill from Dorset, Hamilton and Leslie both originally from Scotland, Westenra from the Netherlands, Lucas, Dawson, and Blayney.

The market town and borough of Monaghan, the chief town of the county, and the market-towns of Carrickmacross, Castleblayney, New-bliss, Clones, and Ballybay, were the principal urban communities of the county. The county, which was once thickly wooded, is hilly, but the majority of the land is cultivable. There are several attractive lakes in the county of which the largest is Lough Muckno, dotted with wooded islets. Due to its geographical position the climate is liable to be both damp and windy. The soil is very varied, with moors in the low-lying areas while there is good land in the central part of the county across the baronies of Trough, Monaghan and Dartry from Glaslough to Clones, and the most productive land in the county is to be found in the south in the barony of Farney.

As in many other counties, wheat, potatoes, flax and oats were the principal crops and almost every farmer kept dairy cows. In the north of the county sheep were raised, and all over the county, pigs, in greater numbers than elsewhere, mostly destined for the provision merchants of Belfast, Drogheda and Newry. Linen was made and bleached in Co. Monaghan in considerable quantity, woollen cloth was manufactured at Carrickmacross, and the county also had, early in the 19th century, two iron mills where agricultural implements were made, and two tanneries.

COUNTY OFFALY

FORMERLY called King's County, the inland Leinster county of Offaly is bounded by the counties of Westmeath and Meath to the north, by Co. Kildare to the east, by Co. Leix, formerly called Queen's County, and by Co. Tipperary to the south, and to the west by Co. Tipperary and the Shannon River separating the county from the Connacht counties of Galway and Ros-common; it is, therefore, surrounded, as is Co. Meath, by seven other counties. The county was carved, in fact, out of an ancient territory which included parts of the present counties of Meath, Westmeath, Kildare and Leix. In the southern part of the territory, known later as Ely O'Carroll, the O'Carroll sept was powerful along with the O'Delany sept, while in the

OFFALY *The graveyard and round tower overlooking the Shannon at Clonmacnoise*

northern part the principal families were O'Connor, O'Molloy and McCoghlan, until the Crown extended its power into the region. In the 16th century the Irish chiefs submitted to the Crown and the land was shired. The King's County was thus created, named in honour of King Philip the consort of Queen Mary I, while to the south the Queen's County was created. The fort at Dangan, the stronghold of the O'Connor Faly chieftain, was made into the chief town of the new King's County and renamed Philipstown. English settlers were put into the county, but as the old Irish landowners only relinquished their claims to their lands after stiff fighting the new incomers did not have an easy time.

Today O'Connor is no longer among the most populous names in Co. Offaly, but Molloy and O'Carroll or Carroll are. The commonest name in the county is now Kelly and O'Kelly followed by Dunne (an old Irish midland name originally belonging to what is now Co. Leix where it is still the commonest surname), Daly, Egan, Molloy, Mooney, O'Carroll and Carroll, Walsh, Kenny, Murray, Dempsey, Kennedy, and Maher. The new names of landowners who came into the county in the 16th and mostly the 17th century, were the families of Parsons (Earls of Rosse) and Moore, later Bury (Earls of Charleville), the Digby family, whose estates in the county came through marriage to a Fitzgerald heiress (the daughter of Lord Offaly and granddaughter of the 11th Earl of Kildare), the Lloyd and Vaughan families from Wales, the Goodbody and Stoney families from Yorkshire, the Rolleston family from Staffordshire, the Darby family (whose seat was Leap Castle, an old stronghold of the O'Carrolls), and the families of Drought, Odlum, Dames, Bennett, and Bernard.

Tullamore, the chief town of the county was a market town, as were the boroughs of Banagher and Philipstown each of which sent two members to the Irish parliament before the Act of Union. The county had four other market towns, Birr, which was renamed Parsonstown (after the family which made its seat at Birr Castle) and then reverted to Birr, Clara, Edenderry and Frankford. The Slieve Bloom mountains rise in the south-west of Co. Offaly along the border with Co. Leix, but save for this, and hilly country in the north-east, the land is mostly flat. The best soil is in the south of the county in the barony of Ballybritt between the foot of the Slieve Blooms and Birr, a region noted for its fine breed of large, strong, working bullocks, and in the barony of Clonlisk which juts into Co. Tipperary. Wheat, potatoes, barley, rape, and oats were the main crops, green crops on any of the small holdings being rare; sheep were bred in the hills. Timber felled in the county fetched good prices on the Dublin market, especially ash which was particularly prized. Many of the countrywomen owned a spinning-wheel, but the textiles produced in the county were mostly, if not all, destined for local use, worsted, frieze and serge.

The women of Co. Offaly had a reputation for being industrious: it was said that young men from other parts went there to seek a bride on that account. The woollen weaving and combing industry at Birr which employed several hundred hands failed in the 18th century as did the glass manufacture there. In the 19th century, save for those engaged by the whiskey distillery or the brick factory at Tullamore or in the two less famous distilleries at Birr, or in the county's few flour mills, most of the population depended for a living on agricultural pursuits.

COUNTY ROSCOMMON

The inland Connacht county of Roscommon is bounded on the north and east by Co. Leitrim, on the east also by the counties of Longford, Westmeath and Offaly, on the south and south-west by Co. Galway, and on the north-west by the counties of Mayo and Sligo, so that like Co. Offaly it has borders with no less than seven other counties. The O'Conors were the most important sept of the region before the Anglo-Norman incursions, the centre of the present county being their principal seat of power; to

the north the McDermots held sway, to the south the O'Kellys. All three surnames still figure today among the half-dozen commonest in Co. Roscommon, O'Kelly and Kelly holding the first place by a wide gap, McDermot in second place, and O'Connor and Connor in sixth place. While the O'Conor Don whose seat is at Clonnalis in the county (and who traces his descent from the O'Conor kings of Connacht and high-Kings of Ireland) retains the spelling of his surname as O'Conor with a single 'n', this name is commonly and more frequently found now as O'Connor or Connor. The other most populous families in Co. Roscommon in modern times are O'Beirne and Beirne trailing McDermot in third place and followed closely by O'Regan or Regan and Flanagan. In seventh place, after O'Connor and Connor, comes McDonagh followed by Quinn, Murray, Brennan, Higgins and O'Higgins, Towey, Kenny, and Flynn.

In the reign of King Henry III most of the county of Roscommon was granted to the de Burgo or Burke family but later, through the marriage of the heiress of that family with a prince of the English royal house, their estates reverted to the Crown. In any case the alien control of the territory appears to have been nominal; the branches of the O'Conors, with their principal strongholds at Ballinafad Castle and Ballintober Castle, and the other Irish chiefs, remained in effective control of most of the area. In the English subdivision of Connacht in 1565, the present county was erected and its limits defined, the McDermot territory became one of its baronies (Boyle), the O'Conor Don's territory became another barony (Ballintober), the O'Conor Roe's territory became the barony of Roscommon and the territory of the O'Kellys became the barony of Athlone and the half-barony of Moycarnon at the southern tip of the county. The native Irish chiefs were compelled to submit and swear allegiance in return for which the Crown re-granted them their ancestral lands but subject to inheritance according to English law. During the upheavals of the 17th century, however, after a period in which the old families regained supremacy, they were eventually dispossessed. The family of the O'Conor Don contrived to retain 10,000 acres or so without renouncing their religion. Some of the others were less fortunate although in the last century a McDermott Roe held 2500 acres in the county, an O'Kelly 1200 or so, and others named O'Conor several estates of between 2000 and 7000 acres. Only a Mr. Wills of Castlerea, Mr. Tenison of Kilronan Castle, Mr. Pakenham-Mahon of Strokestown, the King-Harman family

ROSCOMMON *Interior of the Cistercian abbey, Boyle*

of Rockingham and the family of French (represented principally by Lord de Freyne at Frenchpark) owned more land in the county than the O'Conor Don, a situation of retention of their property by the ancient Irish proprietors which is very rare in that this family did not conform to the Established Church in order to retain their estates, in the penal times, one other example being the O'Connells of Derrynane, Co. Kerry.

COUNTY SLIGO

THE Connacht maritime county of Sligo, which is bounded on its north side by the Atlantic, is bounded on the east by the county of Leitrim, on the south-east by Co. Roscommon, and on the west and south by Co. Mayo. The chief town, which has the same name as the county, is a seaport, situated in the north of the county, and was also a borough and market town. There were

SLIGO *Landscape with cairn at Knocknarea Mountain, reputedly the burial place of Queen Maebh*

three other market towns in the county – Coolaney, and Collooney, with such similar names and close to one another, and Ballymote. The linen industry was introduced into Co. Sligo in 1749 by Lord Shelburne who settled a colony of weavers at Ballymote on a housing estate where each had a cottage and a rood of land for a potato garden and to graze one cow. Subsequently, as that industry flourished, a fabric of mixed linen and cotton was manufactured; four bleach-greens were established where linens purchased at the Sligo market and other markets in the vicinity were bleached. Although the industry diminished in the 19th century, it continued to be the staple one of the county. Fishing was not without importance to the economy, herring, cod, haddock and turbot being taken off the coast, but this industry was scarcely exploited and until the present century the vessels available were mostly inadequate.

Early in the last century the waters of the River Moy were rendered navigable for cargo ships as far as Ballina by a Mr. Levington, an enterprising merchant of that town.

The country people of Co. Sligo, for the greater part, lived miserably until recent times. In the last century, and into the present one, many still lived in wretched dwellings built of sods and roofed with the most elementary sort of thatch. Potatoes, until the disastrous famine years of the 1840's, were their staple diet, with occasionally oat bread, milk, eggs, and salted herring, but even this last, save in the harbour regions, was almost a luxury. The people dressed in homespun stuffs, chiefly frieze.

Of the ancient families of the county the only one which retained any prominence after the 17th century upheavals was a branch of the O'Hara family which managed to retain its estates and fulfil public offices in the penal times having conformed to the Established Church; the head of this family had his seat in the county at Annaghmore and Cooper's Hill. Other branches of the O'Haras, along with the other old native families of the region, were supplanted by the incoming settlers whose descendants became the new landowners and leading gentry of Co. Sligo, the families of Wynne from Wales, Duke from Suffolk, Perceval, Phibbs, Palmer, ffolliott, Cooper, Knox, Hillas, Gore, Gore-Booth and Ormsby-Gore. Today the most numerous surname in the county is Brennan, followed fairly closely by McLoughlin, Gallagher, and Kelly or O'Kelly. Next in descending numerical order come Hart(e), McGowan, Walsh, Kennedy, Durkan, Henry, Flynn, Gilmartin, Leonard, Scanlon, Connolly, O'Hara, Feeney, Stenson, Conway, and Sheridan.

COUNTY TIPPERARY

THE inland Munster county of Tipperary is second only in extent in Ireland to the Ulster county of Donegal, covering as it does over one million acres. The county is bounded on the east and north-east by the province of Leinster, having boundaries with the counties of Offaly, Leix, and Kilkenny. On the south side Co. Tipperary has a boundary with Co. Waterford, marked for some distance by the River Suir. On the south-west Co. Tipperary has a boundary with Co. Cork, on the west with Co. Limerick and Co. Clare, and on the north-west with the Connacht county of Galway, thus being adjacent to seven other counties. The county contained three boroughs, each of which sent two members to the Irish parliament before the Act of Union, Clonmel, Fethard and Cashel, and all three were market towns; Cashel enjoyed a special importance also as the seat of the Archbishop. The other market towns of the county were Carrick-on-Suir, Cahir, Clogheen, Killenaule, Nenagh, Roscrea, Templemore, Thurles, and the town of Tipperary. Even taking into account the extent of the county, the number of its market towns – twelve – indicates the amount of mercantile activity in the area which enjoyed much very fertile land as well as coal mines in the baronies of Slievcardagh and Eliogarty, including what was in the middle years of the 19th century the most extensive coalfield in Ireland at Boulintlea. The community which mushroomed beside one rich colliery opened early in the 18th century, and one of the earliest to be exploited in the county, was named Coalbrook. Ironstone metal was also found in the pits there. In the county there were also a number of productive slate quarries, while near Silvermines copper and lead were found after the expiration, in the 18th century, of the lease of the company which extracted silver from the ore. Copper was also mined near Newport and elsewhere in this county which is fairly rich in mineral deposits.

Otherwise by the 19th century industry in the county was limited; the once-flourishing woollen industry at Carrick-on-Suir and at Clonmel had failed at the end of the 18th century when the government promoted the manufacture of woollens in England. Those two towns attempted to replace their lost business by the manufacture of flannel and blankets and a twilled woollen material called ratteen, but after the Act of Union that industry also failed, creating consequent unemployment and distress in those formerly-prosperous places. Some of

TIPPERARY *Kiltinan Castle incorporating the medieval stronghold of the Butlers with the Georgian mansion of settlers called Cooke*

the county landowners attempted to remedy the situation by promoting the linen industry, but without success. On its principal rivers, the Shannon, the Suir, and the Nore, and their tributaries, the county had, however, about sixty large flour-mills in the 19th century. It was, too, in this county that Mr. Bianconi initiated his service of postal cars which spread through the country, his first run having been established in 1815 between Cahir and Clonmel, the town which was the chief mart for the abundant agricultural produce of the county, sending it down the Suir to Waterford for export.

As this county covered a large territory it accommodated anciently a number of septs; by the time of the arrival of the Anglo-Normans branches of several Dalcassian septs from Thomond had also established themselves in the area. Subsequently the area fell under the sway of the powerful Butler family, of Anglo-Norman origin, who dominated a great palatinate with strongholds across the county, the principal ones being at Carrick-on-Suir, Kiltinan, Cahir, Nenagh and Kilcash.

The commonest Irish surname today in Co. Tipperary is Ryan and O'Ryan, borne by descendants of a sept which was in this region prior to the Anglo-Norman conquest. There are now about four times as many persons named Ryan in the county as there are with any one of the next three commonest names – Maher, O'Brien, and Kennedy. In descending order of numerical strength after those four surnames come Dwyer and O'Dwyer, Hogan, Hayes, Gleeson, McGrath, Walsh, Kelly and O'Kelly, and Lonergan.

COUNTY TYRONE

THE inland Ulster county of Tyrone derives its name from the Irish, Tir Eoghain, having been anciently the territory of the Cinel Eoghain. To the north, the county is bounded by Co. Derry, to the east by Co. Armagh and the waters of Lough Neagh, to the south by Co. Monaghan and Co. Fermanagh, and to the west by Co. Fermanagh and Co. Donegal. It is thus positioned very firmly within the province of Ulster, not having a boundary with a county of any other province. The O'Neills were the magnates in this region and retained their importance until the Flights of the Earls and the sequestration of the estates of the Earl of Tyrone at the beginning of the 17th century. Tullaghoge in the barony of Dungannon, in the east of Co. Tyrone, was the stronghold of the O'Hagans, and there the O'Neill chief was inaugurated; the inaugural stone throne was smashed in 1602 by Mountjoy, the Elizabethan general, bent on vanquishing the power and authority of the first family of Ulster whose chiefs had been styled King of Tyrone long before they acquired the English title of Earl of Tyrone.

O'Neill is still among the most populous names in Co. Tyrone but comes only in tenth place in order of numerical strength, outnumbered even by two settler surnames, Campbell and Wilson, which came to the county when the O'Neills' power was suppressed and their property confiscated. The commonest surnames in the county, in about equal numbers are Quinn, Mullan and Kelly, fairly closely followed in number by Donnelly, Gallagher, McKenna, Campbell, Hughes, Wilson, O'Neill, McLaughlin,

TYRONE *Beatling Mill at Wellbrook, Co. Tyrone*

Doherty and O'Doherty, Smith, and the Scottish settler surname Hamilton.

The presence among the commonest names in Co. Tyrone today of three Scottish surnames, Campbell, Wilson, and Hamilton, and a fourth, if one includes some, at least, of the name Smith, is an indication of how heavily the county was resettled by immigrants attracted from Scotland and England by grants of land and leases. A glance at the list of landowners in the county in the last century immediately reveals the prevalence of Scottish surnames, Aiken, Alexander, Anderson, Baird, Beatty, Buchanan, Caldwell, Campbell, Crawford, Galbraith, Hamilton, Houston, Irvine and Irwin, Johnston, Knox, Maxwell, Montgomery, Scott, Stewart, Warnock, Wilson, and others, far outnumbering the native Irish surnames. Two among the commonest of Irish surnames in the county, Doherty and Gallagher, are not represented on the list of landowners of one acre or more at all, showing that after three centuries many of the Irish had not risen above the situation of tenants of the new landlords to which they were reduced at the time of the Plantation. The principals of the Plantation were the class of grantees called undertakers. The surnames of the new patentees in a list of 1618 were Hamilton, Stewart, Newcomen, Drummond, Davies, Ridgway, Lowther, Leigh, Stewart, Cope, Parsons, Touchet, Heyburn, Sanderson, Lindsay, Richardson, Keneday, Chichester, Balfour, Caulfield, Annesley, Wingfield, and there was a solitary Irishman, Sir Tirlogh O'Nial.

The county had four boroughs, its chief town Dungannon, and three others, Strabane, Clogher, and Augher, each of which sent two members to the Irish parliament before the Act of Union while two others represented the county at large. All four boroughs were also market towns and there were nine other market towns in the county, Omagh, Aughnacloy, Caledon, Ballygawley, Castlederg, Moy, Cookstown, Stewartstown, and Newtonstewart, the last three named for the settler families who founded them. Wheat was grown extensively in the county, save in the mountainous districts, along with the usual Irish crops – potatoes and flax. Due to the extensive division and sub-division of the land there was an exceptionally large number of small farmholdings in the county, but the farmers generally were reputed for their skilful management and industry. Dairy farming was not widespread; the butter that was produced in the county was mostly exported, salted, to Scotland. The staple manufacture of Co. Tyrone was linen, made and bleached there for export to England, but from the end of the 18th century this industry declined; by the 1830's it was reported that two-thirds of the bleach-greens in the county were not in use. Home-woven woollen cloth and blankets for domestic use were usually also dyed at home, blue being the favourite colour for clothing. There was a brewery at Donaughmore and a few mills in the county but none offering great employment.

COUNTY WATERFORD

THE maritime Munster county of Waterford is bounded on the north by County Kilkenny, beyond the River Suir, and by Co. Tipperary, on the east by Co. Wexford, beyond the estuary of the Suir which forms Waterford Harbour, on the west by Co. Cork, and on the south side the boundary is the coastline. The chief city, Waterford, with its fine natural harbour, was founded by Vikings who settled there in the 9th century, fortifying the city, extending the power of their little city-state into the hinterland, and sometimes making forays into the country as far as Kildare and Meath. Their potentate was described by the Irish annalists as 'King of the Danes of Waterford'. The power of this dynasty was not broken effectively until the walled city fell with great loss of life to the Anglo-Normans led by Strongbow and Raymond le Gros in 1171. Thereafter, Waterford grew in importance because of its situation as a centre of communication with England, and of trade with England and continental Europe. King John granted the city a charter of incorporation in 1206 and coinage was struck there in his reign. In the 15th century King Edward IV established a mint in the city. The county had three other boroughs, the market towns of Dungarvan, Lismore, and Tallow, and other market towns, Tramore, and Dunmore. Besides busy Waterford, there are ports at Dunmore, Tramore, and Dungarvan.

The varied scenery of the county is often very beautiful, ranging from the Comeragh mountains dotted with corrie lakes, to the vale of the Suir, the glens descending from Knockmealdown to

WATERFORD *Townscape of the city of Waterford across the River Suir*

the lovely valley of the Blackwater, and the beautiful coast with its long sandy stretches, deep bays, and lofty cliffs and headlands. About two-thirds of the land in the county was tilled, the general crops being wheat, barley, and potatoes, with oats in the more mountainous parts. The remaining third, which was not unimproved land, or bog, was meadow and pasture. Some cotton factories established in the county had but a short life and failed, save that established by the longsighted, socially-aware Malcolmsons which employed up to 1000 people in spinning and weaving before the famine. The owners of the enterprise built not only a large factory fitted with the best type of machinery at Portlaw but also neat well-constructed slate-roofed cottages for their employees, a dispensary with a resident surgeon, and a school. As many as two to three thousand jobs were created in connection with the industry and the requirements it generated. There was also a paper-mill in the county, and a glass factory and breweries with a busy export trade in

the city of Waterford where a succession of other industrial enterprises were established and failed, among them a linen thread factory, a bottle factory, and the manufacture of japanned ware. The port provided employment, shipping live cattle, agricultural products, and beer for export, and bringing in a great variety of imported goods. That over 100,000 flitches of bacon, 50,000 barrels of wheat, 1500 head of cattle, 15,000 pigs and 3000 sheep were exported annually through the port of Waterford in the 1830's gives some idea of the quantity of traffic handled there.

The two commonest surnames in the county today, Power and Walsh, came with the Anglo-Norman invasion, the former originating in France as le Poer, and the latter denoting a settler from Wales. Powers are found now in every walk of life in the county, from great landowners and prosperous businessmen, to farmers, shopkeepers, and down to the poorest and humblest inhabitants. Next in numerical strength comes the surname O'Brien, followed by Murphy, Ryan, McGrath, Foley, Flynn, Morrissey, Kelly, Phelan and Whelan, Sullivan, McCarthy, Butler, and Tobin.

COUNTY WESTMEATH

THE inland Leinster county of Westmeath was created late in the reign of King Henry VIII by hiving off the western part of Meath. Co. Westmeath is thus bounded on the east by Co. Meath; its southern boundary is with Co. Offaly. On the north Westmeath is bounded by the counties of Meath, Cavan, and Longford, and on the west by Co. Longford and Co. Roscommon. In the Irish parliament, before the Act of Union, ten members sat from Co. Westmeath: two for the county, and two for each of the four boroughs in the county, Mullingar, Kilbeggan, Athlone and Fore. The three former were market-towns, but Fore lost its former importance after the dissolution of its Benedictine monastery and dwindled to a village of about only twenty small houses. The little market town of Collinstown is, however, in the parish of Fore. Besides the four already named, the county had other market-towns, Moate, Rathowen, Castletown-delvin, Clonmellon, and Ballinacargy.

Prior to the Anglo-Norman occupation, the principal families of what is now Co. Westmeath were McGeoghegan, O'Brennan, O'Colley, O'Mulleady or O'Melody, O'Daly, McAwley or Magawly, McGann or Magan, and O'Fenelon or O'Finlan. Due to the upheavals of the ensuing centuries not one of these names now ranks among the twenty commonest in the county where a great assortment of surnames are found today and no single one in very significant numbers. However, the old surnames Coffey, Daly and Magan do appear on lists of 19th century landowners in the county. Most of the land had, however, passed to incomers; the resident large landowners by that time were Handcock, Chapman, Fetherstonhaugh or Fetherston, Pakenham, Levinge, Marley, Nugent, Boyd-Rochfort, Smyth, Cooke, Temple, Tuite, and Urquart, with only five of native origin, Ennis, Magan, Malone, Murphy, and Tighe. Of the others, only Tuite and Nugent were of very long standing in the county, having come with the Anglo-Norman settlers, while the rest came in the 17th century or later. The other

WESTMEATH *Tyrellspass*

prominent Anglo-Norman settlers in the region were Dillon, de Hosey (which became Hussey), d'Alton (which became Dalton), de la Mare (which became Delamer), Petit (which became Petty), Ledwich, and d'Ardis (which became Dardis). The family of Hope came about the 14th century, and the Piers family from Yorkshire in the 16th. The most frequently occurring surnames now in Co. Westmeath are Lynch, O'Farrell and Farrell, O'Reilly and Reilly, Daly, Murray, Duffy, McCormick, Walsh, Dalton, Kelly, Smith, Byrne, Carey, Dunne, Fagan, Flynn, Leavy, and O'Neill. A custom which persisted in this county in the last century was the retention of their maiden surname by married women.

Situated on the marches of the English Pale between the Irish dominated regions in Connacht and the east of the country where the Crown writ obtained, the county of Westmeath was often the scene of fighting and was subject to both influences.

The county has some very fine lakes; Lough Ennel, the scene of battles in the Civil War in the 17th century, is the largest. The eastern part of the country has good, very fertile land, much of which was devoted to grazing. In the west the soil is lighter and there are stretches of bogland, extensions of the vast Bog of Allen. Oats and potatoes were the chief crops grown in the county and, on a lesser scale, flax, barley, wheat, and rape. There was scarcely any commercial enterprise in the county a hundred years ago save for the sale of agricultural produce, and, at Mullingar, two tanneries, and a brewery and malting establishment. The home-manufactured frieze and flannel was made only for domestic·use.

COUNTY WEXFORD

THE south-east Leinster maritime county of Wexford which, because of its high level of cultivation, gained the name of 'the garden of Ireland', is bounded by the sea on its southern and eastern sides, by Co. Wicklow on the north, and on the east by the counties of Carlow and Kilkenny and the estuary of the Suir separating it from Co. Waterford. The chief town of Co. Wexford, which has the same name as the county, was founded by the Vikings who gave it its name. It was besieged by the Anglo-Normans after they landed in Bannow and was the first town in Ireland to fall to them; the town was granted its first charter early in the 14th century. The county had no fewer than seven other boroughs besides Wexford, each of which sent two members to the Irish parliament before the Act of Union; Clonmines, Enniscorthy, Fethard, Gorey, New Ross, Taghmon, and Bannow. Of those places, Enniscorthy, Gorey, and New Ross, were thriving market towns, but Clonmines has long been a ghost-town with a silted-up harbour and the ruins of medieval buildings. The old town of Bannow also disappeared long ago; Fethard shrank to a place of fifty houses or so, and the little town of Taghmon shows no trace of former importance except the ruined tower of a castle and the ruins of two medieval churches.

In the wake of the Anglo-Norman conquistadors immigrants flowed into this region, attracted by its rich land and by its proximity to the western coast of Wales, an easy sea-crossing and one still much in use today between Rosslare in Co. Wexford and the Welsh ports of Fishguard and Pembroke. Of these early settlers, several are still represented in the county like the Rossiter family in the barony of Forth (where they have been established for seven centuries although not big landowners), the families of Codd, Stafford, Synott or Sinnott, Hore, and Talbot, and the once-powerful family of Devereux. Today the commonest surname in Co. Wexford is the ubiquitous Murphy, in this case borne, no doubt, by many who descend from the McMurrough (Mac Murchada) sept of Leinster. The next commonest surname in the county, after a considerable drop in numbers, is Doyle. Walsh follows Doyle after another big drop and is only half as numerous; then, in descending numerical order come Byrne and O'Byrne, Cullen, Kavanagh, O'Brien and Brien, Roche, Kelly, Redmond, Nolan, Connor and O'Connor, Kehoe, Ryan, Bolger and Whelan.

There is attractive scenery in the county along the River Slaney and the River Barrow, and an interesting landscape along its western boundary where the lofty chain of the Blackstairs and Mount Leinster dominate the surroundings. Altogether, the south-eastern part of the county resembles the countryside of Devonshire or parts of rural South Wales across the channel, not only because of the similar landscape but also because of the similar appearance of many of the neat farmhouses and the well-fenced and well-cultivated fields where barley, the chief produce, was grown extensively, and to a lesser extent, beans, oats, wheat, rape, potatoes and turnips; 19th century observers noted that the Wexford farmers were more interested in crops than cattle. They raised excellent poultry including turkeys and other domestic fowl which were fattened by cramming them on potato waste and barley meal for sale in Dublin and export to England. At Ballyhack there was an annual poultry fair every autumn with a large attendance and much trading. Beekeeping was another branch of husbandry in Co. Wexford where some of the honey produced was used to make mead.

Rabbits were abundant in the sandy warrens and about 200 reached the markets each week from the burrows near Rosslare alone. There was an extensive manufacture of linen, diaper and woollens at Tintern with its own yarn market but by the 1830's the buildings had fallen into decay although weavers in the neighbourhood still made some textiles for local domestic use. Fishing was mostly restricted to grounds close to the shore, cod and herring being the main catch; oysters and lobster from Wexford were prized on the Dublin market.

WEXFORD *The mill race at Foulkesmill*

THE Leinster maritime county of Wicklow has the sea as its eastern boundary and is bounded on the north by Co. Dublin, on the south by Co. Wexford, and on the west by the counties of Carlow and Kildare. There were four boroughs in the county, Baltinglass, Blessington, Carysfort and Wicklow, of which all but Carysfort were market towns, and seven other market towns: Arklow, Bray, Carnew, Dunlavin, Rathdrum, Tinahely and Stratford-upon-Slaney. The last-named little town was founded in the 18th century by the Earl of Aldborough, whose family name was Stratford, and a cotton and calico printing works established there in 1792 was employing 1000 persons fifty years later. Another landowner in the county, Earl Fitzwilliam, built a flannel hall at Rathdrum for marketing flannel which used to be manufactured extensively in the area, but the industry declined after the 18th century and the building was in disuse early in the 19th century. The Earls Fitzwilliam, whose seat was at Coollatin near Shillelagh, were the biggest landowners in the county, holding, in the last century, 90,000 acres. Near Shillelagh the 4th Earl, who had served as Lord Lieutenant of Ireland in 1796, made many improvements, reclaiming bog and wasteland by draining and trenching, and building flour-mills, carding-mills, bone-mills, a bleaching-green and a multi-denominational school. Superior dwellings were built also for the employees of the estate. Unfortunately such examples of enlightened landlordism were rare.

The county is rich in minerals. Lead was once mined on Carrigeenduff and near Glendalough at Ballinafinchoge; alluvial gold was found in 1796 in the barony of Arklow causing considerable excitement, but it was only in modern times that the mineral wealth has been commercially exploited to any extent, causing as it has ugly scars on the landscape of such beautiful places as the Vale of Avoca.

In the upland and mountain pastures of the county store cattle and sheep were fed and even some of the bogland provided good sheep pasture having a covering of soft grass; otherwise tillage was the chief agricultural pursuit but much of the land in the county is stony and much is wild bog, heath and mountain. Co. Wicklow was rich, however, in woodland and was probably the most thickly wooded county in the country. Because of the wild nature of the landscape and the fastness of Wicklow's romantic glens, it was possible for the original Irish inhabitants to resist the influence of the English Pale. Although the north of Co. Wicklow is so close to the capital, Dublin, it remained for centuries after the Anglo-Norman conquest of the country the lair of descendants of Irish septs long belligerent to the Crown and apt to descend from their hideouts and ravage the surrounding areas, so that only the accessible parts of the county, mainly on the coast, could be colonized.

The intransigent Irish of the county were mostly O'Tooles and O'Byrnes. The former have diminished in numbers although still among the ten most numerous family names in Co. Wicklow today. Byrne and O'Byrne is today by far the most populous surname in the county. The next most common surname in Co. Wicklow is Doyle, followed by three surnames, Murphy, Kelly and Kavanagh, each only half as numerous as Doyle. After these in descending numerical order come Nolan, O'Brien and Brien, Kehoe, Lawler, O'Toole and Toole, Dunne, Farrell and O'Farrell, and Redmond.

WICKLOW *The Sally Gap*

MAP OF IRELAND – SHOWING LOCATIONS OF FAMILY NAMES

This map of Ireland shows the location of the Gaelic septs (and in red) of the principal Hiberno-Norman families in the period after the Anglo-Norman invasion and before the upheavals of the seventeenth century. It has been redrawn and lettered for this book by Kirkham Studios with the permission of the copyright holders, Johnston & Bacon (division of Cassell Limited) from a map prepared by Edward MacLysaght, D. Litt, M.R.I.A. The armorial shields were drawn by Myra Maguire, heraldic artist to the Geneological Office, Dublin Castle. The map shows many of the names mentioned in the text and also includes many others.

Belfast
Dublin

Miles
0 20 40
0 20 40 60
Kilometres

O Roarty
O Kernagha
Mc Swee
Mc Coyle
Mc Sweeney
O Friel
O Toner
O Breslin
O Duffy
Mc Conigle
O Dallaghan
O Begley
O Laverty
O Shryhane
(Straban)
D O N E G A L
Mc Cool
L O B
O Farren
Mc Ward
O Mulligan
O Cannon
O Ga
Mc Fadden
O Kenny
O Boyle
N O Pattan
(Peyton)
Mc Sweeney
O Mooney
Mc Meramin
N Mc Glinchy
Mc Gillespie
Mc Crossa
Mc Nelis
O Gallagher
U
Donegal Mc Roarty
D
Mc Donlevy
Mc Nulty Lynch (chan)
M
O Mulhollan
O Cor
Mc Ward
Mc Grath
Ballyshannon
O Slevin
O Clery
Mc Almon
O Muldoc
Hayes
(Hughes)
O En
O Corc
Meehan
O Goldrick
O Flanagan
O Hart
O Corrigan
O Boland
O Finn
Mc Claney
O Scanlon
O Connolly
Hayes
(Hughes)
Mullover
(Milford)
Sligo
O Scannell
O R O U R K E
O Cosey
O Ronan
O Flannery
Counachtan O Colman
O Noone
O Keenan
Mc Corry
O Canny
O Comane
(Commons)
O Spelman
Meeney
O Curneen
Mc Auley
Mc Gilpin
Mc Hale
Rafferty Loughrey
Mc Erlean
Mc Cunneen
O Mulrennan
Mc Firbis O Conboy
O Consuave
(Ford)
O Drum
O Connigan
O Garvine
(Garvey)
Linnane
(Leonard)
Mc Breslin O Tarpey
D O W D
Somahan
Mc Cabe
Mc Gannon
O Murray
Mangan
C O N O R
S L I G O
O Hely
Mc Govern
O Crehan
O Gaughan
Clery
Mc Firbis
O Finan
O Donagh
Mc Donagh
Mc Coogan
O Gilleen
O Dugan
Derig
O H A R A
O Kanavaghan
(Conway)
Mt
Dermotroe
Mc Keon
O Rodehan
(Roddy)
O Flynn
Mc Andrew
Mc Kilbane
Mc Breheny
O Lavan
Mc S
Barrett
O Flannelly
Mc Keribly (White)
Mc Alary
Taaffe
O Molloy
Mc Gilhooly
O Gallon
O Loughane
(Lofts)
Mc Durkan
Higgins
O Mullaney
Mulvey
Mc Gourtey
O Keevane
O A R A
Conway
O Devlin
Feeheny
Mulvanaghty Mc Dorcy
O Fergus
Jordan
Mohan
French
O Giblin
Mc Greevy
Mc Rannall
(Reynolds)
Mc Mo
Rolan
M A Y O
O Brogan
O Coolahan Killeen
Mc D E R M O T
Mc Weeney
O Beirne
Mc Shanley
Castlebar
B
O Dowd
(Kearns)
O Kerin
Carney
O Flanagan
O Duignan
Mc Culroy
(Gilroy)
Mc Gayr
O Quigley
U
R
K
O Cooney
Mc Brannon
Mc Manus
Mc Cranh
O Tierney
Mc Evilly
E
O Gormley
Mc Gilna
Mc Gibbon
Mc Kerrigan
O Henaghan
Mc Costello
R O S C O M M O N
Mulvihill
Longford
O Mc
Mc Nicholas
O Horan
O C O N O R R U A
O Coyne
O Gormley
O Flynn O Murphy
O Duffy
O Mulconry
O Quinn
O Dorcy
O Beirne
Mc Aneeny
O H
O Hanley
Mc Quill
L O N G F O R D
Mc Morris
N Prendergast
A
O Mulroy
O M A L L E Y
Mc Davie (Burke)
O Moran
Mulrenan
Malkerin
Hayes
O Quinn
Joyce
O Mulrooney
Bermingham
O Clabbymon
Mc Conneely
Dillon McDowell
O Tolleran
Mc Egan O C O N O R
O Devaney
O Kirwan
O Mullally
D O N Mc Geraghty
Grow ney
Jennings Tuam
O Divilly
O Mannion
O Finaghy
Mc Carron
Callanan
Mc Hugh
O Moran
O F L A H E R T Y
Mc Henry
McRedmond
(Burke)
K E L L Y
O Concannon
Mc Dockery
Mc Glyn
Dillon
Athlone
O Feeney
O Mulready
Mc Meaghlin
G
Mc Conry
(King)
O Faherty
W
O Lyne
(Lyons)
A
Mc Egan
Mc Keogh
Furey Mc Auley
O Casey
Mc
O Canavan
Tribes
of
Galway
O Dally
O Haverty
O Touhy
L
L
E
Y
O Murray
O Carberry
C
O Donnell
Mc Kilduff
O Fallon
Mc Aneave
(Forde)
O Halloran
O Daly
Ballinasloe
O Mulkerran
O Breen
O Naughton
O Malone
Tulla
Mc Kilkelly
Bermingham
Mc Ward
O Donnellan
Mc Coghlan
O Rigney
Galway
O Ruane
O Coffey
O Flattery
O Mohan
(Mahon)
O Kenny
O Larkin
Mc Coolahan
C
O Fahy
Mc Kowge
M A D D E N
O Horan
Mc Colgan
O M
B
U
R
K
E
LO Downe
O Drennan
O Tracy
O Dullehanty
(Delahanty)
O Hok
O Heyne
Mc Egan
O Cahill
O Cunnegan
O Larkin
(Delahanty)
Bro Flanagan
Mc N
O Daly O Divily (Deeley)
O Doorly
O Gormican

O Kernaghan
Mc Sweeney
O Toner
O Breslin
O Laverty
O Mulhall
O Doherty
O Harkan
O Dever
O Shiel
Mc Devitt
O Dermond
Mc Gilligan
Coleraine
O Mullan
Mc Quillan
Ballycastle
O Hara
Mc Donnell
O Quinn
Mc Cleary
O Connor
Mc Closky
O Deery
Mc Colgan
Londonderry
O Carolan
O Mulvenna
DERRY
Mc Crilly
O Dimond
ANTRIM
Mc Neill
Mc Keown
Ballymena
Mc Cracken
Mc Alister
Strabane
O Quinney
O Hegarty
O Mellan
Mc Rory
O Corr
O Mulhollan
O Kelly
Antrim
O Neill
Bangor
Belfast
Mc Gee
Mulcreevy
Mc Gilmore
Savage
Lynn
Linchy (Lynch)
Lisburn
O Lavery
Mc Murray
White
Mc Keelaghan
Mc Cann
Mc Sherry
O Heron
O Devaney
O Garvey
Mc Donegan
Mc Cartan
O Rooney
Mc Dutlevy
Mc Govern (Magennis)
O Mulcreevy
Mc Alinden
Newry
O Hoey
O Gowan

DOWN

MEATH

Dublin

Miles
0   10   20   30
0   10   20   30   40   50
Kilometres

53

Miles
0   10   20   30

0   10   20   30   40   50
Kilometres

RURAL IRELAND *Bringing in the hay*

AHERNE

THE territory of the Ó hEachthighearna sept was in south-eastern Clare, in the Barony of Bunratty Lower, around Sixmilebridge, whence at the end of the Gaelic period they moved southwards into County Limerick and County Cork where this surname is now principally found.

AHERNE *Cottage at Sixmilebridge, Co. Clare*

ALEXANDER

FAMILIES of this name are found principally in Ulster and in particular in the south-east of the province in the counties of Down and Antrim where settlers of the name came from Scotland in the 17th century. A number of persons bearing this surname are descendants of the Reverend Andrew Alexander, a Presbyterian minister from Scotland who came to Ulster in 1618.

ALLEN

THIS surname, among the fifty commonest in both England and Scotland, is now widespread in Ireland where it was brought by settlers. It is found in all four provinces but much more frequently in Ulster.

ANDERSON

THIS common Scottish and northern English surname is also common in Ulster, where settlers of the name came with the 17th-century plantation schemes. Families of the name were established, in lesser numbers, at least since the last century, in the other three provinces.

ARCHBOLD

Persons of this name (a varient of Archibald) from England or Scotland settled in the Pale in the medieval period. Their descendants are still to be found concentrated in the Dublin area and around what were the southern extremities of the Pale.

ARMSTRONG

FAMILIES bearing this Scottish or northern English surname are to be found principally in Ulster where settlers of the name established themselves in the 17th century, mainly in the counties of Fermanagh, Tyrone and Cavan. Dr. MacLysaght reported that it was borne also by members of the Lavery family (q.v.) as a mistranslation of their Irish sept name.

ARTHUR

THIS is one of the very few surnames in Ireland of Norse origin, brought by Viking settlers before the Norman conquest. Families of the name are now scattered, but some still live in the Limerick area where the Arthur family was prominent in the medieval period. The arms of the Limerick Arthurs are: Gules, a chevron argent between three clarions or.

AYLWARD

FAMILIES of this name, living mostly in Waterford and in the south-eastern part of Co. Kilkenny, still reside in the region where their ancestors settled in the wake of the Anglo-Norman conquest of Ireland. Their ancient seat was the townland named Aylwardstown in the parish of Kilmakevoge, Barony of Ida, County Kilkenny. The Aylward arms are: a Fleur-de-lis between two estoiles of six points in dexter bend, and as many increscents in sinister bend or.

BAGNALL

PERSONS of this name are still living principally in Leinster where Bagenalstown (now Muine Bheag) in the Barony of Idrone East, Co. Carlow, commemorates an early area of settlement of the family which descends from Sir

BAGNALL *The Mill, Bagenalstown (now Muine Bheag)*

Nicholas Bagenal, who came from Staffordshire and was Marshal of the Army in Ireland in the reign of Elizabeth I. In the 19th century the surname was mostly confined to Co. Offaly but Bagnalls are now established also in Dublin and in Co. Kildare.

BANNON

ONE sept named Ó Banáin had its territory in Co. Tipperary where families named Bannon still

reside; another Ó Banáin sept was from Co. Fermanagh. The name Bannon is also found in Co. Westmeath where a branch of the family bore the arms: Vert, an Irish wolfhound courant argent between three trefoils slipped or.

BARR

Now a fairly common name in Ulster, particularly in the counties of Donegal and Derry, this surname is of English or Scottish origin.

BARRETT

FAMILIES of this name came to Ireland with the Anglo-Norman invasion. It is said that those who settled in Co. Cork were originally Barratt, while the Connacht settlers were always Barrett; but the name is now usually spelt Barrett everywhere in Ireland. In Cork, where the name is still found most frequently, the family established themselves in what became the Barony of Barretts, whence they spread out into the counties of Kerry and Limerick. The Connacht Barretts held the territory of Tirawley in north-western Mayo where, Gaelicized, they formed themselves into a sept with a chief like the indigenous inhabitants. Their descendants still live in Co. Mayo and Co.

59

Galway but are not nearly so numerous as the Munster family.

BARRETT *Port-na-hally Bay – Achill Island, Co. Mayo*

BARRON

PERSONS of this name in Ulster will mostly descend from the MacBarrons, a branch of the O'Neills, although some may have their origin in settlers of the name from Scotland. The southern families of Barron, mostly established in Co. Waterford and Co. Wexford, are of Anglo-Norman origin, being in reality Fitzgeralds, descended from a branch of that family who were barons of Burnchurch in Co. Kilkenny and who assumed Baron (Barron) as their surname.

BARRY

THIS is now one of the hundred commonest surnames in Ireland and can be found in all the four provinces but overwhelmingly within Munster and still mainly in Co. Cork where, about 1183, the first of the name came to Ireland from Wales. This Philip de Barri, received a grant of three cantreds. He was connected, through his mother, to the principal Anglo-Norman conquerors of Ireland; his brother, Gerald, is better remembered as Giraldus Cambrensis, the historian of the invasion. Branches of Philip's descendants formed septs according to the ancient Irish tradition, two of them being established in the baronies of Barrymore and Barryroe in Co. Cork.

BARRY *Entrance gates, Fota House, with the motto of the Barry family whose home it was*

BEATTY

THIS is a Scottish surname, principally found in Ulster where it is often also spelt Beattie. Dr. MacLysaght has pointed out that families of the name in other parts of Ireland might, in some cases, descend from old Irish stock named Betagh (Biadhtach).

BEGLEY

FAMILIES of this name still live in Co. Donegal, the ancient home of the Ó Beaglaoich sept, and in Co. Kerry where Begleys from Donegal went as mercenaries in the 15th century and settled and spread into Co. Limerick.

BEHAN

THIS Leinster sept is still to be found mainly in that province today, in Dublin and in Co. Kildare. Families of the name in Co. Kerry are presumably of the same origin.

BEIRNE

EASILY confused with Byrne and O'Byrne, the surname Beirne and O'Beirne is of entirely different origin, being a Connacht sept with branches in Co. Roscommon, still a principal habitat of the family, and in Co. Mayo. Later, families of the name spread into Co. Leitrim where the name is still found also. By the end of the last century the majority of persons of this name had lost the prefix O', but now, many of them have reassumed it.

BELL

ONE of the hundred commonest surnames in Ireland and principally found in Ulster where it was brought by settlers from Scotland, where it is among the fifty commonest surnames, and northern England, in the 17th century. Outside of Ulster it is most prevalent, not surprisingly, in Co. Louth.

BERGIN

THE ancient territory of the O'Bergins was the Barony of Geashill in Co. Offaly whence they spread south and west into Co. Leix and Co. Tipperary where most of the families of this name still live. This surname is one of those now rarely, if ever, found with its original prefix O'. Berrigan is a variant.

BERMINGHAM

Now distributed fairly widely in Leinster and Munster, less frequent in Connacht, where one branch of the de Berminghams were Lords of Athenry, families of this name are of Anglo-Norman descent.

BLAIR

SETTLERS from Scotland were the ancestors of the Blair families, now fairly numerous in Ulster where they are to be found in most of the nine counties of the province but most frequently in Co. Antrim.

BLACK

This surname, common in Ulster where it is widely distributed, was brought by settlers from Scotland and the north of England.

BLAKE

ONE of the so-called 'Tribes of Galway' the Blakes were prominent in that city since the 14th century and were landowners in many parts of the county. Their ancestral name was originally Caddell, of Welsh origin, but was supplanted by Blake, first used as an alias by their common ancestor Richard Caddell alias Niger (or Blake) who was Sheriff of Connacht in 1303 and owned an estate in the Barony of Dunkellin. The Blakes in Co. Kildare, where there are three Blakestowns, also descend from the Galway Blakes.

BLENNERHASSET

AN English settler from Flimby in Cumberland who came to Co. Kerry in the reign of Elizabeth I with the Munster Plantation of the forfeited Desmond estates, brought this name to Kerry where it is still to be found, especially in the neighbourhood of Tralee. The Registrar of Births reported in the last century that Hassett and Blennerhasset were used interchangeably by some families in Co. Kerry. The Blennerhasset coat of arms is: Gules, a chevron ermine, between three dolphins, embowed, argent.

BOHAN

THIS surname which seems to have now completely lost its suffix, O', is found today in all four provinces but its main concentration used to be in Connacht in Co. Leitrim and Co. Galway. The variant Bohane was confined to Cork where it is still found.

BOLAND

ANOTHER surname which has lost its prefix, O', the name Ó Beollain was formerly rendered O'Bolan, but is now always found spelt with a final 'd' and is widely distributed. The Munster Bolands come from the O'Bolans whose territory was on the banks of Lough Derg, in the Barony of Clonderalaw, Co. Clare; this sept claimed descent from a brother of Brian Boru. The seat of the Connacht sept of O'Bolans was at Doonaltan in the Barony of Tireragh, Co. Sligo. In the same county, O'Bolans were erenaghs of the Church of St. Columban at Drumcliff in the Barony of Carbury. The name is now also found frequently in Leinster where it was already established in Co. Offaly by the 17th century.

BOLGER

UNTIL recent years this surname was rare outside Leinster where it was found principally in Co. Wexford. It is still to be found predominantly in that county and is concentrated around Graiguenamanagh in the region where the counties of Carlow, Kilkenny and Wexford meet.

BONAR

THE name of this Co. Donegal family, found principally in the neighbourhood of Ballybofey and Stranorlar, is a pseudo-translation of the Irish Ó Cnaimhsighe, also anglicized as Crampsy, which is also found in Co. Donegal.

BOWE

THIS surname, formerly found mostly in Co.

Kilkenny but now also farther south in Waterford, is an anglicized form of the Irish Ó Buadhaigh.

BOWLER

SEEMINGLY of English origin this surname was, until recently, found exclusively in Co. Kerry, where the majority of families of the name still live, and where it has been established for a very long time, giving its name to the townlands of Ballybowler North and Ballybowler South in the Barony of Corkaguiny.

BOYD

THIS is a Scottish surname, common in Ulster, whence it was introduced by settlers from Scotland in the 17th century.

BOYLAN

THE O'Boylan sept came from Oriel, having their principal stronghold in the barony of Dartry, Co. Monaghan. They soon spread to reach eastern Co. Fermanagh across Co. Monaghan and southern Co. Armagh into the northern part of Co. Louth. They also established themselves to the south of their original territory, in Co. Cavan and Co. Meath. The name is still found most frequently in those areas but invariably without the prefix O'.

BOYLE

THE majority of families of this name in Ireland descend from the Irish sept, Ó Baoighill, whose territory was in southern Co. Donegal whence they spread out, but the name is still most prevalent in Ulster. In recent years a number of families have reassumed their abandoned prefix O' but

BOYLE *The town wall and gate of Youghal, Co. Cork, once the estate of the Earls of Cork* frequently soggy and the best results were not obtained. Much of the bogland waited until recent years to be reclaimed but rape was grown quite extensively on boggy soil where it thrived.

The Royal Canal, which linked Co. Longford by water with the markets and ports of Dublin and Drogheda, was a great advantage to the area after its completion, providing facilities for transporting produce to the ports. Of the agricultural pursuits in the county the most notable was pig fattening; the bacon cured in Longford, and the pork, were exported to England. The standard of living of the ordinary people of Co. Longford was deemed by an early 19th century observer to be better than in many other parts of Ireland, meat, fowl and freshwater fish being abundant and moderately priced in the markets. The small farmers rarely ate meat, their staple diet being potatoes, and some who raised pigs never tasted their own produce, being obliged by necessity to sell it all. Nevertheless, this observer found the people, on the whole, to be healthy and robust, and given to sports such as hurling, wrestling and football, as well as dancing, which was the chief Sunday amusement.

COUNTY LOUTH

THE Leinster maritime county of Louth on the eastern seaboard of Ireland is the smallest county in the island. It is bounded on the north by Carlingford Bay, which separates it from Co. Down in Ulster, and by the Ulster county of Armagh, on the west by the Ulster county of Monaghan and also on the west and on the south by Co. Meath. By far the greatest part of the land in the county is good, a very small proportion having remained unimproved or uncultivable. Curiously, like many of the more fertile counties, the population growth in the first forty years of the 19th century was much less than in the very underprivileged areas where the population explosion contributed greatly to the awful misery wreaked by the famine of the 1840's.

Although Co. Louth was not infrequently overrun by Irish chieftains and their followers from the 13th to the 16th centuries, it was mainly influenced by its situation within the Pale, and by the importance of the mercantile town of Drogheda, with its sea-port which is the chief town of the county. Carlingford and Dundalk, like Drogheda, were also boroughs, market-towns and sea-ports, although of lesser importance. There were two other boroughs in the county, Dunleer and Ardee. Each of these boroughs sent two members up to the Irish parliament and two were sent also by the county at large.

A great proportion of the land in the county was under pasture. Wheat, flax and barley were grown in large quantities also, the flax being supplied in the last century to the industrial towns of Leeds and Bolton in England for spinning. The existence of the eastern seaboard ports in the county greatly facilitated the export

LOUTH *The ruins of 13th century Castleroche*

of its produce while residents in the north of the county could also use Newry for that purpose. The towns also provided employment; Dundalk had a pin factory established in 1836 which

33

employed a work force of six hundred persons within one year of its foundation, also an iron and brass foundry, breweries and distilleries. Drogheda, situated at the mouth of the River Boyne which divides the town, had places of manufacture of coarse linen and calico, a mill for spinning flax, a tannery, soap and candle factories, two iron foundries, salt-works, a distillery, three breweries, flour and corn mills, and a very busy port.

The commonest surnames in Co. Louth in descending numerical order are Byrne and O'Byrne, Kelly and O'Kelly, Murphy, Smith, Clarke, Duffy, McArdle, Reilly and O'Reilly, Carroll and O'Carroll, Mathews, Martin, Donnelly, Farrell and O'Farrell, Morgan, Rice, Hanratty, McCourt, McKenna, Boyle, Connor and O'Connor, Lynch and O'Hare. The English or Welsh surnames Smith, Clarke, Mathews, Morgan, Rice, Boyle and Lynch are all known to have been adopted also by Irish families, respectively Ó Gabhann and Mac Gabhann, Ó Cleirigh, Mac Mathghamhna, Ó Moghrain, Ó Maolchraoibhe, Ó Baoighill and Ó Loingsigh, as well as being borne by descendants of immigrants from across the Irish Sea.

COUNTY MAYO

THE maritime Connacht county of Mayo is bounded on the north and west by the Atlantic, on the south by Co. Galway, on the east by Co. Sligo and Co. Roscommon. According to the Ordnance Survey reports made in the decade prior to the famine years of the 1840's, about one-third of the land in the county, over 400,000 acres, was unprofitable mountain and bog; a further 57,000 acres were under water. The appearance of the county varies from tracts of bleak, rugged mountains to lakeland, heath, flat rocky ground, bogland and fertile plains. Clew Bay, dotted with drumlin islets, is remarkable

MAYO *The bridge at Burrishoole*

the name is much more frequently found without the prefix. Of quite distinct ancestry are the descendants of the English adventurer Richard Boyle and of other members of his family who followed him to Ireland at the close of the 16th century. This Boyle, who became Earl of Cork, acquired vast estates in Co. Cork and western Co. Waterford. Settlers from Renfrewshire in Scotland also brought the name Boyle to Co. Derry with the 17th century plantation of Ulster.

BRACKEN

THIS family descend from the sept Ó Breacáin which was established in the area between Edenderry and Rathangan around what is now the border of Co. Offaly and Co. Kildare. The surname, invariably without the O', is now scattered in various parts of the country but some Brackens still survive in the neighbourhood of their early territory, and particularly around Tullamore, Co. Offaly.

BRADLEY

THIS common English surname is now widely distributed throughout Ireland although it is found most frequently in Ulster. While some Bradley families will be descendants of English settlers many Irish Bradleys will descend from the sept, Ó Brollacháin, whose name was anglicized both as O'Brallaghan (a form which has disappeared) and Bradley. The sept was seated near the borders of Co. Tyrone, Co. Donegal and Co. Derry whence a branch emigrated southwards and established itself in Co. Cork.

BRADSHAW

THIS common English surname, brought to Ireland by settlers from England, mostly in the 17th century, is now found in all four provinces, but predominantly in Ulster. In the south, outside Dublin, it is found most often in Co. Tipperary.

BRADY

AMONG the hundred commonest surnames in Ireland, Brady, formerly Mac Brady, but now usual without the prefix, is mostly heavily distributed in Ulster and Leinster. The territory of the MacBradaigh sept was in eastern Breffny, in the eastern part of the Barony of Loughter Upper, Co. Cavan, close to Lough Oughter, and there is still a heavy concentration of Bradys in

Co. Cavan. Dr. MacLysaght has noted that the Brady families in Munster mostly descend from O'Gradys of Co. Clare who, for some reason, adopted the surname Brady in lieu of O'Grady in the 16th century.

BRANNIGAN

PERSONS named Branigan and Brannigan are now to be found mainly in and around Drogheda, Co. Louth, whence a number have moved south to Dublin. The name is also now established in Co. Kilkenny whence, presumably, some of this family came from their home further north. The territory of the Ó Branagáin sept was, in fact, the area where the counties of Louth, Monaghan and Armagh meet.

BREEN

AT the beginning of this century Breens were to be found in the majority in Leinster, in lesser but roughly equal numbers in Munster and Ulster, not at all in Connacht. Some descend from the sept Mac Braoin, whose seat was in the Barony of Knocktopher, Co. Kilkenny, whence they were dispersed after the Anglo-Norman invasion; many seem to have settled in Co. Wexford where the name is still prevalent although it is now widely distributed elsewhere also. Breens not of the MacBreen stock would descend from the sept O'Braoin, whose territory was the Barony of Brawny in Co. Westmeath.

BREHENY

A Connacht family, confined exclusively to that province at the beginning of this century, the Brehenys still reside mostly in the counties of Sligo, Roscommon and Galway.

BRENNAN

NOT surprisingly, this surname is among the fifty commonest in Ireland as it is borne by the descendants of six distinct septs, four of which were Ó Braonáin, one Ó Branáin, and one Mac Branáin. The name is now widely distributed in all four provinces but as always, is still found predominantly in Leinster where the principal sept of Ó Braonáin once held a territory called Idough, a vaguely defined hilly area in the north of Co. Kilkenny. Carrigan, the Ossory diocesan historian, identified Idough with the rural deanery of Odagh, comprising 21 parishes, the greater portion of which was described in the 16th century as the Barony of Fassadinin and Idough. These O'Brennans were, themselves, divided into four septs by the 17th century, each with its own sept centre. The other distinct Ó Braonáin septs held territories in east Co. Galway, Co. Kerry and Co. Westmeath. The Ó Branáin sept originated in Co. Fermanagh. Descendants of those septs have usually abandoned their prefix O' although a small minority has retained or reassumed it, while the descendants of the Mac Branáin sept, whose territory was in eastern Co. Roscommon, have entirely lost their prefix Mac.

BRESLIN

DESCENDANTS of the brehon family called Ó Brisleáin, none of whom seem to have reassumed the prefix O', still reside mostly in Co. Donegal, a region with which they have always been associated.

BRIEN See O'BRIEN

BRIODY

FAMILIES of this name, now invariably in use without the prefix O', were long established in northern Co. Longford and western Co. Cavan whence they have spread out also into Co. Westmeath.

BRODER

IT has been suggested that this family could be of Norse origin but Dr. MacLysaght has pointed out that their name was Ó Bruadair and Mac Bruadair, and that while Bruadar was a common Scandinavian name it was also recorded in Ireland before the Viking invasions. At the beginning of this century Broder families were found mostly in Co. Kerry and Co. Limerick, presumably descendants of the Ó Bruadair sept anciently situated in the Barony of Barrymore, Co. Cork. It has been used interchangeably with Broderick and Brothers.

BRODERICK

WHILE some Broderick families may be descendants of settlers with the Welsh patronymic surname Broderick (Ap-Roderick) there is evidence that most Irish Brodericks are descended from Ó Bruadair septs, once established in Co. Cork, Co. Kilkenny, and Co. Galway, the anglicized form of their name, Broder (q.v.) having undergone a further curious anglicization in being changed to Broderick, now much more common than Broder, and more widespread.

BROGAN

DESCENDANTS of the northern Connacht sept, Ó Brogáin, settled in Co. Mayo and farther north in Co. Donegal where they were mostly congregated at the end of the last century, since which time there has been a general dispersal although the name is still well represented in those two counties. None of the branches of the Brogans appear to have reassumed the prefix O'.

BROPHY

Descendants of the Leinster sept O Bróithe, whose territory was in Co. Leix, are still to be found mostly in mid-Leinster and southern Leinster, especially in Co. Carlow and Co. Kilkenny. This is yet another name where the prefix O' has been abandoned.

BROSNAN

THIS family was established in Co. Kerry, the only county where the name was found at the end of the last century. Some Brosnans have since settled in the capital and in other counties but the great majority are yet to be found in Co. Kerry. Some who settled in Co. Limerick have adopted the variant spelling, Brosnahan. Other spelling variations resulted in Bresnan which seems to have been preferred by those who settled in Co. Cork, and Bresnahan.

BROWN(E)

SETTLERS from England and Scotland brought over to Ireland the name Brown(e). Among the ten commonest surnames in England and among the five commonest in Scotland it now ranks among the fifty most common surnames in Ireland. The first to bring the name over were Anglo-Normans (Le Brun) who established themselves in Galway where they left descendants. The English family of Browne which settled in Co. Kerry in the reign of Elizabeth I also has a large progeny. Others of the name came to Ireland in the 17th century including Scottish Browns who established themselves in Ulster, the province where this surname is still most frequent.

BRUNTY *See PRUNTY*

BRYAN

WHILE Bryan was occasionally and confusedly adopted by descendants of the O'Briens, it is the distinct surname of a Leinster family of Anglo-Norman descent long established in that province and particularly in Co. Kilkenny.

BUCKLEY

AT the end of tha last century the vast majority of the numerous families of this name in Ireland was concentrated in the province of Munster and today, although Buckley is one of the hundred commonest surnames in the country it is still to be found predominantly in Co. Cork and Co. Kerry. Buckley is an anglicization of the Irish Ó Buachalla.

BUGGY

IN use invariably without its prefix O', the surname Buggy belongs to Leinster where it is still found principally in Co. Kilkenny and Co. Leix, the region which has long been its home.

BURKE

WITH its variant spelling, Bourke, this surname, which now ranks as one of the twenty commonest in Ireland, was brought to Ireland with the Anglo-Norman conquest of the country. It is now distributed through all four provinces but is least numerous in Ulster and most numerous in Connacht where the family, then known by a Latin form of their name, de Burgo, obtained vast estates at the end of the 12th century. Burgh also survives as a version of this surname while some of the family reverted to de Burgh when it was fashionable to boast Norman ancestry.

BURKE *Entrance front of Portumna Castle, Co. Galway, built in the 17th century by the Burkes, Earls and later Marquesses of Clanricarde*

BURNS

THIS common Scottish surname is also common in Ulster where it was brought by settlers in the plantation schemes of the 17th century. In the other provinces, where it occurs less frequently, it often results from a corruption of the Irish Beirne or Byrne.

BUTLER

THIS surname, prominent in Irish history, can be traced back to the appointment of Theobald FitzWalter, one of the Anglo-Norman invaders, as Hereditary Chief Butler of Ireland. His son, also Theobald, adopted the surname le Botiler or Butler and it became the family surname of his descendants. The first Theobald acquired the baronies of Ormond Upper and Ormond Lower in Co. Tipperary; his descendants extended the family possessions in that county and in Co. Kilkenny where the largest of the Butler castles eventually became the seat of the head of the family but there were numerous other Butler strongholds, among them the great medieval castle at Cahir, Nenagh Castle, Kiltinan Castle, Kilcash Castle, Roscrea Castle, Terryglass Castle, and the castle at Carrick-on-Suir, all in Co. Tipperary. Now most frequently found in Leinster and Munster, the name Butler is borne by several thousand persons in Ireland, a number of whom still live in close proximity to the medieval seats of the family.

BYRNE

BYRNE and O'Byrne (both forms are in use) is one of the ten commonest surnames in Ireland, borne by about one percent of the population of the Republic. The ancient territory of the O'Byrnes was in Co. Kildare but as the Anglo-Normans extended the Pale they were displaced and found a new home in the hills of southern Co. Wicklow with the sept centre at Ballinacor in the barony of Ballinacor South. Dublin and Co. Wicklow account for the largest number of Byrnes and O'Byrnes today and there is still a substantial representation of the name in Ballinacor South barony, in and around Aughrim and Tinahely.

CADOGAN

IN Ireland this surname with its variant spelling Cadigan is distinct from the Welsh surname Cadogan which was brought over by settlers. The Irish family was a sept, Ó Ceadagáin, in Co. Cork, to which county the name was still confined at the end of the last century; and where most persons of the name still live, particularly in the area around Skibbereen, barony of West Carbury.

CAFFERKY See McCAFFERTY

BUTLER *Kilcooly Abbey, Co. Tipperary, with the tomb of Piers Fitz Oge Butler*

CAFFREY *See McCAFFREY*

CAHALANE

THIS Munster surname, in Irish Ó Cathaláin, is one of the many that has lost its prefix O'. Several variant spellings have been noted in the past of which Cahalan has survived (favoured by families in the north of Co. Tipperary around Ballinderry) and Cahillane. Births of Cahalanes and variant spellings were reported in the last century in Co. Cork and Co. Kerry. While the name has not vanished entirely in Co. Kerry it is now found mostly in Co. Cork and prevalently in the west of that county.

CAHILL

ONE O'Cahill sept held territory in the barony of Eliogarty, Co. Tipperary, where two townlands named Ballycahill commemorate their presence. A more powerful O'Cahill sept once held sway in southern Galway. Ballycahill, near the southern shore of Galway Bay, in the barony of Burren, Co. Clare, and Ballycahill, near Portumna in Longford barony, Co. Galway, may have been seats of that sept or of distinct septs of the name. Yet another O'Cahill sept was anciently situated in the barony of Magunihy, Co. Kerry. It is, therefore, not surprising that the surname Cahill, invariably in use without the

CAHILL *The Burren, Co. Clare*

prefix O', has a wide distribution; it is most prevalent in Munster.

CAIRNS

THIS Scottish surname was introduced into Ulster, and particularly to its south-eastern counties of Antrim, Down and Armagh, by settlers from Scotland in the 17th century. Some families in Ireland named Cairns adopted this spelling for the surname more usually spelt Kearns, which is of Irish origin, deriving from Ó Ciaráin, Ó Ceirin, Kieran.

CALDERWOOD

THIS Scottish surname was brought over in the 17th century to Ulster where it is most prevalent in Co. Antrim. Catherwood, also established in Co. Antrim, is a variant of this surname.

CALDWELL

THIS Scottish surname was brought to Ulster by settlers in the 17th century and its distribution is still largest in that province. Dr. MacLysaght has noted that in Co. Tyrone, where it is found, it has also been used as an anglicization of an Irish name Ó hUarghuis or Ó hUairisee, and that in Co. Cavan it was also used as an anglicization of the Irish MacConluain.

CALLAGHAN See O'CALLAGHAN

CALLAN

THE Ó Cathaláin sept belonged to Oriel and their descendants are still to be found in the region of that ancient territory, in Co. Louth and in Co. Monaghan.

CALLANAN

THIS surname with its variant spelling, Callinan, is found principally in south-west Munster among descendants of the sept, Ó Callanáin. It is also found in Co. Galway among descendants of an erenagh family of the same name in that county.

CAMPBELL

ONE of the ten commonest surnames in Scotland, Campbell was brought to Ulster first by galloglass and later, in much larger numbers, by settlers in the 17th century plantation schemes. It is now among the fifty commonest surnames in Ireland. Dr. MacLysaght has noted that some of this name may be of ancient Irish origin, however, descended from a Co. Tyrone sept

that bore the name Mac Cathmhaoil.

CANAVAN

THE O'Canavans were the hereditary physicians of the O'Flahertys in Connemara where the surname survives, without its prefix O', in the neighbourhood of Clifden as well as elsewhere in Co. Galway.

CANNING

ENGLISH settlers from Warwickshire brought this surname to Co. Derry, where the name survives, early in the 17th century. They can hardly account for all the Cannings to be found today also in the other three provinces. Many of these, and particularly those in Co. Donegal and Co. Leitrim, may descend from members of the Ó Canáin sept from Co. Donegal who adopted the anglicization Canning rather than the more usual Cannon.

CANNON

THE distribution of this surname is heaviest in Co. Donegal where descendants of the Ó Cananáin or Ó Canáin sept of that county adopted it as an anglicization of their Irish name, and in Co. Galway where descendants of the sept Ó Canáin, whose territory was in the southern part of that county, took the same uncommon surname in English but some families of the name in Ireland could be of settler descent.

CANTWELL

THIS name, originally de Kentwell, was brought to Ireland with the Anglo-Norman invaders and established in Co. Kilkenny. Eight centuries later families of the name are still to be found today in that county and in the adjacent counties of Tipperary and Waterford as well as a good number settled in the capital.

CARBERRY

FAMILIES named Carberry or Carbery may descend from one or the other of two septs. It appears that the majority today derive from the sept Ó Cairbre whose territory was in the barony of Clonlonan, Co. Westmeath. The erenagh family of the name at Galloon, barony of Coole, Co. Fermanagh, belonged to that sept. The other sept, Mac Cairbre, had their centre in the Knockmealdown mountains of north-western Co. Waterford, at Ballymacarbry in the barony of Glenahiry.

CANTWELL *Tomb of an Anglo-Norman knight of the Cantwell family at Kilfane, Co. Kilkenny*

CAREW

THIS name is of Anglo-Norman origin. It is not clear at what date it was brought to Munster where, for several centuries, families of the name are recorded in Co. Waterford and Co. Cork. By the last century most of the Carew families in Ireland were living in Co. Tipperary which is still the county where the name is commonest. The Carew coat of arms is: Or, three lions passant sable.

CAREY

THIS surname is widely distributed throughout Ireland but is most prevalent in Munster. It can be of English origin, brought over by settlers, or it can be of Irish origin. Descendants of the sept Ó Ciardha, whose ancient territory was Carbury barony in Co. Kildare, adopted Carey and Keary as anglicized forms of their name. Dr. MacLysaght has noted that Irish surnames, Ó Céirin, Ó Ciaráin, Mac Giolla Céire, have

also been rendered in English as Carey. The Registrar of Births reported in the last century that in Caherciveen Union, Co. Kerry, Carey was used interchangeably with Curran.

CARLETON

THIS surname, in Ireland, with its variant spelling Carlton, can be of settler origin or of Irish origin having been used as an anglicization of Ó Cairealláin and Ó Cearbhalláin, which were more usually rendered O'Carolan, q.v.

CARLIN

THIS surname is found mostly in Co. Tyrone and Co. Derry where it is an anglicization of Ó Cairealláin, and Ó Cearbhalláin, the septs whose name was more usually rendered O'Carolan, q.v.

CARMODY

THIS surname has long been in Co. Clare, Co. Kerry and Co. Limerick, where it is still concentrated, being more prevalent now in the latter two counties.

CARNEY

DESCENDANTS of the O'Cearnaigh sept whose territory was in the barony of Carra, Co. Mayo, have adopted Carney as an anglicization of their name, and families of the name are still to be found today in the neighbourhood of Castlebar. However, the form Carney was also adopted sometimes rather than the much more frequent form Kearney (q.v.) by descendants of the Mac Carnaigh sept of Ballymacarney, barony of Dunboyne, Co. Meath, of the Ó Catharnaigh sept who once held sway in the barony of Kilcoursey, Co. Offaly, and of an Ó Cearnaigh sept anciently established at Cashel, Co. Tipperary.

CAROLAN

DESCENDANTS of both the Ó Cairealláin sept, whose seat was in the parish of Clondermot, barony of Tikeeran, Co. Derry, and of the Ó Cearbhalláin sept from Co. Cavan and Co. Monaghan, have adopted the surname Carolan. The heaviest distribution of this surname today outside of the capital is in western Co. Cavan around Kingscourt and Bailieborough in Clonkee barony and in the adjacent regions of Co. Meath, Co. Monaghan and Co. Louth. Occasionally it is now found in use with the original prefix O'.

CARR

FAMILIES of the name Carr, found in all four provinces, but predominantly in Ulster, are of diverse origins. Some descend from Scottish settlers named Kerr, one of the fifty commonest surnames in Scotland, who came to Ulster with the 17th century plantations. The Scottish Kerr being, in fact, pronounced Kar, was easily rendered as Carr. Other families will descend from English settlers named Carr. Still others, are of Irish origin, their ancestors having adopted the form Carr as an anglicization of an Irish name such as Ó Carraigh (more often rendered as Carry), Ó Maoilchéire (Mulcair), and of Mac Giolla Chathair in Co. Donegal, where the Registrar of Births noted in the last century that in Milford Union Carr was used interchangeably with McIlhair and in Donegal Union with McElhair.

CARRIGAN *See CORRIGAN*

CARROLL *Mill at Birr, Co. Offaly*

CARROLL

ALTHOUGH many families descended from Ó Cearbhaill septs now use the prefix O', the majority has not resumed the prefix. There were, anciently, several septs of the name and today their descendants are numerous; many thousands of Irish bear the name in Ireland and also many abroad in the Irish diaspora. The heaviest concentration of the name in Ireland has always been in Leinster where the sept who ruled Ely O'Carroll (which was partly in modern Co. Offaly) and the sept from Oriel (which comprised part of modern Co. Louth) must have a large descent. Some Carroll families, even some who have recently assumed the form O'Carroll, in fact descend from the Mac Cearbhaill sept from Ulster where, with its prefix, Mac Carroll has survived mainly in Co. Derry.

CARSON

THIS Scottish surname, found principally in Ulster where its heaviest distribution was in Co. Tyrone, was brought to the province by settlers in the 17th century.

CARTY

OCCURRING principally in Leinster and in Connacht, but found also in the other two provinces, Carty, deriving from Ó Carthaigh, became unavoidably confused with, and thus interchangeable with, the much commoner Carthy and McCarthy which are, in fact, Mac Carthaigh in Irish. Two distinct distributions of families named Carty may be noted, however, in areas not associated with McCarthys, one in Co. Wexford and one in Connacht.

CASEY

PREDOMINANTLY found in Munster but also found in considerable numbers in the other provinces, the surname Casey, sometimes in use with its prefix O', is borne by families descended from a number of unrelated Ó Cathasaigh septs. One of these septs held sway in the barony of Balrothery West, Co. Dublin, but was displaced in the Anglo-Norman settlement of the Pale and scattered. Another sept of the name was established in Co. Limerick with a sept centre near Bruff, another in the barony of Condons and Clangibbons in northern Co. Cork near the Co. Limerick border, and others in Connacht in Co. Mayo and in Co. Roscommon.

CASHIN

A few families of this name still live in Co. Leix the ancient home of the Mac Caisin family but the name is now fairly widely scattered through other parts of the country.

CASHMAN

THIS surname is found almost exclusively in Co. Cork where it was adopted as an anglicization of Ó Ciosáin which in the adjacent county of Kerry was rendered as Kissane, q.v.

CASSERLY

THE surname Casserly or Casserley, in Irish Mac Casarlaigh, was formerly most concentrated in Co. Roscommon but is now found also

CASSIDY

THIS surname is still commonest in Ulster where the Ó Caiside family were hereditary ollavs and physicians to the rulers of Fermanagh, the Maguires, who had their stronghold at Enniskillen in that county.

CATHERWOOD See CALDERWOOD

CAUGHEY See Mc CAUGHEY

CAULFIELD

CAULFIELD *The ruins of Castle Caulfield, Co. Tyrone*

73

THIS English surname was brought to Ireland in the 16th century from Oxfordshire, but Dr. MacLysaght has noted that it was also adopted as an anglicization of Irish surnames such as Mac Cathmhaoil (also rendered as Mac Call and as Campbell), Mac Gafraidh (usually rendered as Caffrey), Gaffney, and others. In the last century, the Registrar of Births reported that in Kilkeel Union, Co. Down, Caulfield was used interchangeably with McKeown, MacCavanagh and Kavanagh!

CAWLEY

A variant of Mc AULEY, q.v.

CHAMBERS

THIS surname, introduced by settlers from England, is found in all four provinces, but more prevalently in Ulster.

CHRISTIE

THIS Scottish surname was brought over by settlers in the 17th century to Ulster where it was established most prevalently in Co. Antrim.

CHERRY

THIS English surname was brought over by settlers in the 17th century to Ulster where it was established most prevalently in Co. Down.

CHRISTOPHER

THIS surname has been established in Co. Waterford since the 17th century; in the 17th century it was concentrated in the barony of Decies and is still found in Co. Waterford and the adjacent county of Cork.

CLANCY

THIS surname, which should have its prefix Mac, is Mac Fhlannchaidh in Irish. It is found today in small numbers as Mc Clancy, but as Clancy without the prefix it is widely distributed in all four provinces. One Mac Fhlannchaidh sept came from north Co. Clare where their sept centre was Cahermaclanchy in the barony of Corcomroe. Another sept of the name held the barony of Rosclogher in Co. Leitrim where their stronghold in the 16th century was a castle built on a crannóg in Lough Melvin.

CLARKE

ONE of the twenty commonest surnames in Scotland and among the thirty commonest in England, Clark, spelt with and without a final e, is now among the forty commonest surnames in Ireland. This is due largely to the fact that it was brought over by settlers in large numbers but also because some descendants of the Irish sept Ó Cleirigh adopted Clark as an anglicization of their name rather than Cleary, see below. This interchangeability of Clarke and Cleary was noted by the Registrar of Births in the last century in several districts, among them Tuam Union, Co. Galway, and Enniskillen Union, Co. Fermanagh. By far the heaviest distribution of Clarkes is in Ulster but even there families of the name will be of settler descent and also of

Henry Clarke, Duc de Feltre, a Napoleonic hero of Irish descent

Ó Cleirigh stock as a branch of that sept settled in Co. Donegal and Co. Derry and another settled in Co. Cavan when they left their homeland in Co. Galway. Similarly, while the second heaviest distribution of Clarkes is in Leinster where settler descent is also likely, it must be noted that a branch of the Ó Cleirigh sept settled in that province too, in Co. Kilkenny.

CLEARY

 THE Ó Cleirigh sept, from which present-day Cleary families descend, originally held sway in southern Co. Galway near the border of Co. Clare and close to Dun Guaire (Dungorey) the stronghold of the 7th century King of Connacht, Guaire the Hospitable, from whom they claimed lineal descent. Dispersed from their territory in the wake of the Anglo-Norman conquest, branches of the sept established themselves in western Ulster in Co. Donegal and Co. Derry, in southern Ulster, in Co. Cavan and in southern Leinster, in Co. Kilkenny.

CLIFFORD

SOME families of this name in Ireland may descend from settlers who brought it from England but in Co. Kerry, where it has been and is still found predominantly, it was used as an anglicization of the Irish, Ó Clúmháin. In the last century the Registrar of Births reported that in Dingle Union and Killarney Union, Clifford was used interchangeably with Cluvane, which it has now supplanted, although at least one family in Kerry has reassumed the Irish form Ó Clumháin.

CLOHERTY

THIS surname is still found mainly in Co. Galway which was its only home until the present century.

CLOHESSY

THIS surname is now found predominantly in Co. Limerick whence it was brought by descendants of the family (in Irish Ó Clochsaigh) from their home in southern Co. Clare at Ballycloghessy in the barony of Islands.

CLOONAN

THIS surname, in Irish Ó Cluanáin, belonged to Co. Galway where families of the name survive, others having settled in other parts of the country in recent times.

CLOSE

FAMILIES of this name in Ireland may be either descendants of an English family which came from Yorkshire to Co. Monaghan in the first half of the 17th century and then settled in Co. Antrim, or of Irish stock, their ancestors in the same area having adopted Close as an anglicization of their Irish name, Ó Clusaigh.

CLUNE

THIS surname is still found predominantly in Co. Clare and some of the name still live around Quin, close to the early home of the Mac Clúin family which was the townlands of East, North, and West Ballymacloon in Quin parish, Bunratty Upper barony.

COAKLEY

THE English surname Colclough, pronounced Colkly and eventually Coke-lee, was brought by a settler in the 16th century from Staffordshire to Co. Wexford where he was granted sequestrated monastic property at Tintern in 1565. Descendants of this family in Co. Wexford, and generally in Leinster, tended to retain the spelling Colclough although still pronouncing their name Coke-lee, while those who migrated westwards to establish themselves in Co. Cork, mostly found themselves recorded by the way their surname was pronounced. Their descendants have thus inherited their surname as Coakley. The commonness of this name in Co. Cork, however, is largely due to the fact that members of the family whose name in Irish was Mac Caochlaoich adopted Coakley as an anglicization of their name as well as Kehelly and Kehilly. The interchangeability of Coakley, Kehelly and Kehilly was noted by the Registrar of Births in the last century, in West Cork in Bandon Union and Dunmanway Union where Kehelly, Kehilly and Coakley have all survived to the present time.

COCHRANE

THIS Scottish surname is usually borne in Ireland by descendants of settlers from Scotland who brought it to Ulster in the 17th century. However, in the last century, the Registrar of

Births noted that Cochrane was used interchangeably with Corcoran, a name of Irish origin, in Newry Union, Co. Down, and Balrothery Union, Co. Dublin.

CODD

THIS English surname was brought by settlers to Co. Wexford at least as early as the century following the Anglo-Norman invasion and it is still predominantly found in that county today.

CODY

DESCENDANTS of the family named Archdeacon, which settled in Co. Kilkenny from England at least as early as the century following the Anglo-Norman conquest, adopted an Irish name, Mac Óda, which became Cody and Coady, a surname still found predominantly in southern Co. Kilkenny.

COEN

THIS surname in Ireland, also sometimes spelt as the Hebrew name Cohen, is found mostly in Connacht and particularly so still in Co. Galway and Co. Roscommon where it came into use as an anglicization of the Irish Ó Cadhain which was also rendered as Coyne and Kyne. In the last century the Registrar of Births reported the interchangeability in Banbridge Union, Co. Down, of Coen with Cowan, a surname which usually derives from the Irish Ó Comhdháin; but is also a Scottish surname brought to Ulster by settlers from Scotland.

COFFEY

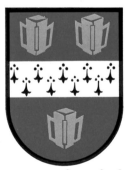

FAMILIES of this name, invariably in use without its prefix O', will descend from one of the Ó Cobhthaigh septs. One was from southwestern Co. Cork, another belonged to Co. Westmeath and another to Co. Roscommon; the first of these appears to have the largest progeny as Coffey families are most numerous in Munster.

COGAN

THIS surname can be a variant spelling of Coogan deriving from the Connacht sept Ó Cuagáin, it is found more frequently in the south

76

where families of the name may trace their ancestry to Anglo-Normans named de Cogan who settled in Co. Cork at the end of the 12th century. The name still survives in that county where some families now use the medieval form, de Cogan, having reassumed the particle, de, which had been lost.

COGHLAN

THIS surname derives either from the Mac Cochláin sept whose territory was the barony of Garrycastle, Co. Offaly, or from the Ó Cochláin sept from Co. Cork where their descendants are numerous, usually now preferring the spelling Coughlan.

COLCLOUGH See COAKLEY

COLEMAN

As Coleman is an English surname, some who bear this surname in Ireland may descend from settlers but most will descend from the Irish sept, Ó Colmáin which was located in Co. Sligo. However, the surname spelt both Colman and Coleman, is twice as prevalent in Munster as in Connacht which may be accounted for by the fact that while Clifford was adopted in Co. Kerry instead of Cluvane by descendants of the Ó Clúmháin family, many descendants of this family in Co. Cork took the name Coleman.

COLGAN

FAMILIES of this name may descend either from the sept Ó Colgan (which was later known also as Mac Colgan) from the barony of Tirkeeran, Co. Derry, whence they spread into the Inishowen peninsula of Co. Donegal, or from the Mac Colgan sept who were established in the barony of Garrycastle, Co. Offaly. The townlands of Kilcolgan Beg and Kilcolgan Mór in the north of that barony near the present border of Co. Westmeath, commemorate their sept centre and families of the name still survive nearby in Co. Offaly in the neighbourhood of Tullamore.

COLL

THIS surname is most numerous in Ulster and particularly in Co. Donegal where it derives from the name of the gallowglass family, Mac Colla. The name Coll has also been established for centuries in Co. Limerick where its origin is, however, uncertain and where it survives only in small numbers.

COLLINS

THIS is yet another common English surname borne in Ireland both by descendants of settlers and to a greater extent by descendants of Irish families who adopted it as an anglicization of their Irish surname, which accounts for it now being among the fifty commonest surnames in Ireland. It is over three to four times as prevalent in Munster as in the other provinces because it was adopted by descendants of the Ó Coileáin sept from Co. Limerick and of the Ó Cuilleáin sept from Co. Cork.

COMERFORD

THIS surname was brought from England early in the 13th century by settlers who established themselves in Co. Kilkenny; the principal representation of the name is still in that county and in Dublin.

CONATY

THIS surname, which derives from the Irish Ó Connachtaigh, is found predominantly in its old homeland, Co. Cavan.

CONBOY

DESCENDANTS of the Connacht sept Ó Conbhuidhe bearing the name Conboy survive in that province, thinly scattered through Co. Galway, Co. Sligo, Co. Mayo and Co. Roscommon.

CONCANNON

THE territory of the Ó Concheannáinn sept was in the parish of Kilkerrin, barony of Tiaquin, Co. Galway. For centuries their descendants remained in that neighbourhood and today (apart from a number of Concannon families who have migrated to the capital) the name is still found predominantly in Co. Galway.

CONDON

THIS family which actually only arrived in Ireland with the Anglo-Norman invasion became a sept according to Irish custom. They held the barony of Condons in northern Co. Cork, close to the Limerick and Tipperary county borders. The name is found today predominantly in those three counties.

CONDRON

THIS surname is borne by descendants of a Co. Offaly sept Ó Conaráin. Some of the name are still living in that county whence the family spread into adjacent counties. The variant spelling Conran is in use and presumably the Condren families now living in Co. Wexford also share the same ancestry.

CONEFREY

THIS Co. Leitrim family name derives from the Irish Mac Confraoich.

CONLON

THE surname Conlon and the less numerous variant Conlan, both found in all four provinces, derive from the Ó Conalláin and Ó Coinghiolláin which are occasionally also rendered as Connellan.

CONNAUGHTON

FROM the Connacht sept Ó Connachtáin descend the families named Connaughton of Co. Galway and Co. Roscommon. Some are still living in Co. Galway but the dispersals of persons of this name over the last hundred years have resulted in its appearance in several other parts of the country.

CONNEELY

THIS Co. Galway surname derives from the Irish Mac Conghaile. It was exclusively a Co. Galway name and is still rarely found outside that county.

CONNELL

See O'CONNELL and McCONNELL

CONNERY

THIS Munster surname, found predominantly in Co. Limerick and now with a particular concentration in Kilmallock barony, derives from the Irish Ó Conaire but has confusedly been used interchangeably both with Conry (q.v. and Conroy (q.v.).

CONNOLLY

THIS surname, among the thirty commonest in Ireland, is most heavily distributed in Ulster and in approximately equal numbers in the other three provinces. This distribution tallies with its derivation from three different septs, Ó Conghalaigh from Connacht, Ó Conghaile which was established in Ulster in Co. Monaghan, and Ó Coingheallaigh from West Cork in Munster.

after the Williamite victory in the War of the Two Kings at the end of the 17th century and the establishment of Protestant ascendancy. Of humble background, his father was a blacksmith or a publican, he or his parents became Protestants and due to his acumen and extraordinary intelligence, after success at the bar he soared to power, serving ten times as a Lord Justice between 1716 and 1729, was chief commissioner of the Irish Revenue 1709–10 and 1714–1729 and Speaker of the Irish House of Commons 1715–1729. He commissioned the building of Ireland's greatest mansion, Castletown, at Celbridge, Co. Kildare, and left, at his death, a very considerable fortune. The Rt. Hon. William Conolly, M.P., his nephew, was his heir.

CONNOR *See O'CONNOR*

CONROY

THIS surname should be borne by descendants of the septs Ó Conraoi, which belonged to eastern Co. Galway and southern Co. Roscommon, and Mac Conraoi of Moycullen barony in western Co. Galway, but due to similarities in pronunciation and spelling it has been confusingly used interchangeably with Conry (q.v.) deriving from Ó Maolconaire, with Conrahy which derives from Ó Conratha and Mac Conratha, and Connery which derives from Ó Conaire.

CONRY

THIS surname Conry, abbreviated from Mulconry, derives, in principle, from the sept Ó Maolconaire which had its sept centre in the parish of Clooncraff in the barony and county of Roscommon. Conry families may still be found living in the neighbourhood of Castlerea and Lanesborough, Co. Roscommon, not many miles distant from their ancient family seat. As Mulconry the name has survived in Co. Clare. Because of the similarity in spelling and pronunciation the surname Conry has also been used interchangeably with the more numerous Conroy which derives from Ó Conraoi and Mac Conraoi, with Connery which derives from Ó Conaire, and with the rarer Conrahy which derives from Ó Conratha and Mac Conratha.

William Conolly was the epitome of the successful nouveau-riche of the new society created in Ireland

CONSIDINE

THE name of this old Co. Clare family derives from Mac Consaidín. The heaviest distribution of families of this surname is still in the south of Co. Clare and in Co. Limerick.

CONVERY

THIS surname, concentrated in Co. Derry, where it belonged mainly to the neighbourhood of Magherafelt, derives from the Irish Mac Ainmhire.

CONWAY

THIS surname, which is found in all four provinces, most usually denotes descent from the sept Mac Conmheadha, or Mac Connmhaigh, from Co. Clare, some of whose members were recorded with the prefix O' rather than Mac. In the 16th century members of a Welsh family named Conway came to Ireland where they settled mainly in Co. Kerry with estates at Killorglin and also in Co. Dublin. Undoubtedly some minority of Conways in Ireland today will descend from these settlers.

COOGAN

THE descendants of the Co. Galway sept Ó Cuagáin are now most heavily distributed in Leinster, particularly in Co. Kilkenny and Co. Carlow. The second heaviest distribution is in Ulster, particularly in Co. Monaghan.

COOK(E)

THIS surname, among the fifty commonest in England, was brought to various parts of Ireland by settlers and is now established in all four provinces with the heaviest distribution in Ulster. One prolific settler family of the name which came first to Co. Cork proliferated in the 17th century in Co. Tipperary where one branch was seated at Kiltinan Castle and others at Castle Cooke and at Cordangan. Dr. MacLysaght has noted that Cook was also adopted in Connacht as an anglicized form of Mac Hugo (in Irish Mac Uag), more usually rendered Mac Coog, and used by a branch of the Burkes.

COONEY

THE sept Ó Cuana from south-west Ulster established themselves in Connacht where the townland of Ballycooney in Loughrea barony, Co. Galway, commemorates their presence in the south of the county whence they spread into Co. Clare. Subsequently their descendants seem to have been widely dispersed and are now found in all four provinces. In the last century the Registrar of Births reported that in Dunmanaway Union in West Cork, Cooney was used interchangeably with two other surnames, the West Munster surname Coonihan or Counihan (which derives from the Irish Ó Cuanacháin) and with a Cork surname Coumey or Comey.

CORCORAN

FAMILIES of this name may be descended either from the Ó Corcráin sept whose homeland was around Lough Erne in Co. Fermanagh, or the Mac Corcráin sept which belonged to Co. Offaly. The Connacht Corcoran families, mostly in Co. Mayo, are more likely to descend from the Fermanagh sept while the Leinster and Munster families of the name would appear to be descendants of the Offaly sept. There is evidence also that in Co. Kerry Corcoran was used interchangeably with Corkery or Corkerry which derive from Ó Corcra. As both Mac Corcráin and Ó Corcra ultimately derive from the same Irish word, corcair, meaning purple or ruddy, it may well be that quite a number of Corcorans from south-west Munster descend, in fact, from an Ó Corcra rather than from the Ó Corcráin or Mac Corcráin septs.

CORKERY

FAMILIES of this name are mostly confined to south-west Munster, mostly in Co. Cork, in lesser numbers in Co. Kerry. The spelling Corkerry is also in use, which makes the surname seem like an amalgamation of the names of the two counties where it is found. In fact, in Irish it is Ó Corcara which has caused confusion between this name and Corcoran which derives from O' or Mac Corcráin, the root of all these names being the Irish word corcair, meaning purple or ruddy.

CORMICAN

FOUND predominantly in Co. Galway this name derives from a sept Ó Cormacáin of which there were several. The distribution of surviving families of the name indicates descent from the septs once located in Co. Galway, Co. Clare and Co. Roscommon and possibly also from one that was in Co. Derry.

CORR

THIS name, which originated in northern Ulster,

derives from the Irish Ó Corra. It is now most heavily distributed in Ulster, the second heaviest distribution being in Leinster, where, besides a substantial number of families of the name in the capital, it is found in Co. Kilkenny and Co. Louth. In Ulster the main homeland of the name at present is in Co. Tyrone, Co. Cavan and Co. Monaghan. Families of this surname in Co. Cork may be among those whose ancestors used Corr interchangeably with Curry.

CORRIGAN

THE Ó Corragáin sept which belonged to Co. Fermanagh gave rise to the surnames Corrigan, Currigan, Courigan and Carrigan. Some descendants of the sept migrated southwards settling in Co. Monaghan and Co. Louth, in Co. Offaly, and into north Co. Tipperary where their presence is commemorated by the name of Ballycorrigan townland, in the barony of Owney and Arra. Today, as Carrigan it is found predominantly in southern Co. Tipperary in the baronies of Iffa and Offa East and Iffa and Offa West. The more numerous families of Corrigan are very scattered, but with the exclusion of families of the name settled in the capital, the heaviest distribution is in other counties of Leinster, Co. Louth, Co. Carlow, Co. Kildare and Co. Westmeath.

CORRY

FAMILIES of this name settled in Ulster from Scotland with the 17th century plantation of the province. It is still predominant in Ulster. The presence of Corry families in Munster, particularly in western Co. Clare, appears to be due to the adoption of this spelling of their surname by descendants of the Thomond sept Ó Comhraidhe, more usually rendered as Curry.

COSGRAVE

THIS surname and its variant, Cosgrove, which are in use in about equal numbers, are borne by descendants of the Mac Cosgraigh and Ó Cosgraigh septs of Co. Monaghan, an Ó Cosgraigh sept from south-eastern Leinster and another Ó Cosgraigh sept from Connacht. Consequently the two modern versions are widely scattered, Cosgrave predominating in Leinster and Cosgrove in Ulster and Connacht.

COSTELLO

THE barony of Costello in Co. Mayo takes its name from this family which was established there. The Costello families descend from a branch of the Anglo-Norman family of de Nangle in Connacht which adopted the Irish name Mac Oisdealbhaigh. Costello families are now widely dispersed but the heaviest representation of the name is still in Connacht.

COSTIGAN

THIS surname derives from the Ossory sept Mac Costagáin (Mac Oistigin). The name is still mainly confined to Leinster and is most prevalent in Co. Tipperary.

COTTER

THIS Munster family, most heavily represented in Co. Cork, derives its name from the Irish Mac Coitir (Mac Oitir); their medieval homeland was in the barony of Imokilly, Co. Cork, where they gave their name to the townland of Ballymacotter.

COUNIHAN

THIS surname, which was confined to Co. Kerry until the present century, derives from the Irish Ó Cuanacháin. Descendants of the family have scattered in recent times but are still represented in their ancestral county.

COURNANE

THIS Co. Kerry surname derives from the Irish Ó Curnáin. Until very recent times in that county it was used interchangeably with the English surname Courtney which is now borne by many more families of Ó Curnáin ancestry than is Cournane.

COURTNEY

THIS surname was brought from England to Ireland by settlers from Devonshire who were among the principal adventurers who acquired parts of the sequestrated Desmond estates in Co. Limerick and Co. Kerry at the end of the 16th century. The majority of families of the name in Ireland today, however, descend from the Ó Curnáin family of Co. Kerry, their progenitors having adopted the name Courtney in lieu of Cournane. As recently as the early years of the present century there is record of families in Co. Kerry who used the two surnames interchangeably.

COYLE

FAMILIES of this surname have been distributed across the northern half and the east of the country since the dispersal of their ancestors from Ulster where, nevertheless, Coyle families are still more than twice as prevalent as in Leinster and much more so than in Connacht. Coyle, like the less common surname McCool found principally in Co. Donegal and Co. Tyrone, and the much rarer form Mac Ilhoyle which survived around Ballymoney, Co. Antrim, derives from the Irish MacGiolla Choille and Mac Giolla Comhghaill.

COYNE

THIS Connacht name, which has spread into Leinster, derives from that of the sept Ó Cadhain whose territory was in Co. Mayo and also, seemingly, from that of the north Connacht sept Ó Comhdháin. Descendants of a family whose Irish name was Mac Giolla Chaoine adopted the surname Coyne as well as Kilcoyne in Co. Mayo, while Coen and Kyne are also on record as variants of Coyne.

CRAIG

THIS Scottish surname was brought by settlers from Scotland in the 17th century to Ulster where the great majority of Craigs in Ireland are to be found. It has, however, also very occasionally been confused with Creagh (q.v.).

CRAMPSY

THIS family, which belongs to Co. Donegal, derives its name from the Irish Ó Cnáimhsighe. Crampsie and Crampsey are variant spellings. Kneafsey has survived as another variant of this surname. Bonar was adopted as a surname by some Ó Cnáimhsighe descendants according to a report of the Registrar of Births who remarked the interchangeability of Bonar and Crampsie in Inishowen Union, in Co. Donegal, in the nineteenth century.

CRAWFORD

THIS Scottish surname is found predominantly in Ulster where it was brought at the time of the 17th century plantation schemes by settlers from Scotland, some of whom gave their name to the town of Crawfordsburn in Co. Down, others to Crawford's Hill in the parish of Devenish, Co. Fermanagh, others to Crawfordsland in the parish of Kilbride, Co. Antrim; others acquired land farther west in Co. Donegal.

CREAGH

THIS Co. Clare family, whose name is a transliteration of the Irish Craobhach, traces its lineage to a branch of the O'Neills of Thomond which adopted this surname. It is now found more often in the southern counties of Munster, particularly Co. Cork.

CREAN

DESCENDANTS of the Ó Croidheáin sept from Co. Donegal which spread into Co. Sligo, took the name Crean and its variant Crehan. The form O'Crean was in use into the 17th century after which the prefix O' was lost. Crean later occurred more frequently as a surname in Co. Kerry and Co. Cork, where it derived from a corruption of the Irish name Ó Cuirin.

CREGAN

THIS surname may derive either from Ó Croidheagáin or Mac Riagáin. In Connacht, where the spelling Creegan has been favoured, descent from the former is most likely while the Munster and Leinster families, more often Cregan, more probably descend from the latter family, this deduction being based not on the difference in spelling but on the original homeland of the respective ancestral families.

CREHAN See CREAN

CREMIN

THIS surname and its variant Cremen belong to Co. Cork and Co. Kerry where they derive from the Irish Ó Cruimin, although the Registrar of Births reported in the last century that in Bantry Union, Cremin, Cremeen and Crimeen were used interchangeably with the commoner local name M'Carthy. Cremen is found today mostly in Co. Cork and Cremin is found more frequently in that county now than in Co. Kerry. Today Cremins and Crimmins also exist as variants of this name.

CRILLY

THE Crilly families are said to descend from an Oriel sept Mac Raghallaigh. Crillys are still to be found mainly in that region, in Co. Louth and Co. Monaghan, and also in Co. Derry where their early association with that county is commemorated in the name of the parish of Tamlaght O'Crilly where there was an erenagh family of that name.

CRONIN

AT the end of the last century the name Cronin was almost exclusively confined to Co. Cork, Co. Kerry and Co. Limerick with the majority of families of the name in Co. Cork where the sept Ó Cróinín was originally located, one of its branches having been erenaghs of St. Finbarr's foundation at Gougane Barra. Population movement in the present century has brought many Cronin families to the capital and dispersed a number to other counties but the heaviest distribution of the name by far is still in Co. Cork where Cronin families are numerous. The name is still well represented, too, in Co. Kerry and Co. Limerick.

CROSSAN

THIS family, found principally in Co. Derry in the last century, derives from the north Ulster sept Mac an Chrosáin. Crossans are now established in the adjacent counties of Donegal and Tyrone and in Co. Leitrim.

CROTTY

THIS Munster surname derives from the Thomond sept Ó Crotaigh which migrated to eastern Munster. Families of the name today are found principally in Co. Cork and Co. Waterford while some of the name are established in Co. Kilkenny.

CROWLEY

FAMILIES of this name descend from the sept Ó Cruadhlaoich which originated in Co. Roscommon. A branch of this sept migrated to West Cork, establishing itself in the neighbourhood of Dunmanaway where, distant from the rest of the sept, it became autonomous with its own chief.

The name became vastly more numerous in Co. Cork than in the earlier home of the sept in Connacht, the branch that moved to the south having multiplied and flourished while the sept in Connacht rapidly dwindled. Today, a very few Crowley families survive in Co. Galway, presumably descended from those of the sept who remained in Connacht while the name is common in Co. Cork with a number of families still living in and around Dunmanaway. The prefix O' has been reassumed by a very small number of families.

CUDDIHY

THIS Co. Kilkenny surname derives from the Irish Ó Cuidighthigh. The variant spellings Cudahey, Cuddahy, Cuddehy and Quiddihy have all but vanished in Ireland. Apart from the Cuddihy families settled in the capital, the majority of families of the name still reside in Co. Kilkenny with a few scattered in adjacent counties.

CULHANE

SAVE for the families of the name who have settled in the capital in the present century, Culhanes are found almost exclusively in Co. Limerick with a particular concentration in the neighbourhood of Glin. The name derives from Ó Cathaláin which is also rendered Cahalane (q.v.).

CULLEN

THIS surname ranks among the hundred commonest in Ireland. Most Cullen families will descend from the sept Ó Cuilinn which held Glencullen in the south of Co. Dublin on the border of Co. Wicklow whence some moved south in the late medieval period and established themselves in Co. Wexford where two townlands named Cullenstown commemorate their presence, one in the barony of Bargy and the other in the

CRONIN *Gougane Barra, Co. Cork, in the area where the sept originated*

adjacent barony of Shelmalier West. Several hundred Cullen families now reside in Dublin while Co. Wexford, Co. Kildare and Co. Wicklow can count the largest number of the hundreds of Cullen families living in the rest of

Bridget, née Finucane, wife of Lt. Col. John Cullen J.P. of Skreeny, Co. Leitrim

the country. Some who bear this name may derive from less prominent septs with similar names, the Ó Cuileamháin sept, which was also located in South Leinster, the Mac Cuilin sept of Leitrim, and an Ó Cuileannáin sept in Co. Donegal whose descendants adopted Cullen in lieu of Cullinan as their surname.

CULLIGAN

THIS surname and its variant Quilligan derive from the Co. Clare sept Ó Cuileagáin. Both forms of the name survive being found predominantly in southern Co. Clare and northern Co. Limerick.

84

CULLINAN

AT the end of the last century the majority of Cullinan and Cullinane families lived in Munster with a few of the name, which derives from Ó Cuileannáin, in each of the other three provinces. The predominance of the name in Munster, where it was found mostly in Co. Cork, Co. Waterford and Co. Clare, indicates a descent of these families from the sept Ó Cuileannáin whose territory was in Barryroe barony in Co. Cork. The heaviest distribution of Cullinans and Cullinanes is still in Munster and some families of the name are still to be found in Barryroe barony in and around Clonakilty. Quillinan is a variant spelling (favoured in Co. Tipperary) which has survived.

CULLOTY

THIS Co. Kerry family, still found mostly in that county in the neighbourhood of Tralee, Ballymacelligott and Killarney, derives its name from the Irish Ó Codlata.

CULLY

THIS Ulster surname derives from the Irish Ó Colla and Mac Colla, some families of the latter descent having retained the prefix and remained McCully. In the last century the Registrar of Births reported also that in Trim Union, Co. Meath, there was evidence of the use of Cully interchangeably with the much commoner surname Cullen.

CUMISKEY

THIS curiously foreign-sounding name, also rendered Comiskey, Comaskey, Comeskey, Cumesky, Cumaskey, in fact derives from the Irish Mac Cumascaigh, the prefix Mac having invariably been lost. This family was originally located in Co. Monaghan whence they spread into north Leinster. Families spelling their name Comiskey are found today still in Co. Monaghan, Comaskey has survived in that county, too, and also in Co. Cavan and Co. Westmeath, Cumiskey has also survived in Co. Monaghan, in the adjacent counties of Louth and Cavan and in Co. Longford. These three spellings are all represented today in Dublin as well as Cumaskey. In the last century the Registrar of Births reported the use of the normally quite distinct surname Comerford interchangeably with Cumiskey and its variants in Cavan Union and in Granard Union, Co. Longford.

CUMMINS

THE English surname Cummings was brought to Ireland by settlers but most Cummins families in Ireland are of Irish stock, descended from Ó Coimín or Ó Comáin. An Ó Coimín sept in Connacht provided erenaghs for the church of St. Cuimín, Kilcummin, a parish in its homeland, the barony of Títawley, Co. Mayo. The present distribution of the name is thinnest, however, in Connacht, and even allowing for a wide dispersal of that sept it appears more likely that the numerous Cummins families in Leinster and in Munster (where the Irish name was Ó Comáin) descend from one or more other distinct sources of the name. There is, incidentally, a Kilcummin parish in Co. Kerry, in the barony of Magunihy, indicating a devotion to St. Cuimín in that area also and in Pubblebrien barony, Co. Limerick, there is a townland named Ballycummin.

CUNNANE

THIS surname, deriving from the Irish Ó Cuineáin, belongs to Connacht. Until recently it was located exclusively in Co. Roscommon and Co. Mayo and it survives along with its variant spelling, Queenan, in both those counties.

CUNNINGHAM

NORMALLY a Scottish name, Cunningham was brought to Ulster (the Irish province in which it is most prevalent) by settlers from Scotland in the 17th century. It was then adopted in lieu of their original names by descendants of the Irish families Ó Connagáin and Mac Cuinneagáin which were otherwise transliterated as Cunnigan, a name which disappeared, replaced by Cunningham. The very considerable number of Cunningham families in Connacht will be descendants of Ó Connagáin and Mac Cuinneagáin. Cunningham has also been adopted as their surname by persons with similar sounding Irish surnames such as the Co. Kerry surname Counihan, and the Co. Donegal surname Conaghan and the Co. Down surname Conegan or Mac Conegan, itself a corruption of Mac Donegan. The total collection of Cunningham families in Ireland from all these sources, settler and native, place

this surname today among the hundred commonest in the country.

CURLEY

BOTH Curley and Turley (which is less numerous) derive from Mac Thoirdealbaigh (Mac Turlough) and both are found in Connacht, principally in Co. Galway and Co. Roscommon, although population movement in this century has displaced a number of families of both names from their original location. The townlands of Ballymacurly South and Ballymacurly North in Ballymoe Barony, Co. Roscommon, on the border of Co. Galway, indicate an early homeland of the family some of whom are still in that immediate neighbourhood.

CURRAN

FAMILIES of this name are distributed throughout Ireland, the heaviest distribution being in Ulster, the thinnest, but nevertheless numerous, being in Connacht. Persons of the name must descend from one of several Ó Corráin or Ó Curráin septs, one of which was located in Co. Galway and another presumably in south Leinster whence it spread into Co. Waterford where families of the name were particularly numerous in the 17th century. Those of the name in Co. Kerry, where the variant Currane obtains also, would appear to descend from yet another Ó Corráin or Ó Curráin stock.

CURRID

THIS surname, which derives from the Irish Ó Corthaid, was concentrated in Co. Sligo. It is still represented in that county and in the capital where several families of the name have settled.

CURRY See CORRY

CURTIN

THE sept Mac Cuirtin or Mac Cruitin, from which the Curtin, Mac Curtin, and Mac Curtain families derive their name and descent, belonged to the neighbourhood of Ennistymon in the barony of Corcomroe in northwestern Co. Clare. The name remained almost exclusively in Munster until the present century when Curtins, Mac Curtins and Mac Curtains settled in the capital and less frequently in other provinces. Outside Dublin the heaviest distribution is still in Munster, in Co. Limerick and Co. Cork where descendants of the Co. Clare sept established themselves.

CUSACK

THIS surname, originally de Cussac, was brought to Ireland by Anglo-Norman settlers who acquired lands in the Pale, principally in Co. Meath, early in the 13th century. Their descendants dispersed and are found today in all four provinces with the heaviest distribution of the name outside the capital now being in Munster and particularly in Co. Limerick.

CUSSEN

CUSSEN families are found mainly in Co. Limerick around Newcastle West and Broadford, and in Co. Cork. Their name is believed to be of Anglo-Norman origin; it is recorded in north Co. Cork and in Co. Limerick early in the 14th century. A Cussen then held the lands of Farrahy in Fermoy barony on which the castle was still in the possession of the family in the 17th century. Cussen has also been used interchangeably with the English surname Cousins which survives principally in Co. Wexford.

DALTON

DERIVING from d'Alton, this is a name of Norman origin brought by settlers who came at the beginning of the 13th century in the wake of the Anglo-Norman invasion, and acquired lands first in Co. Meath and then in Co. Westmeath. The name is still most frequently found in Leinster but is numerous in Munster and comparatively uncommon in the other provinces.

DALY

This surname is among the thirty commonest in Ireland; it is most heavily distributed in Munster and then in Leinster with about half the number in that province living in Ulster and in Connacht. The Ó Dálaigh sept had its territory in Co. Westmeath in the barony of Magheradernon which now forms part of the barony of Moyashel and Magheradernon. Branches of the sept established themselves in other parts of the country, notably in Co. Galway, Co. Clare, Co. Cavan and Co. Cork where they flourished and multiplied, accounting for the numerous Daly descendants to be found today – about 15–17,000 in Ireland, and many thousands more in Britain, Canada, the United States of America, and other countries of the Irish diaspora. There are a few O'Daly families in Ireland who have reassumed the prefix O' as the returns of the Registrar of Births in the last century only show this surname in use without its prefix.

DANAHER

FAMILIES of this name are found predominantly in Co. Limerick but some are living in Co. Tipperary, the ancient location of the sept O'Danachair from whom they descend. Danagher is a variant. At least one Danaher family has reassumed the prefix O'.

DARCY

SOME families of this name will descend from a family of Norman origin, d'Arcy, which settled in Co. Meath in the 14th century. The use of the apostrophized particle d' was not widely retained although it was resumed. The present use of the apostrophized particle does not, however, necessarily denote descent from the Norman family of d'Arcy. Descendants of two Ó Dorchaidhe septs, one from around Lough Mask in Co. Mayo, the other from eastern Co. Galway, adopted Darcy as well as Dorcey as their surname and some of these Darcys then fancifully adopted the form d'Arcy.

DARMODY

THIS surname, which derives from the Irish Ó Diarmada, is found principally in Co.

Tipperary. The variant spelling Dermody is more numerous and more widely dispersed. Due to its derivation (Diarmada = Dermot) this surname has been interchanged with Dermott and MacDermott in various parts of the country.

DARRAGH

THIS Ulster surname, located principally in Co. Antrim, derives from the Irish Mac Dubhdara (Mac Dara).

DAVIS

THIS extremely common Welsh patronymic surname Davis or Davies (deriving from David) is found in Ireland where it was brought by settlers, in all four provinces but predominantly in Leinster and in Ulster, a heavy distribution of the name being remarkable in the east coast counties of Dublin and Antrim. It seems generally not to have been confused with any native Irish names although an instance of such was noted in the last century by the Registrar of Births who reported the use of Davis in Dungannon Union, Co. Tyrone, interchangeably with McDaid which derives from Mac Daibhaid (Mac David) which is more usually Davitt or Devitt (q.v.). The surname Davis was also assumed by descendants of a branch of the McMurroughs which was distinguished by the name MacDavie Mor.

DAVITT *See DEVITT*

DAVOREN

SOME families named Davoren still survive in Co. Clare, the home of their ancestral sept Ó Dabhoireann, whose sept centre was near Lisdoonvarna in the Burren. The stone fort of Cahermacnaghten was their home in the medieval period and the site of their famous law school. In the 17th century it was known as 'O'Davoren's town'. The variant spelling Davern is now more common than Davoren; it is found mainly in Co. Tipperary and in eastern Co. Limerick.

DEA *See O'DEA*

DAVOREN *Bridge at Lisdoonvarna, Co. Clare*

DEANE

FAMILIES of this name may be of settler origin, this surname being common in England, but by translation it became the surname of descendants of the sept Ó Deaghain (déaghan – dean, deacon) from Co. Roscommon, and also as a translation of Mac an Deagánaigh, the latter likely to be true of the Deanes in Co. Donegal, the former of the Deanes in Co. Mayo.

DEASY

THE Deasy families in Co. Cork, one of the two locations of the name at the end of the last century, derive their name from the Irish Déiseach, signifying 'of the Decies', baronies in West Waterford. The lesser number of Deasys coming from the other location, Co. Mayo, appear to derive from Mac an Déisigh which Father Woulfe reported as having been found in

87

Co. Sligo. Deasy is found today very predominantly in Co. Cork but, though rare, is not
extinct in Co. Mayo.

DEEGAN

THIS surname derives from Ó Duibhginn, a sept
which was located in the barony of Clandonagh,
Co. Leix. Deegan families still reside in that
county and in adjacent counties.

DEELY

THIS Co. Galway surname and its variants
Deeley and the rarer Devilly derive from the
Irish Ó Duibhghiolla.

DEENEY

THIS surname, which is found in eastern Co.
Donegal and western Co. Derry, derives from
the Irish Ó Duibhne. Due to a misunderstanding
of the meaning of the Irish name it was confused
with the similarly pronounced Irish word
daoine (duibhne = disagreeable; daoine =
people) and rendered in English as People. Both
Deeney with its variant spelling Deeny and
Peoples have survived and are represented today
in Co. Donegal.

DEERY

THIS Ulster family from Co. Monaghan and Co.
Tyrone derives its name from the Irish Ó
Daighre.

DEEVY

THIS surname and its variant Devey derive from
the Co. Leix sept Ó Duibhidhe. Deevy is still
represented in that county whence it has spread
into Co. Kilkenny, Co. Waterford and Co.
Tipperary and to Dublin but nowhere in any
considerable numbers. Devoy is also found
today still in Co. Leix as well as in Co. Carlow,
and there are families of the name in the capital.
The fanciful spelling De Voy also appears.

DELAHUNTY

THIS surname (locally pronounced Dullanty)
derives from the Offaly sept Ó Dulchaointich. It
is now found mainly in an area radiating out from
its original homeland, in Co. Leix, Co. Tipperary,
Co. Kilkenny, Co. Waterford. The variant
Dulanty is rare but not extinct in Ireland;
another variant, Delanty, also survives.

DELANEY

THE Ó Dubhshláine sept, whose territory was in

Upperwoods barony, Co. Leix, were the ancestors of the families named Delaney and
Delany which are still well represented in that
county despite a dispersal of the name into other
regions and the settlement of a considerable
number of Delaneys in the capital.

DEMPSEY

THE surname Dempsey
is now both numerous
and widespread but its
heaviest concentration
is still in Leinster where
the sept Ó Diomasaigh
(from which it derives)
held sway on the
borders of Co. Leix and
Co. Offaly. In a very
few instances persons
of the name Dempsey have reassumed the
prefix in recent years.

DEMPSEY *Houses in the town of Kinnitty, Co.
Offally*

DENNEHY

AT the end of the last century the surname Dennehy was confined to West Munster, to the counties of Cork and Kerry where it is still found predominantly although there has been an inevitable dispersal with the population movement of this century and the urban drift has brought a number of families of the name to the capital. Dennehy derives from the Irish Ó Duineacha. It has on ocasion been confused with Denny, the name of an English settler family in Co. Kerry.

DESMOND

THIS Cork surname derives from the sept Ó Deasmhumhnaigh which was originally located in West Cork whence it moved westwards. The majority of Desmond families are still to be found in Co. Cork today.

DEVANE

Two Ó Dubháin septs, one from Co. Kerry and one from south Connacht, are the ancestors of families who bear the surnames Devane (the form favoured in Co. Kerry), Duane (the form favoured in Co. Galway) and Dwane.

DEVEREUX

THIS Norman surname, originally d'Evreux (which pinpoints its ultimate homeland in Normandy), was brought to Ireland following the Anglo-Norman conquest by settlers who established themselves in Co. Wexford. Despite the establishment of many of the name in the capital, Co. Wexford can still count the largest percentage of Devereux families in the country. Deveraux, Devereaux, Devery (favoured in Co. Offaly) and Deverell (favoured in Co. Leix and Co. Offaly), are variants which are still represented in Ireland.

DEVINE

THIS South Ulster surname derives from the Ó Daimhin sept whose territory was in Co. Fermanagh, which, with Co. Tyrone, long remained the homeland of its descendants. The branches spread into Leinster and were well established in Dublin before the massive migration towards the capital in this century, as well as in Co. Monaghan, Co. Cavan and Co. Louth.

DEVITT

DEVITT, often in use with its prefix as McDevitt, and its variant Davitt (which was favoured in Co. Mayo), derive from Mac Daibheid which in its original location in Co. Donegal was rendered as McDaid which also survives, most families of that name still being resident in that county.

The founder of the Irish National Land League, Michael Davitt (1846–1906), was born in Co. Mayo. In the wake of the famine his family suffered eviction and emigrated to England but Michael remained fiercely attached to his native land and sensitive to the deprivation of its peasantry; he entered parliament in 1882, devoting his energies to fight landlordism and advance the cause of Irish independance.

DEVLIN

THIS predominantly Ulster surname is borne by descendants of the sept Ó Doibhilin whose territory was in the east of Dungannon barony, Co. Tyrone, along the western shore of Lough Neagh. The family has dispersed through the counties of Ulster, the adjacent counties of Leinster and beyond but is still strongly represented in Co. Tyrone.

DIAMOND

THIS north Connacht and north-west Ulster surname derives from Ó Diamáin in Co. Derry. It is now found (but nowhere in large numbers) in that county, in Co. Donegal, and in Co. Mayo, as well as scattered families farther afield including several in the capital.

DICKSON

THIS English and Scottish surname was brought to Ulster, particularly by settlers, early in the 17th century. The spelling Dixon, now widely scattered, was favoured in Western Mayo where a number of families seem to have arrived from an earlier home in Co. Donegal. Descendants of the Irish family Ó Diochon also are on record as having adopted the surname Dickson/Dixon.

7th century monument at Carndonagh, Inishowen peninsula, the country of the Mac Daibheid sept

DILLON

THIS surname arrived in Ireland at the end of the 12th century with the Anglo-Norman settlement which accompanied the invasion. These Dillons acquired a vast territory which comprised much of Co. Westmeath whence they extended westwards into Connacht, branches taking root in Co. Mayo and Co. Roscommon. The name is now widely distributed.

DINNEEN

FAMILIES of this name, the majority of whom still reside in Co. Cork, descend from the West Cork sept Ó Duinnin. Some descendants of this sept adopted as their surname the English settler surname Downing which is found still in Co. Cork and Co. Kerry.

DIRRANE

THIS Co. Galway surname still belongs almost exclusively to that county where it is also represented in the Aran islands but is nowhere numerous; it dervies from the Irish Ó Dearáin. Dirane and Derrane exist as variants.

DISKIN

THIS Galway surname, still predominantly borne by families residing there, derives from Ó Discin. According to Dr. MacLysaght the family was formerly located in Co. Sligo.

DIVER

SAVE for a handful of families settled in the capital this surname is still found exclusively in its original home county, Donegal. The Diver families descend from the Donegal sept Ó Duibhidhir. A branch which settled in Co. Mayo adopted the spellings Dever and Devers which both survive in that county.

DOBBIN

THIS English surname was brought to Ireland by settlers. Its heaviest distribution is in Co. Antrim where families of the name were settled around Carrickfergus early in the 17th century, whence some of the name established themselves at the end of that century in Co. Armagh. At a much earlier date, at least from the 14th century, a Dobbin (Dobbyn) family had made its home in Co. Waterford.

DOBBS

THIS English surname was brought to Ulster by a settler from England as early as 1596, a few years prior to the great wave of immigration which accompanied the plantation of Ulster. Descendants of that family are still living near Carrickfergus, Co. Antrim, where their ancestors settled. Their coat of arms is: Per pale sable and argent a chevron engrailed between three unicorns' heads erased all countercharged. The presence of Dobbs families in Leinster may be accounted for by descent from the Ulster settler family or from independent settlers of the name from England where it is not at all rare.

DOCKERY

THIS surname, which is found mainly in Roscommon, is in Irish Ó Dochraigh which itself ultimately derives from the more complicated Mac Dháil Ré Dochair, the name of an east Connacht sept which was attached to the O'Connors.

DOHENY

THIS name is borne by descendants of the West Cork sept Ó Dubhchonna. They are to be found today to the east of their original location, in Co. Tipperary and Co. Kilkenny. There is evidence that some Dohenys adopted in lieu of their own name the English surname Dawney.

DOHERTY

THE Ó Dochartaigh sept was originally located in Raphoe barony, Co. Donegal. In the 14th century they held sway over the whole Inishowen peninsula. Doherty and O'Doherty, the name borne by their numerous progeny, is among the twenty commonest names in Ireland today. A minority of descendants of the sept retained their prefix O'; in the present century a considerable number have reassumed the prefix although the Dohertys still slightly outnumber the O'Dohertys. Despite the commonness of the

91

name, which must be borne today by around 20,000 persons in Ireland, it is still to be found very predominantly in its original home county of Donegal and then mostly in the adjacent counties.

DOHERTY *Rainbow beyond Malin Head, Co. Donegal*

DOLAN

THE Ó Dobhailen sept originated in the barony of Cloumacnowen in eastern Co. Galway and in the adjacent barony of Athlone, Co. Roscommon. Their descendants, bearing the name Dolan, are still to be found in those counties and, due to a north-eastward migration of branches of the sept, also in considerable numbers in Co. Fermanagh, Co. Leitrim and Co. Cavan as well as dispersed farther afield.

DONAGHY *See McDONAGH*

DONEGAN

FAMILIES of this name and its many variants (such as Donagan, Dunnegan, Dunnigan etc.) derive from one or other of a number of distinct Ó Donnagáin septs. One of these originated in Co. Cork, another in Co. Tipperary, another in Co. Monaghan. Consequently the name is widely distributed and found in all four provinces but it is rare in Connacht and commonest in Leinster. There are still a good number of Donegan families in Co. Cork and Co. Kerry, apparently descended from the Cork sept. Dunican, which could easily be confused with variants of Donegan, is, in fact, a distinct surname deriving from Ó Duinacháin in Co. Offaly.

DONNELL *See O'DONNELL*

DONNELLAN

THE Ó Domhnalláin sept was located in south-eastern Co. Galway. Their stronghold was in the barony of Kilconnell at Ballydonnellan where they remained through the late medieval period. Their descendants, of the name Donnellan, Donelan, Donelan, Donlon, are still most numerous in Connacht. Some Donnellan families still survive in the immediate neighbourhood of the ancient lands of their ancestral sept.

DONNELLY

THIS surname is among the hundred commonest in Ireland. Most, if not all, who bear the name will descend from the sept Ó Donnghaile which was first located in Co. Donegal but migrated eastwards and established itself in Co. Tyrone where their sept centre was at Castle Caulfield, formerly called Ballydonnelly, in Dungannon Middle barony. From this area branches moved farther east and settled in Co. Antrim. Despite the proliferation of the name the heaviest distribution by far is still in Ulster.

DONOGHUE *See O'DONOGHUE*

DONNELLY *Woodland near Ballydonnelly, Co. Tyrone*

DONOHOE *See O'DONOGHUE*

DONOVAN *See O'DONOVAN*

DOODY *See O'DOWD*

DOOGAN *See DUGGAN*

DOOLAN

THIS surname, which is commonest in Leinster and Munster, where it is widely distributed, derives from the Irish Ó Dubhlainn. It has been confused on occasion with Dolan which has a separate derivation and in the last century the Registrar of Births reported that in various parts of the country such as Co. Kilkenny, Co. Offaly and Co. Tipperary, the surname Dowling was used interchangeably with Doolan.

DOOLEY

THE Ó Dubhlaoich sept was originally located in south-eastern Co. Westmeath close to the present border of Co. Meath but migrated southwards and re-established itself in Ballybritt barony, Co. Offaly. Their descendants are still present in Co. Offaly, in the adjacent part of

Co. Tipperary in the neighbourhood of Roscrea, and in Co. Leix as well as being scattered farther afield.

DOONAN

THIS name, which derives from Ó Dúnáin, seems to have its source in an erenagh family, Ó Dúnáin from Co. Fermanagh, but it became more prevalent in east Connacht in Co. Roscommon and Co. Leitrim where it is still found.

DORAN

DORAN families in Ulster are likely to be descendants of an Ó Deoradháin (Ó Deoráin) sept which was located in south-eastern Ulster in Co. Down and Co. Armagh where the name is still found. There was, however, another sept of the name in Co. Leix which was scattered and engendered branches which established themselves in regions as far apart as Co. Wexford (where they settled mainly in Bantry barony) and Co. Kerry.

DORGAN

THIS surname, found principally in Co. Cork, derives from the Irish Ó Deargáin. The name of Ballydorgan townland in the barony of Condons and Clangibbon indicates an early home of the family. The variant form Dargan is found in Leinster.

DOWD *See O'DOWD*

DOWLING

ALTHOUGH it may appear to be a name of English origin, in fact Dowling derives from the Irish sept Ó Dúnlaing which was located in the west of Co. Leix along the banks of the River Barrow. From there they spread southwards into Co. Kilkenny and westwards into Co. Carlow and Co. Wicklow. Many settled in Dublin before the massive migration to the capital in this century and there are now roughly as many Dowlings in Dublin as in all the rest of Ireland but the name is still numerously represented in Co. Kilkenny, Co. Carlow, Co. Wicklow and Co. Leix.

DOWNEY

ONE or the other of two Ó Dúnadhaigh septs provide the ancestry of the families named Downey. One of those was located in the area where the counties of Cork, Kerry and Limerick meet. The numerous Downeys descended from this sept are still found largely in that area. There is evidence that some Downey families in West Munster adopted the surname Downing in lieu of Downey. In the last century the Registrar of Births reported instances of the interchangeability of these names in various places in Co. Kerry and Co. Cork. He also noted the interchangeability of Downey in Newry Union, Co. Down, with the name Gildowney, Mc Gilldowney and Muldowney, the two former being, in fact, derivants of Mac Giolla Domhnaigh, more usually rendered as Mc Eldowney, and the latter deriving from Ó Maoldomhnaigh.

DOYLE

AMONG the twenty commonest surnames in Ireland, the name Doyle is borne by approximately one half of one per cent of the total population of the island today. It has always been found predominantly in south-eastern Leinster and it is there, with Dublin, that the majority of Doyles is still to be found. Doyle derives from the Irish dubh-ghall, meaning literally 'dark foreigner' but the term was applied generally to describe the Norsemen who settled on the east coast of Ireland from the 9th to the 11th centuries. This, of course, explains the commonness of the name as Doyles may descend from a number of distinct ancestors who were dubbed dubh-ghall, this sobriquet then being carried as a surname by their descendants.

DRENNAN

THE Ó Draighneán sept originated in Co. Galway but their descendants, the Drennans, are widely scattered, being found as far off from their ancient homeland as Co. Antrim, Co. Kilkenny and Co. Leix, and Co. Cork.

DRISCOLL See O'DRISCOLL

DROHAN

THIS South Munster surname, found mostly in northern Co. Waterford and in south-eastern Co. Tipperary, derives from the Irish Ó Druacháin.

DRUMM

AT the end of the last century this surname was found mostly in Co. Fermanagh along with its variant spelling Drum. It derives from Ó Droma, the name of an erenagh family whose home was on the Cavan-Fermanagh border in the barony of Knockninny, Co. Fermanagh, and Tullyhaw, Co. Cavan, in the territory called Kinawley. Dr. MacLysaght has noted that the name Drummy, which is found in Co. Cork, is of the same derivation, the Drummys being descended from a branch of the Ulster sept which established itself in the south far from its original home. The Registrar of Births reported instances in the last century of the Scottish surname Drummond being used interchangeably with Drumm in Ulster (Co. Cavan) and with Drummy in Munster (Dungarvan Union, Co. Waterford).

DUDDY See O'DOWD

DUFFY

DUFFY *The High Cross at Clones in the south-west of Co. Monaghan, the county where the name is commonest*

SEVERAL distinct Ó Dubhthaigh septs provide the ancestry of the Duffys and O'Duffys, whose surname is one of the fifty commonest in Ireland. Duffy is found predominantly in Co. Monaghan (where it is the commonest single surname), and the adjacent counties. It is difficult to determine, however, whether they belong to the Ó Dubhthaigh sept which was located in the barony of Boylagh in the extreme west of Co. Donegal (where Duffy families are still to be found) or to the Ó Dubhthaigh sept whose sept centre was Lissonuffy in Roscommon barony, Co. Roscommon. The latter would seem more likely. In Co. Cork and Co. Kerry Duhig was generally used for Ó Dubhthaigh instead of Duffy and has survived there as a surname.

DUGGAN

THE Irish Ó Dubhagáin has been transliterated as Duggan, Dugan and Doogan. The best-known Ó Dubhagáin sept was located in Fermoy barony in northern Co. Cork. Another was located in southern Co. Galway. Dugan and Dougan were the favoured spellings in east Ulster where families using that form of the name predominate. Doogan is the spelling found most often in Co. Donegal. The more numerous Duggan families predominate in Munster where their noticeably heavier distribution in Co. Tipperary denotes descent from the Fermoy sept.

DUHIG *See O'DUFFY*

DUIGNAN

FROM the sept Ó Duibhgeannáin of eastern Connacht descend families with the surname Duigan and the less frequent variants Duignam, Dignan (favoured in Co. Westmeath) and Dignam.

DULLAGHAN

THE majority of families of this name is still found in its homeland in Co. Louth. It derives from the Irish Ó Dubhlacháin. In the last century the Registrar of Births reported the use of the name Dullaghan interchangeably with

Dillon in Ballymoney Union, Co. Antrim.

DUNLEAVY

THIS surname and its variants, Dunlevy and the rarer Donleavy, derive from the sept Mac Duinnshléibhe which belonged to south-eastern Ulster where they were displaced at the end of the 12th century and re-established themselves in Co. Donegal. The heaviest distribution of the name in North Connacht, particularly in Co. Mayo and Co. Sligo whence it spread to Co. Galway, must be due to further migrations.

DUNN(E)

WHILE a few Dunn and Dunne families in Ireland could be descendants of settlers from England, where this surname is common, the vast majority of those of the name in Ireland, where it ranks among the fifty commonest surnames, is of native Irish stock, being descendants of the sept Ó Duinn or Ó Doinn whose territory was in the barony of Tinnahinch, Co. Leix, Brittas in that barony being their stronghold. The heaviest distribution by far of the name has always been in Leinster where it is about five times as numerous as in Ulster or Munster. The family is still represented in its ancient ancestral territory by Dunnes living in the neighbourhood of Rosenallis, Co. Leix.

DUNPHY

THIS south Kilkenny name derives from an Ossory sept named Ó Donnchaidh, distinct from the other septs of the same name and whose descendants adopted Dunphy instead of Donoghue as their surname. It is still found mainly in Co. Kilkenny and in the adjacent county of Waterford.

DURKAN

THIS North Connacht name and its variants, Durcan and Durkin, derive from the Irish

95

Ó Duarcáin or Mac Duarcáin. It is still strongly represented in Co. Mayo where it was always most prevalent.

DWYER See O'DWYER

EGAN

THIS surname derives from Mac Aodhagáin, a sept which originated in Co. Galway but became widely dispersed, some settling in Co. Tipperary, Co. Offaly and Co. Kilkenny, so that Egans were to be found in roughly equal numbers at the end of the last century in Connacht, where they originated, and in Leinster, where they settled, with a substantial representation in Munster. Keegan, another surname deriving from the same sept, is far commoner in Leinster than in the other provinces. The name is rarely, if ever, now found with its prefix as McEgan.

ENNIS

THE Leinster surname Ennis, which is found mainly in Co. Dublin, Co. Kildare, Co. Meath and Co. Westmeath, derives from the same source as Hennessy (q.v.).

ENRIGHT

THE Munster surname Enright is commonest in Co. Limerick where, at the end of the last century, about one half of all the families of the name in Ireland were living. With very few exceptions the other half were all in the adjacent counties of Cork, Kerry and Clare. Save for the Enright families, who have established themselves in the capital, the present distribution is roughly the same. The variant Enraght seems only to have survived in Ireland, at least, with one family. The Irish form of the name, from which Enright and Enraght derive, is MacIonnrachtaigh.

EUSTACE

THE surname of the Eustace family was introduced to Ireland as FitzEustace by a settler who established himself in Co. Kildare at the time of the Anglo-Norman conquest. The town and parish of Ballymore Eustace in Naas South barony, Co. Kildare, marks the area of the family's influence. Today families of the name are found mainly in the capital, and scattered through Leinster from Co. Louth in the north to Co. Wexford in the south, with a few of the name dispersed further afield outside the province. The main branch of the Eustace family

has as its coat of arms: Or a saltire gules.

FAGAN

THE origin of the Fagan family remains doubtful. The published pedigree of the Fagans of Co. Kerry, who descend from the Fagans of Feltrim, Co. Dublin, used to trace their lineage to the O'Hagan sept. However, recent versions of the pedigree begin only with an ancestor born in Dublin in 1492. Dr MacLysaght has mentioned that a Fagan is recorded in Dublin in 1200 soon after the Anglo-Norman invasion. He opines that the name Fagan was brought to Ireland about that time by an Anglo-Norman settler or settlers but he recognizes that descendants of the O'Hagans who became Fegan (q.v.) also used the spelling Fagan. Now, and for centuries past, Fagan families have been most heavily distributed in and around Dublin where they are numerous. The Registrar of Births in the last century noticed a number of variants used interchangeably with Fagan, some of which, like Fegan (q.v., which derives from Ó Faodhagáin and ultimately from the same source as O'Hagan, q.v.) and Feehan and Feighan (q.v., which derives from Ó Féichin or Ó Fiacháin) can also be distinct surnames in their own right.

FAHERTY

THIS surname is still found predominantly in Co. Galway. The Fahertys descend from the sept Ó Fathartaigh whose territory was in Clare Barony, Co. Galway, along the eastern shores of Lough Corrib. From the mainland the name reached the Aran Islands where several Faherty families are living today. The more numerous Flahertys and O'Flahertys, descendants of the more important sept Ó Flaithbheartaigh, from the same part of Co. Galway, have absorbed a number of Fahertys. The two names in the same region being similar, confusion was unavoidable, especially in the times of widespread illiteracy; there is evidence of their use interchangeably and, Flaherty being the commoner name by far, inevitably some Fahertys were recorded as Flaherty and that name stuck to their descendants.

FAHY

FAMILIES of the same Fahy and its variant Fahey descend from the sept Ó Fathaigh whose territory was in the northern part of Loughrea barony in southern Co. Galway. At the end of the last century at least half of the Fahy and

Fahey families in Ireland were still located in Co. Galway and of those that were not there was a considerable number dispersed, not far off, in the north of Co. Tipperary. Due to population movement in this century the dispersal of the name is now greater and more widespread but there is still a considerable representation of the name in Co. Galway and it is still found in and around Loughrea.

FALLON

THE surname Fallon is now widely dispersed in Ireland, families of the name being found from Co. Donegal in the north to Co. Cork and Co. Kerry in the south-west and Co. Wexford in the south-east. There remains, however, a noticeably heavier concentration of the name in Co. Galway and Co. Roscommon and in the counties adjacent to Co. Roscommon, Co. Westmeath and Co. Longford. The Fallons descend from the sept Ó Fallamhain whose territory was in the south of Athlone barony in southern Co. Roscommon; in the townland of Milltown in Dysart parish are the ruins of their castle stronghold. Fallon families are still residing today in the immediate area of their ancestral lands. There have been some isolated instances of the resumption of the prefix O' with the surname Fallon. Falloon, a variant spelling, seems to have been confined to Co. Armagh where it survives.

FALVEY

THIS surname, which derives from the Irish Ó Fáilbhe, seems to have originated in Co. Kerry whence it spread to Co. Cork where most families of the name are now found.

FANNING

THIS surname was brought to Ireland by settlers in the wake of the Anglo-Norman conquest of the country. From their principal place of settlement in Slievardagh barony in the south-east of Co. Tipperary they dispersed south-eastwards as far as Co. Wexford and westwards into Co. Limerick where the name became firmly established. Fanningstown in Iverk barony, Co. Kilkenny, and three town-lands of the name in eastern Co. Limerick, one in Smallcounty barony and two in Coshlea barony, indicated places of settlement of some of these dispersed branches. Fanning families, however, still survive in the region close to their ancestral lands in Co. Tipperary, being found in the neighbourhood of Littleton. In general, Fannin is a variant favoured in Co. Cavan.

FARRAGHER

THE surname Farragher, which is found mainly in Co. Mayo and Co. Galway, and the surname Fraher, which is found in Munster, mainly in Co. Cork and Co. Waterford, both derive from the Irish Ó Fearchair, but it is not clear whether they are ultimately of the same stock.

FARRELL

THE Ó Fearghaill sept held sway over the territory called Annaly, in Co. Longford, their seat being where the town of Longford grew up. At the end of the last century families with the name O'Farrell were outnumbered by about fifteen to one by the Farrells who had lost the prefix. Today, the Farrells are still more numerous than the O'Farrells but as many families have reassumed the prefix in this century, now about one-quarter to one-third of the descendants of the Ó Fearghaill sept are O'Farrell but the majority is still Farrell. This surname is among the fifty commonest in Ireland and is widely distributed throughout the country. However, about two-thirds or more of all the Farrell and O'Farrell families in Ireland are in Leinster and the name is still well represented in Co. Longford. Ferrall is a variant also found in that county.

FARRELLY

THE territory of the sept Ó Faircheallaigh was in Loughter Lower Barony in northern Co. Cavan where they were erenaghs of the Abbey at Drumlane which became an Augustinian priory. The distribution of Farrelly families in Ireland in the last century which, save for the capital, was exclusively in Co. Cavan and the adjacent counties, particularly Co. Meath, indicates their descent from the Cavan sept. In the last century the Registrar of Births reported the interchangeability of the Scottish or English surname Farley with Farrelly in at least three different unions in Co. Cavan.

FARREN

THIS surname, which belongs to Co. Donegal and Co. Derry, derives from Ó Faracháin. However, Dr. MacLysaght has reported that some Farrens adopted this name in lieu of Fearon and these are, therefore, really of a separate lineage.

FARRISSEY

THIS surname, which is now extremely rare in Ireland, is borne by descendants of the sept Ó Fearghusa which belonged to Co. Mayo and Co. Leitrim. It is known to have survived in the Irish diaspora where at least one family in the United States uses a variant phonetic spelling Faricy.

FAY

IN principle Fay is a name brought as de Fay with the Anglo-Norman settlement following the invasion at the end of the 12th century and soon established in Co. Westmeath. The heaviest distribution of the name is still in Leinster, especially in Dublin, with a spill over into the southern counties of Ulster. In the latter area it is likely that some, perhaps all, the Fay families are not of the Anglo-Norman stock but bear the name as a less usual derivant of the Irish Ó Fiaich more widely rendered in southern Ulster as Fee or Foy.

FEE

THIS is the most usual transliteration of the Irish Ó Fiaich and as such found mainly in the south of Ulster. Foy is a variant found also in Connacht.

FEEHAN

IT appears that in Munster this surname must derive from the name of the sept Ó Fiacháin which was located in south-eastern Co. Tipperary where the name is still found as well as dispersed to other parts. The Feehan families in Co. Louth, however, more probably descend from the same source as those named Fegan (q.v.). Feighan is known to have occurred as a variant of Feehan but may also derive from the Irish Ó Féichin. See also Fagan.

FEELY

FAMILIES of this name, and its variants Feeley, Feehely, Feehily, Feehilly, deriving from the Irish Mac Fithcheallaigh, are to be found mainly in northern Co. Roscommon and the adjacent counties of Leitrim and Mayo. Families of the same surnames and its variants in Munster will most likely descend from the West Cork sept Ó Fithcheallaigh and are found predominantly still in Co. Cork. The Feehely, Feehily, Feehilly variants are much more frequent in Munster but do also occur in Connacht, while Feely and Feeley are more frequent in Connacht but do also occur in Munster.

FEENEY

FAMILIES of the name Feeney (with its less common variant Feeny) and Finney, a variant favoured in Ulster, may descend either from the north Connacht sept Ó Fiannaidhe which was located in Co. Mayo and Co. Sligo, or from the south Connacht sept Ó Fidhue which was located in Co. Galway and Co. Roscommon. In the latter county two townlands named Ballyfeeney, one in Ballintober North barony and the other only a few miles distant in the adjacent barony of Roscommon, indicate an area of settlement of the Ó Fidhue sept.

FEERICK

THIS surname, which derives from the Irish Mac Phiaraic, has always been found predominantly in the south of Co. Mayo whence it spread into Co. Galway. Families of the name are still residing today mainly in and around Ballinrobe, Co. Mayo.

FEGAN

THIS name, found in Dublin and north of Co. Dublin in Co. Louth and up into Co. Armagh, derives usually in that area from Ó Faodhagáin which itself is a corruption of the name of the Co. Tyrone sept Ó hAodhagáin (which is usually rendered as O'Hagan – q.v.). There is considerable confusion regarding the real connection, if any, between Fegan and Fagan (q.v.) other than their use interchangeably, which has been noticed by the Registrar of Births in the last century along with the use of Feehan (q.v.) and Feighan interchangeably with Fegan and Fagan.

FENNELL

FAMILIES of this name in Ireland may be of

either English or native Irish stock. English settlers brought the name from England to Co. Tipperary at least by the 16th century and their descendants spread into Co. Cork, where some were early adherents to the Society of Friends (Quakers). The majority of Fennell families in Ireland, however, will bear the name as an anglicization of the Irish Ó Fionnghaill. Today, although the name is fairly widely dispersed, there is a noticeable concentration of Fennells in Co. Carlow and in the barony of Decies-without-Drum, Co. Waterford, in the neighbourhood of Dungarvan and Stradbally.

FENNELLY

THIS surname, which derives from Ó Fionnghalaigh, is found mainly in the west of Co. Kilkenny and across the county border in the east of the adjacent county of Tipperary and in Co. Leix, which is also adjacent.

FENNESSY

FAMILIES of this name, which derives from the Irish Ó Fionnghusa, are found mostly concentrated in the neighbourhood of Clonmel in southern Co. Tipperary on the Tipperary and Waterford border.

FENTON

THE number of Fenton families in Ireland is due to this English surname having been adopted instead of Fenaghty and Finaghty and Finnerty (which derive from Ó Fionnachta) and instead of Feighney (which derives from Ó Fiachna). Evidence of the interchangeability of these surnames in Co. Cork and Co. Kerry is given in reports of the Registrar of Births in the last century. As a distinct English surname Fenton was introduced to Leinster by settlers, at least by the 16th century and to Ulster in the 17th century, so some Fenton families in Ireland may be true Fentons, that is to say of settler descent.

FERGUSON

THIS Scottish surname, among the forty commonest in Scotland, was brought to Ulster by settlers, most of whom came with the plantation schemes in the first quarter of the 17th century.

FERRITER

AN English surname brought to Co. Kerry in the 13th century where Ballyferriter in the barony of Corkaguiny, Dingle Peninsula, was their seat.

FERRITER *Ferriters Cove, Dingle Peninsula, Co. Kerry*

FERRY

THIS surname belongs to Co. Donegal, where the majority of Ferry families still live. They descend from the Donegal sept Ó Fearadhaigh.

FINAN

FAMILIES of this name, descended from the north Connacht sept Ó Fionnáin, are still mostly found in Connacht, in Co. Sligo, Co. Mayo, Co. Roscommon and Co. Galway.

FINN

AT the end of the last century Finn families were distributed in almost equal numbers in Leinster, Munster, and Connacht and, with a much lesser frequency, in Ulster (about one to every five in any one of the other provinces). Nevertheless two of the three known Ó Finn septs were located in Connacht and the third in the south of the region called Oriel which took in parts of southern Ulster and Co. Louth in Leinster. The considerable presence of Finns in Munster could be due to an early migration of a branch of one of these northern septs or to descent from a distinct source of the name there, of which no evidence has been found. Of the two Connacht Ó Finn septs, one was located in Co. Sligo in a territory called Calry, which is in the north of the county in Carbury barony along the northern shore of Lough Gill, but they gave their name to a barony in the south of the county, Coolavin (Cúil Ó bhFinn). The other sept Ó Finn in Connacht was located in Dunkellin barony in Co. Galway.

FINNEGAN

AT the end of the last century the surname Finnegan, with its variants, Finegan, Finigan and Finnigan, was distributed in about equal numbers in Leinster, Ulster and Connacht with only about one-quarter to one-third the number in Munster as in any one of the other provinces. Families of this widespread name descend from one or the other of two Ó Fionnagáin septs. One of these septs was located in the north-east of Co. Roscommon in the barony of Ballymore in that county and the adjacent barony of Ballymoe in Co. Galway. The other sept of the name was on the borders of the ancient Kingdoms of Breffny and Oriel in the region where the counties of Cavan, Monaghan and Meath now meet. At the present time some Finnegan families, descendants of these septs, may still be found living in the neighbourhood of the ancient home of their ancestral sept.

FINNERTY

THIS surname, with its variants, Fenaghty and Finaghty, derives from the Irish Ó Fionnachta. Families of these names are found mainly in Connacht in Co. Galway but there is also a fair distribution in Munster. See also Fenton.

FINUCANE

THIS family derives its surname from the Irish Mac Fionnmhacáin. Finucanes are still living in the original homeland of their ancestors in Co. Clare but the family has spread from that county also, mainly into Co. Limerick and Co. Kerry. Kinucane was recorded as a variant in Ennis Union, Co. Clare, by the Registrar of Births in the last century but this form appears now to be extinct, at least in Ireland. (*see page 84*)

FITZGERALD

THIS surname, one of the commonest in Ireland, is borne by families of all ranks of society there, from the ducal family of Leinster, baronets and knights, down to the humblest persons. It came to Ireland, however, with an aristocratic Anglo-Norman, or more accurately Cambro-Norman knightly family from Wales which played an important role in the Anglo-Norman conquest of the island in the 12th century. Although the name is now such a common one it is by no means equally distributred throughout the country, the great majority of Fitzgerald families being found in Munster where, until the sequestration of their palatinate at the end of the 16th century, the Fitzgeralds, Earls of Desmond, held a vast territory in Co. Limerick, Co. Cork and Co. Kerry, with their principal castle stronghold at Askeaton in Co. Limerick and another important seat at Newcastle West in the same county. Of about 15,000 persons named Fitzgerald in Ireland at the close of the 19th century, 11,500 (almost four-fifths), were living in Munster, and most of these were still residing in Co. Limerick, Co. Cork and Co. Kerry. Save for some families dispersed to

FINNEGAN *Landscape in the barony of Ballymore, Co. Roscommon*

Connacht, where a branch of the family was established in Co. Mayo in the medieval period, and where Fitzgeralds from Co. Kilkenny were transplanted to the same county in the 17th century, and where there were less than one thousand Fitzgeralds in the province, and in Ulster, where there were only about three hundred or so of the name; the rest, around 2500 persons or more, were in Dublin and the other counties of Leinster, where the Fitzgeralds of Kildare held sway for centuries with their principal castle strongholds at Maynooth and Kilkea in Co. Kildare. Of the Fitzgerald nobility, the Dukes of Leinster have sold their splendid 18th century mansion, Carton, Co. Kildare, near their ancient stronghold, Maynooth, and the Knights of Kerry have left their ancestral place at Dingle, Co. Kerry, and gone to live in England but the Knight of Glin is still at Glin Castle in Co. Limerick.

FITZGIBBON *The medieval Blossom Gate at Kilmallock, Co. Limerick, the town that was the seat of the White Knights, a branch of the Fitzgibbons*

FITZGIBBON

IN Ireland, families of the surname Fitzgibbon, which is of Anglo-Norman origin, descend from settlers who came over in the wake of the Anglo-Norman conquest at the end of the 12th century. The establishment of the name in Munster at that time accounts for the majority of Fitzgibbon families being found still in that province and mainly in Co. Limerick. See also Gibbons. The White Knight was the hereditary title of the chief of this Norman settler family in Desmond. Until recently Fitzgibbon families were found almost exclusively still in Munster and predominantly in Co. Limerick. Their particular territory, Clangibbon, forms part of the present barony of Condons and Clangibbon in the north of Co. Cork adjacent to the Co. Limerick border.

FITZHARRIS

THIS Anglo-Norman surname, now found mainly in Co. Carlow, was earlier principally in Co. Wexford. The Registrar of Births reported, in the last century, the use of Fitzhenry in Wexford Union interchangeably with Fitzharris. Fitzhenry survives as a surname in Co. Carlow and Co. Wexford and there are families of both surnames in Dublin. The Registrar also reported an instance at Killeen, Co. Meath, of the use of Feeharry for Fitzharris.

FITZHERBERT

THIS surname was brought from England to Co. Cavan by a settler from Staffordshire in the 17th century.

FITZMAURICE

FAMILIES of this Anglo-Norman name in Ireland can be sorted into two geographically separate groups, the one in Co. Kerry the other in Connacht, originating in Co. Mayo. The Connacht Fitzmaurices, in fact, descend from another Anglo-Norman family, Prendergast, one branch of which in Co. Mayo took Fitzmaurice for their surname. The ancestry of the Kerry Fitzmaurices is ultimately the same as that of the Fitzgeralds whose heraldic device – a saltire gules on an argent field – is incorporated into the Fitzmaurice coat of arms: Argent, a saltire gules, a chief, ermine. The progenitor of the Kerry Fitzmaurices was Maurice Fitz Thomas whose issue took FitzMaurice as their name; he, who was a grandson of Maurice FitzGerald of Maynooth, Co. Kildare, established himself in Co. Kerry early in the 13th century, with his stronghold at Molahiffe in Magunihy barony.

FITZPATRICK

ALTHOUGH this surname is composed with the Norman prefix Fitz it is not of Anglo-Norman origin. The surname Fitzpatrick was adopted by descendants of the Ossory sept MacGiolla Padraig in lieu of the usual translation (Mc) Gilpatrick or Kilpatrick. Both Gilpatrick, which is rare, and Kilpatrick, which was found mainly in Ulster, have survived, however, as surnames, now borne by descendants of those of the sept who did not 'Normanize' their name. Fitzpatrick ranks among the hundred commonest surnames in Ireland and is found everywhere. There is, nevertheless, still a noticeably heavy concentration of the name in Co. Leix, which was the homeland of the important Ossory sept, MacGiolla Padraig. It is possible that Fitzpatrick, meaning simply 'son of Patrick', also became the surname of persons of other families, having been used in the first place to distinguish the person. There are abundant examples of the use of Fitz in this way. For example, two contemporary John Roches, one the son of a John, the other of a Patrick, would be described as John Roche fitz John and John Roche fitz Patrick. The Reports of the Registrar of Births in the last century contain a number of strange variants found to have been used interchangeably with Fitzpatrick. These include Fitch in Ulster, in Banbridge Union, Co. Down, and Irvinstown Union, Co. Fermanagh; Patchy also in Ulster, in Kilkeel Union, Co. Down; Paragon and Parrican in Balrothery Union, Co. Dublin; Patrick in Belfast Union, Co. Antrim, and Gorey Union, Co. Wexford.

FITZSIMONS

THIS Anglo-Norman surname, brought to Dublin early in the 14th century by a settler from Cornwall in England, is distributed almost equally in Leinster, where it is commonest in and around Dublin, and in Ulster, where the heaviest distribution is in Co. Cavan.

FLAHAVAN

FLAHAVAN families, whose name derives from the Irish Ó Flaitheamháin, have long been concentrated in west County Waterford and on the other side of the Blackwater around Youghal in Co. Cork where the variant spelling Flavin has found favour.

FLAHERTY See O'FLAHERTY

FLANAGAN

THIS surname, one of the hundred commonest in Ireland, is in Irish, Ó Flannagáin. It is found in all four provinces, but more frequently in Connacht and least frequently in Munster. The most prominent sept of the name held a territory in Co. Roscommon in Frenchpark barony, another belonged to Co. Fermanagh and yet another to Ballybritt barony in Co. Offaly.

FLANNERY

ONE Ó Flannabhra sept from Killala, Co. Mayo, and another from Upper and Lower Connello baronies in Co. Limerick, are the progenitors of families named Flannery. They are found, in fact, in about equal numbers in Connacht, where there is still a good representation of the name in Co. Mayo, and in Munster, where the name is still well represented in Co. Limerick and has spread from there, particularly to the region around Nenagh in the neighbouring county of Tipperary.

FLATLEY

THIS surname derives from the Co. Sligo sept, Ó Flaithfhileadh (Ó Flaitle). It was found almost exclusively in Co. Mayo by the end of the last century and is still principally represented in that county in the neighbourhood of Knock.

FLATTERY

THIS surname, in Irish, Ó Flaitre, belongs to the region in the north of Co. Offaly in Kilcoursey barony and the adjacent baronies of Upper and Lower Mayfenragh in Co. Meath.

FLEMING

A Fleming is any native of Flanders, so those who bore the name in Ireland will not necessarily have a common ancestor. The most notable Irish Fleming family established itself in Co. Meath in the wake of the Anglo-Norman invasion and the Flemings, Lords of Slane, had their stronghold at that place. Fleming families in Co. Cork may descend from much later settlers and in Ulster, where there is the heaviest distribution of Fleming families in Ireland, most will have come from Scotland at the time of the Plantation of Ulster in the 17th century, being descended themselves from settlers from Flanders who had previously found a new home on the borders of Scotland at the end of the 12th century.

FLOOD

As the surname Flood exists in England it is probable that some families of this name in Ireland will be descendants of English settlers, but there is evidence that Flood was adopted as their surname by native Irish families whose name in Irish was Ó Maoltuile or Mac Maoltuile. The Registrar of Births reported, at the end of the last century, the interchangeable use of Flood and McAtilla (deriving from Mac an Tuile and ultimately from Mac Maoltuile) in Milford Union, Co. Donegal. Flood families are found for the greater part in Leinster and in Co. Cavan in Ulster. The Floods of Burnchurch, Co. Kilkenny, bore as coat of arms: Vert, a chevron, between three wolves' heads erased argent.

FLYNN

FLYNN and O'Flynn rank together among the fifty commonest surnames in Ireland. Families of the name do not have a common ancestry but may descend from any number of distinct persons who became distinguished at a given time by the adjectival descriptive flann, which means ruddy,

and which gave rise to the name Ó Floinn. There were two O'Flynn septs in Co. Cork, where the surname is still widespread, one seated in West Cork in West Carbery barony with a stronghold at Ardagh and the other in East Muskerry barony. In Connacht, there was an O'Flynn sept seated in Castlereagh barony, Co. Roscommon, and in Ulster, another sept of the name held a territory in southern Co. Antrim; some of their descendants have become O'Lynn or Lynn.

FOGARTY

THE Ó Fógartaigh sept, from which the families named Fogarty descend, held a territory named Eile ni Fhógartaigh whence the name of the barony of Eliogarty, Co. Tipperary. Ely O'Fogarty (Eile ni Fhógartaigh) distinguished that part of Ely which was under the Ó Fógartaigh chief from that part which was under the Ó Cearbhaill, known as Ely O'Carroll. There is still a strong representation of the surname Fogarty in Co. Tipperary and in the region of Thurles, close to their former stronghold, Castle Fogarty. See also Gogarty.

FOLEY

THE surname Foley derives from Ó Foghladha, the name of a sept which originated in Co. Waterford. Foley now ranks among the hundred commonest surnames in Ireland but its distributions is very noticeably heaviest in Munster.

FORD(E)

FAMILIES of the name Ford in Ireland may descend from one of the Irish septs, some of whose members adopted Ford as their surname, or from English settlers named Ford, a number of whom came to Ireland at various times and to various parts of the country since the 14th century. Of the native Irish families, whose descendants adopted the name Ford, were the Mac Consnámha and Mac Giolla na Naomh septs in Connacht; in both cases Ford is a mistranslation of the original name. In Co. Cork, Ford(e) was adopted by some descendants of the Ó Fuartháin sept.

FORTUNE

THIS surname is still found principally in Co. Wexford, the county with which it has always been associated in Ireland. It seems unclear whether it derives from the Irish Ó Foirtcheirn or whether the family descends from an immigrant settler. The Registrar of Births also reported at the end of the last century the use of the surname Fortune in Dunmanaway Union, Co. Cork, interchangeably with Farshin and McCarthy. Farshin (from the Irish fairsing, meaning generous) was adopted by some of the McCarthys; its interchangeable use with Fortune was obviously due to the similarity in pronunciation.

FOX

A small minority of Fox families in Ireland will be descended from English settlers of that name; most are of native Irish ancestry being descended from a forebear who was designated by the sobriquet 'sionnach', meaning the fox. The most famous of these was Tadhg Ó Catharnaigh, Chief of Teffia in Co. Meath in the latter half of the 11th century, who was known as Sionnach, and many of whose descendants came to be known as Sionnach instead of their ancestral sept name Ó Catharnaigh, which was usually anglicized as O'Caherny, Carney and Kearney. There is evidence that Fox was also adopted as a surname by other Irish families through mistranslation of their Irish name. One example of this was the use of Fox interchangeably with Shanaghy (which derives from seanchaidhe and not from sionnach).

FOY See FEE

FRASER

As Fraser is one of the twenty commonest surnames in Scotland it is almost surprising that it is not more strongly represented in Ireland. Most of the Fraser families in Ireland are in Ulster where settlers brought the name in the 17th century. Frizell, which is a known variant of Frazer in Scotland, also exists in Ulster and was still used there interchangeably with Fraser in the last century in Co. Antrim.

FRAWLEY

THIS surname, in Irish Ó Freaghaile, is found mainly in the southern part of Co. Clare and in the adjacent county of Limerick.

FRENCH

THE French families in Ireland are of remote Norman origin, Anglo-Norman settlers of the name having established themselves in Co. Wexford where the name survives. From that county a branch of the family went to Galway early in the 15th century where they prospered and multipled so that their descendants soon came to be numbered among the so-called 'Tribes of Galway'.

FRIEL

THE Ó Firghil sept, from which the Friel families descend, claimed lineal descent from a brother of Saint Columcille. Their home was in Co. Donegal where their chief enjoyed the hereditary office of inaugurating the chief of the O'Donnells as lord of Tyrconnell. The distribution of the name today is still mainly in Co. Donegal and in neighbouring Co. Derry and Co. Tyrone.

FUREY

THIS name derives from a branch of the Ó Maoilsheachlainn sept of Co. Westmeath called the Ó Furreidh or Ó Foirreith and who settled in Co. Galway where the name survives, as well as being sparsely scattered in other parts.

FURLONG

THIS surname is still found in Ireland, predominantly in Co. Wexford where settlers of the name from England established themselves in the 13th century.

GAFFNEY

THIS surname, which is distributed in approximately equal numbers in Ulster and Connacht and rather more heavily in Leinster with a considerable representation in the capital, can derive from more than one origin. It has been used as a translation of Ó Gamhna, an Ossory sept, also of Ó Géibheannaigh, a Connacht sept (whose name is more properly anglicized as Geaveney or Keaveney), also of Mac Conghamhna, another Connacht sept, and of Mac Carrghamhna, a sept of the southern Uí Neill (whose name is also anglicized as McCarron). Caulfield was widely adopted as a surname by Gaffney families. In the last century the Registrar of Births reported the use of Gaughney interchangeably with Gaffney in Granard Union, Co. Longford, but Gaughney is also the anglicization of Mag Fhachtna.

GALLAGHER

The Ó Gallchobhair sept, from which Gallagher families are descended, held a territory in the southeast of Co. Donegal in the baronies of Tirhugh and Raphoe with a sept centre at Ballynaglack near Stranorlar. Although Gallagher and O'Gallagher rank among the twenty commonest surnames in Ireland, the distribution is still markedly concentrated close to the original territory of the sept. At the beginning of this century two-fifths of all the Gallaghers in Ireland were still to be found in Co. Donegal. Despite 20th century population movements this pattern is still noticeable, with a predominance of the name outside the capital, in Co. Donegal and the neighbouring Derry, Tyrone and Sligo.

GALLIGAN

This name derives from that of the Co. Sligo sept Ó Gealagáin, also rendered as Gilligan, which is still found in Co. Sligo but also widely scattered. Galligan is found mainly in Co. Cavan and in adjacent counties.

GALLIVAN

Predominantly a Co. Kerry family surname, Gallivan, like the commoner surname Galvin, which is more widely scattered, derives from Ó Gealbháin, a Co. Clare sept, branches of which settled in Co. Kerry and in Co. Roscommon.

GANLEY

This surname derives from Mag Sheanlaoich, more usually rendered Shanly, q.v.

GANNON

This Co. Mayo family derives its name from the Irish Mag Fhionnáin.

GARA See O'GARA

GARVEY

This surname derives from the Ó Gairbith sept which belonged to Oneilland East Barony, Co. Armagh, and was prominent a little farther to the east in eastern Co. Down as well as from Mac Gairbith which seems to have a separate origin in Co. Donegal. Garvey is also in use as a surname as a corruption of Garvin (Ó Gairbhín) in Connacht and of Garvan (Ó Garbháin) in Munster.

GARVIN

The Ó Gairbhín sept, from which Garvin families descend, was originally seated in Co. Meath but migrated westwards in the wake of the Anglo-Norman invasion and re-established itself in Western Co. Mayo where one branch became prominent at Murrisk.

GAUGHAN

This Co. Mayo surname derives from the north Connacht sept, Ó Gáibhtheacháin (Ó Gachain). A variant anglicization is Gavaghan also found mainly in Co. Mayo and Co. Roscommon.

GAVIN

The surname Gavin, and the less common surname Gavan, derive from two Irish septs, the Ó Gábháin, which belonged to North Connacht, and the Ó Gáibhín from southern Munster. At the end of the last century almost all the Gavin families were confined to Connacht, about two-thirds of these being in Co. Mayo and about one-quarter in Co. Galway. The form Gavan seems now to have all but disappeared and one concludes that Gavan families have adopted the spelling Gavin.

GAYNOR

The Gaynor families, now found scattered in various parts of Ireland, were formerly predominantly in northern Leinster in Co. Westmeath and the adjacent counties; their surname derives from the Irish Mag Fhionnbhairr.

GEOGHEGAN

THIS surname, pronounced Gay-gan, derives from the Mac Eochagáin sept of the barony of Moycashel, Co. Westmeath, where Castletown Geoghegan was once a stronghold and seat of the family. Into the 18th century many of the family retained the prefix Mac, being recorded as Mac Geoghegan and a few still use this form. Not surprisingly many variant spellings are recorded, including Gagan, Gahagan, Gegan, Gehegan, Geogan and Houghegan.

GERAGHTY

FROM the Mag Oireachtaigh sept of Co. Roscommon and Co. Galway, whose lineage began with an Oireachtach of the Ó Roduibh sept in the 12th century, descend the Mac Geraghty and Geraghty families whose surname has appeared in records with numerous variant spellings, including Garity, Garrity, Gearty, Gerarty, Geraty, Gerety, Gerity, Gerty, some of which have survived. A number of Geraghty families still reside in the original home counties of their ancestral sept although the name is also now rather widely scattered.

GETTY

THIS surname, found in Ulster, mostly in Co. Antrim but also in other parts of the province, was apparently brought over by settlers from Scotland, where it is a known variant of the Scottish surname Dalgetty.

GIBBONS

OF Norman settler stock like the Fitzgibbon families, the Gibbons families do not, however, share the same ancestry, being in fact lineally descended from the great Burke family of Connacht, of a branch known as MacGibbon Burke and then eventually as Mac Gibbon and Gibbons. Gibbons is still notably a Connacht name, and predominantly from Co. Mayo, where the seat of the Mac Gibbon Burkes was in the townlands of North and South Ballymacgibbon near Cong in Kilmaine barony.

GIBLIN

THIS surname is still found predominantly in Connacht where the early home of the family, in Irish, Ó Gibealáin, was in Co. Roscommon.

GIBNEY

THE majority of Gibney families, since at least the end of the last century, lived in the capital and in Co. Meath; their surname appears to derive from the Irish Ó Gibne.

GIBSON

PREDOMINANTLY found in Ireland in eastern Ulster, Gibson families in Ireland are of settler descent. The majority will be descended from Scottish immigrants who came with the 17th century plantation schemes.

GILGAN

THIS surname derives from the Ó Giollagáin sept whose home was in northern Co. Leitrim and the adjacent region of Co. Sligo. The name survives in that part of Ireland in small numbers.

GILGUNN

FAMILIES of this name survive in Co. Leitrim and Co. Fermanagh. They descend from the Co. Fermanagh sept Mac Giolla Dhuinn.

GILHOOLEY

THE Gilhooley families, some of whom are still living in their ancient homeland region in Co. Leitrim, derive their name from the Irish Mac Giolla Ghuala, the name of a branch of the Ó Maoilmhiadhaigh sept of Co. Leitrim.

GILLAN

THIS surname, found mainly in western Ulster and in the Connacht county of Sligo, with its variant Gillen, derives from the Irish sept Ó Giolláin, whose homeland was in north-eastern Co. Tyrone and western Co. Donegal.

GILLESPIE

GILLESPIE families derive their name from the Irish Mac Giolla Easpuig and so, by translation, some of them adopted the English surname Bishop. Gillespie is predominantly an Ulster surname found in all the counties of that province. A number of variant spellings are recorded, those most widely varying from the normal being Clusby, Glashby and Gillesby, all reported in Ardee Union, Co. Louth, and Glaspy, reported in Westport Union, Co. Mayo.

GILMARTIN

THIS Connacht surname, long concentrated almost exclusively in the counties of Sligo and Leitrim, derives from the Mac Giolla Mhártain sept which originated in Tyrone and migrated westwards.

GILMORE

THIS surname, with its less common variant Gilmour, can derive either from the Irish Mac Giolla Mhuire or Mac Giolla Mhir. It was also brought to Ulster, where it is commonest, by settlers from Scotland, where the name exists with the same Gaelic origin.

GILROY See McILROY

GINTY See McGINTY

GLEESON

THE surname of the Gleeson families comes from the Irish Ó Gleasáin, also written Ó Glasáin. The ancient origins of the forebears of this sept were in Co. Cork but the sept established itself in Owney and Arra barony, Co. Tipperary. At the end of the last century about one-half of all the Gleeson families in Ireland still resided in Co. Tipperary and the greater part of the rest lived in other counties of Munster. Gleeson families are still numerous in the region of Nenagh near their early homeland.

GLYNN

GLYNN families descend usually from the Mag Fhloinn sept which had its territory in Co. Roscommon, near Athlone, although a small minority may descend from Welsh settlers who quite separately brought the Welsh surname Glyn(n) from Wales. The Irish family name is preserved also in the name of a Co. Roscommon lake and town of Loughglynn, a region where Glynn families still reside.

GOGARTY

THIS surname, deriving from the Irish Mag Fhógartaigh, is a cognate of Fogarty, q.v.

GORDON

As Gordon ranks among the fifty commonest surnames in Scotland it is not surprising that it is found frequently now in Ulster whence it was brought by Scottish settlers since the time of the 17th century plantations and whence families of the name have moved on to the adjacent provinces also.

GORMAN

THIS family surname derives from the Mac Gormáin sept whose territory was in the barony of Slievemargy, Co. Leix, until the 12th century when they were ejected by the Anglo-Normans. Some of the sept migrated to Co. Monaghan, where their descendants survive as Gorman and McGorman, and others migrated to Co. Clare, establishing themselves there in Ibrickan barony. One of the descendants of the Clare branch achieved fame and fortune in France in the 18th century. Due to his prominence, and because he adopted the form O'Gorman, other descendants of the sept have adopted the prefix in place of their lost prefix which should rightly be Mac. At the end of the last century there were six Gormans for every one O'Gorman but widespread assumption of the prefix O' by Gormans in the present century has altered the situation and the O'Gormans now outnumber the Gormans. The correct form McGorman has long been rare but is not extinct.

GORMLEY

FAMILIES named Gormley and O'Gormley descend from the Ulster sept Ó Gairmleadhaigh, whose early home territory was in North and South Raphoe baronies in Co. Donegal but which migrated eastwards across the River Foyle in the counties of Derry and Tyrone, re-establishing itself there about the 14th century.

There is still a considerable representation of Gormley families in Co. Tyrone. To the south of Co. Tyrone in the counties of Longford and Cavan, and also in Co. Antrim, where members of the family settled there is evidence that their name was confused with Gorman, while in the home county of Tyrone, in Omagh Union, the Registrar of Births reported in the last century the use of the English surname Grimes interchangeably with Gormley.

GOULD

THIS surname, which is of English origin, is recorded in Cork long prior to the settlement of English immigrants in 16th century and was apparently introduced by settlers who came like the Coppingers by the 14th century. Gould families took a prominent part in the mercantile life of Cork city for centuries and some of the name still reside there at the present time.

GRACE

THE Norman sobriquet le Gras is the origin of the surname Grace borne by descendants of Anglo-Normans who came to Ireland about 1200. The Graces established themselves in Co. Kilkenny, principally in Gowran Barony, and that county and Co. Dublin were long the main areas of distribution of the surname, now more widely scattered. The Graces of Castle Grace, Co. Kilkenny bore as their coat of arms: Gules, a lion rampant, per fesse argent and or.

GRADY See O'GRADY

GRAHAM

As it ranks among the fifty commonest surnames in Scotland, Graham was brought to Ulster by a number of settlers since the 17th century plantations and, in fact, in such numbers that it now ranks among the hundred commonest surnames in Ireland. Over three-quarters of the Grahams in Ireland are found in Ulster and a fair number of the remainder in Dublin.

GRAY

GRAY also ranks among the fifty commonest surnames in Scotland but its importation to Ireland was less than that of Graham by about one-half. The distribution, however, is similar to that of the Graham families in Ireland, about three-quarters in Ulster and most of the remainder in Dublin.

GREANEY

THIS surname, which derives from the Irish Ó Gráinne or Mac Gráinne, is found mainly in two distinct areas, in Munster, in Co. Kerry, whence it spread into Co. Limerick and in Connacht, in Co. Galway.

GREEHY

THIS surname, in Irish Ó Griocha, belongs to an area in West Co. Waterford and across the River Blackwater in eastern Co. Cork.

GREEN(E)

As Green ranks among the twenty commonest surnames in England it, of course, came to Ireland over the centuries, brought by numerous English settlers of the name. The large numbers of Greens in Ireland, where the name is found in all four provinces, may be accounted for, however, by the fact that this common English name was adopted as an anglicization of their name by several Irish families. The Irish uaine, meaning green, usually used to denote things dyed green, was the reason for some members of the Ó hUainín (Honeen, Houneen) family in Co. Clare to take the surname Green. The Irish, glas, also meaning green, was usually applied, as an adjective, to things green by nature. Because of this translation members of the MacGiolla Ghlais (McIllesher, Mc Alesher) family in Co. Fermanagh and of the Mac Glasáin (McGlashan) family in Co. Derry, took the surname Green also. The Irish word faithche, meaning a fair green, being similar to their family name, accounts for the adoption of the surname Green by members of the Ó Fathaigh (Fahy) family in Co. Galway.

GREER

THIS surname was brought from Scotland in the 17th century by settlers who established themselves principally in eastern Ulster in the counties of Antrim, Down and Armagh. Of the descendants of one particular settler Henry Greer, a Quaker, from Alnwick in Northumberland, who came to Ireland in the mid-17th century, some bear the surname Greer and others Greeve, Grieves, and Greeves; their immigrant ancestor himself was known in his lifetime both as Greer and Greves.

GREHAN

THE Grehan families derive their name from the Irish Ó Gréacháin. Before the population movement of the 20th century about one-half of the Grehans in Ireland lived in western Leinster, in Co. Westmeath, and one-half farther west in Connacht, in the counties of Galway, Mayo and Sligo. Some survive in all those places but others are now more widely dispersed.

GRIFFIN

WHILE some Griffin families in Ireland may descend from settlers of that name who came over from Wales and England, the great majority will come from ancient Irish lineage, being descendants of septs named Ó Gríobtha. One of these had its sept centre at Ballygriffin in Glanarought Barony, Co. Kerry. Griffin families are still numerous in Co. Kerry and in the adjacent county of Limerick where there is a Ballygriffin townland also, situated in Coshma barony. It is possible, however, that some, or all of the Co. Limerick Griffins and indeed also some of the Co. Kerry Griffins may descend from the Ó Gríobtha sept whose territory was in Inchiquin barony, Co. Clare, with a stronghold there at Ballygriffy whence branches of the sept migrated to neighbouring counties.

GUINNESS See McGUINNESS

HACKETT

THIS surname derives from the personal name Haket and was brought to Ireland at the end of the 12th century by Anglo-Norman settlers who established themselves in Leinster where their name is commemorated in the townlands of Hacketstown and Ballyhacket Lower and Upper in Rathvilly barony, Co. Carlow, Hacketsland in Rathdown barony, Co. Dublin, and Hacketstown in Balrothery East barony, Co. Dublin. There are also places named Ballyhacket in Ulster, in Co. Derry and Co. Antrim, and places named Hacketstown in Munster, in Co. Cork and Co. Waterford. Castle Hacket in Clare barony, Co. Galway, was once a stronghold of a branch of the family which established itself in Connacht. The name is now rare in Connacht but survives in the other three provinces with the heaviest distribution in Leinster, particularly in Dublin and in Co. Kilkenny.

HAGAN See O'HAGAN

HALL

THIS English surname, which ranks among the twenty commonest in England, is found predominantly in Ulster but also in considerable numbers in Leinster and Munster, although rare in Connacht. It was brought to Munster by settlers as early as the 14th century but came to Ulster with the 17th century planters.

HALLAHAN

THIS surname, and its variant, Hallaghan, which derive from the Irish Ó hAileacháin, are found mainly in eastern Co. Cork and western Co. Waterford.

HALLIGAN

THE Halligan families descend from the Ó hAileagáin sept and are still found in its ancient territory in southern Co. Armagh and Co. Louth as well as in Dublin and in Connacht, where branches established themselves. Because of the similarity between Ó hAileagáin and Ó hAileacháin the surnames Hallahan (Hallaghan) and Halligan have sometimes been confused.

HALLINAN

THE Hallinan families, most of whom live in Co. Cork and the adjacent counties of Limerick and Tipperary, derive their name from the Irish Ó hAilgheanáin.

HALLISSEY

THIS surname is found predominantly in Co. Cork and in lesser numbers in Co. Kerry, the counties which have long been the home of families of the name which derives from the Irish Ó hAilgheasa.

HALL(E)Y

DR. MacLysaght found two derivations for the Munster surname Hally or Halley, either Ó hAilche or Ó hAille, the latter being the name of a sept from southern Co. Clare (possibly ultimately of the same derivation as Ó hAinle). Halley and Hally families are found now predominantly in Co. Waterford spilling over into southern Co. Tipperary.

HALPIN

THIS surname, found predominantly in Dublin and in Munster, in Co. Clare and Co. Limerick, and its variants, Halpeny and Halfpenny which are found mainly in Co. Louth and Co. Monaghan are all derived from the Irish Ó hAilpin.

HAMILTON

ONE of the forty commonest surnames in Scotland, Hamilton was brought to Ulster in considerable numbers by settlers during the 17th century plantation of that province, so that it is among the twenty commonest surnames in Co. Antrim, and among the fifteen commonest in both Co. Down and Co. Tyrone.

HANAFIN

THE strongest representation of Hanafin families is in the neighbourhood of Tralee, Co. Kerry, but prior to the population movements of this century the name, which derives from the Irish Ó hAinbhthin, was found exclusively in Co. Kerry where it was also spelt Hanifin.

HANL(E)Y

THIS surname comes from the name of the Connacht sept Ó hAinle whose homeland was in Co. Roscommon where descendants of the sept are still found as well as being widely dispersed in Munster, where a branch established itself in Co. Cork.

HANNA

THIS Scottish surname is found predominantly in Ireland in eastern Ulster, in Co. Antrim and Co. Down, where it was brought by settlers from Scotland in the 17th century.

HANNIGAN

THIS surname derives from the Irish Ó hAnnagáin. Even before the population movements of the 20th century Hannigan families were scattered in various parts of Ireland, as widely apart as Co. Waterford in the south, Dublin in the east, and Co. Tyrone in the north.

HANNON

IT appears that most Hannon and Hannan families from Co. Limerick derive their name from the Irish Ó hAnáin or Ó hAnnáin but in that county, according to Dr. MacLysaght, Irish Ó hAnnacháin, usually anglicized as Hanahan, also became Hannan. In Co. Galway the surname Hannon is found; it may derive from Ó hAnnáin but Dr. MacLysaght has pointed out that some Galway Hannons bear the name as a corruption of the Irish Ó hAinchín which is more correctly rendered in English as Hanneen. Hannon is also found in Co. Roscommon where it appears to derive from Ó hAnnáin.

HANRAHAN

Hanrahan families are still found principally in Munster, in Co. Limerick, and in lesser numbers in the adjacent counties of Clare, Kerry, Cork and Tipperary. They trace their descent from the Ó hAnracháin or Ó hAnradháin sept whose homeland was in the south of Co. Clare.

HANRATTY

THE territory of the Ó hAnrachtaigh sept, from which the Hanratty families descend, was in Oriel, in the north of Co. Louth whence they moved north-westwards in the wake of the Anglo-Norman invasion, re-establishing themselves in the barony of Cremorne in Co. Monaghan and despite 20th century population movements many of the name still live in the neighbourhood of Dundalk, Co. Louth, and Castleblayney, Co. Monaghan.

HARBISON

THE surname Harbinson or Harbison was brought to Ulster in the 17th century by settlers from the north of England or from Scotland. It has remained predominantly an Ulster name in Ireland where it has been found mainly in Co. Antrim. Harvison and Herbison have been reported as variants, and in the last century the Registrar of Births reported in Newry Union, Co. Down, the use of Harbinson interchangeably with the otherwise quite distinct surname, Herbert.

HARE See O'HARE

HARGADON

THIS Co. Sligo surname, which derives from the Irish Ó hArgadáin, is now found scattered thinly in other parts of Ireland, where it is sometimes spelt Hargaden, but also survives in and around Sligo town.

HARKIN

THIS rather English-appearing surname, in fact, derives from the Irish Ó hEarcáin and belonged originally to the Inishowen peninsula in Co. Donegal. It is still found principally in Co. Donegal.

HARRINGTON

ALTHOUGH the English surname Harrington did come to Ireland with settlers from England, the vast majority of families named Harrington in Ireland today are, in fact, of native Irish lineage, being, for the most part, descended from the Irish sept Ó hIongardail. Members of this sept adopted Harrington as their surname and they are still numerous in its old homeland West Cork. According to Dr. MacLysaght some other Irish names were also anglicized as Harrington, in Connacht Ó hOireachtaigh, more usually Heraghty, and in Co. Kerry Ó hArrachtáin, the name of a sept which originated in Co. Galway.

HARRIS

RANKING among the thirty commonest surnames in England, Harris was inevitably brought to Ireland by a number of settlers and was established in about equal numbers in Leinster (particularly Dublin) and Munster (particularly Co. Cork), in lesser numbers in Ulster (but particularly in Co. Antrim) and hardly at all in Connacht.

HARRISON

LIKE Harris, the surname Harrison ranks among the thirty commonest in England and consequently was brought to Ireland by numerous settlers but principally to eastern Ulster and to Dublin.

HAR(R)OLD

HAROLD is one of the few surnames of Norse origin to be found now in Ireland. It was brought by Norse settlers prior to the Anglo-Norman invasion in the 12th century to two Viking seaports which became Hiberno-Norse settlements, Dublin and Limerick. The name figured prominently in the history of Limerick for centuries and at the end of the last century the largest number of Harold families in the country was still in that city and its environs. Families spelling their name both Harold and Harrold are still living there today as well as in Co. Cork and in Dublin.

HART

WHILE a minority of Hart families in Ireland may be lineally descended from English settlers of the name like the Hart(e)s of Lullingstone in Kent who established themselves in Co. Limerick in the 16th century, the great majority descend from the Irish sept Ó hAirt, one of the so-called Four Tribes of Tara, whose territory was in Co. Meath but who re-established themselves in Carbury barony, Co. Sligo, after migrating westwards in the time of the Anglo-Norman invaders at the end of the 12th century. The Connacht counties of Sligo, Leitrim and Roscommon remained the principal homeland of the Hart(e)s and O'Harts but the name is also found in considerable numbers in the other three provinces. This surname was rarely found with the prefix O' until the present century and the Hart(e)s being among those families who did not move to reassume it, the O'Hart(e)s are still very much in the minority to the Hart(e)s.

HARTIGAN

THE Hartigan families, most numerous in Co. Limerick, long their home, descend from the Thomond sept Ó hArtagáin which was located in the east of Co. Clare and across the Shannon in the north of Co. Limerick.

HARTNETT

FAMILIES named Hartnett, and the less common variant Harnett, derive their name from the Irish Ó hAirtnéada. Harnett has been favoured as a spelling in Co. Limerick mainly and in Co. Kerry; Hartnett has been slightly commoner in Co. Cork but this spelling is also found in Co. Limerick.

HARTY

THE Munster surname Harty, found mainly in Co. Kerry, and in Co. Tipperary and Co. Cork, derives from the Irish Ó hAthartaigh (Ó hArtaigh).

HASSAN

THIS surname, in Irish Ó hOsáin, belongs to the Sperrin Mountains in Co. Derry.

HASSETT

SOME descendants of the planter family Blenner-hassett, in Co. Kerry, adopted Hassett as an abbreviated form of their name but Hassett is borne as a surname also by descendants of the Thomond sept Ó hAiseadha, whose home was in Co. Clare in which county and in the adjacent county of Tipperary most Hassetts of that lineage have resided.

HAUGHEY

THE Haughey families, who derive their name from the Irish Ó hEachaidh, resided in equal numbers in Co. Donegal and Co. Armagh until some were dispersed in the course of 20th century population movement.

HAYES *See O'HEA*

HEA *See O'HEA*

HEALY

ONE of the fifty commonest surnames in Ireland, Healy derives either from the Connacht sept, Ó hElidhe which held sway in the south of the barony of Tirerril, Co. Sligo, where the townland of Ballyhealy commemorates their association with that area, or the Munster sept, Ó hEalaighthe whose sept centre was in the barony of Muskerry, Co. Cork. Heally and Hely are known variants.

HEANEY

HEANEY families, who descend from the Oriel sept Ó hEighnigh, are still to be found mainly in that area, in Co. Armagh and Co. Louth, and are also well represented in Co. Antrim.

HEARN(E)

THE English surname Hearn(e) may be borne in Ireland by some descendants of English settlers of that name but most Hearn(e) families will be of Irish descent, their forefathers having adopted this English surname as an anglicized form of the Irish Ó hEachthigheirn or Ó hEachthighearna, more widely anglicized in Ireland as Ahearn or Aherne. Hearn(e) was the form widely favoured in Co. Waterford where it is still well represented.

HEARTY

THIS surname, in Irish Ó hAghartaigh, belongs to Co. Louth and Co. Monaghan and is distinct from the Munster surname Harty which derives from the Irish Ó hAthartaigh (Ó hArtaigh) although, inevitably outside their homelands, the two surnames are liable to be confused.

HEFFERNAN

THE earliest known territory of the Ó hIfearnáin sept, from which families bearing the surname Heffernan descend, was in the barony of Inchiquin in Co. Clare, whence they migrated southwards and established themselves across the Shannon in Owneybeg barony in the north-east of Co. Limerick where the Slieve Phelim Mountains mark the border of Co. Limerick and Co. Tipperary. Despite the dispersal of Heffernan families in the course of 20th century population movements there is still a considerable concentration of the name in Co. Limerick and Co. Tipperary.

HEFFRON

THE Irish Ó Eimhrín, a surname which originated in Ulster, is most usually rendered in English as Heffron but many variations of spellings are recorded, including Haveron, Havern, Havron and Hefferan. At the end of the last century one-third or more of all the families of this name lived in Co. Mayo but it is now widely scattered.

HEGARTY

THE sept Ó hEigcear-taigh provided the forebears of the Hegarty, O'Hegarty, Hagarty, Hagerty, Heggarty, Higerty, Hegerty families. The early homeland of the sept was in Ulster, along the present border of Co. Donegal and Co. Derry, and those two counties are still today the home of many Hegarty families, including some living close to the early sept centres of their ancestors in Loughinsholin and Tirkeeran baronies in Co. Derry and on the other side of Lough Foyle in Inishowen barony, Co. Donegal.

A branch of the sept, which migrated southward and established itself in Co. Cork, was prolific so that there is a considerable distribution of Hegartys in that county now. Resumption of the prefix O' has been scant among the descendants of the Ó hEigceartaigh sept, only a small minority having favoured its use again.

HEGARTY *Cross-inscribed stone, Duncrun, Co. Derry*

HEHIR

THE homeland of the Ó hAichir sept was in Co. Clare in which county and in the neighbouring county of Limerick most of its descendants are to be found bearing the surname Hehir.

HENCHY

THIS is a variant anglicization of Ó hAonghusa preferred by descendants of that sept in Co. Clare to the commoner form Hennessy, q.v.

HENEHAN

THIS surname, with its variant spellings Heneghan, Henaghan, Henekan, Henihan, derives from the name of the Connacht sept Ó hEineacháin. Until the turn of this century families of this name lived almost exclusively in Connacht and principally in Co. Mayo which still claims the heaviest distribution of families deriving their surname from Ó hEineacháin. In the last century the Registrar of Births reported the use of the English surname Bird interchangeably with Henekan in Tuam Union, Co. Galway, an example of pseudo-translation.

HENNESSY

THE early homeland of one Ó hAonghusa sept, ancestors of families named Hennessy, was in the barony of Lower Philipstown, Co. Offaly, along the present border of that county and Co. Westmeath. Hennessy families still survive in this area and around Kilbeggan, Co. Tipperary, where they settled and where their descendants are still to be found. Another sept of the same name held a territory in West Cork near Rosscarbery and it is from this sept that the Hennessy families, numerous in Co. Cork, trace their descent.

HENRY

THIS surname, found predominantly in Ulster, but also fairly common in Connacht, may derive from the Irish surname Mac Innéirghe or Ó hInnéirghe, or from the Anglo-Norman Fitzhenry imported to Ireland following the invasion in the 12th century and which became Mac Einri in Irish. Some Henry families in Ulster, where the name is commonest in Co. Antrim, descend from 17th century immigrant settlers of the name from Scotland and England, in some cases the present form Henry being a corruption of the Scottish surname Hendry.

HERAGHTY

THIS surname, and its variants, Heraty and Herity, Heraughty, derive from the Irish Ó hOireachtaigh. Formerly found living mostly in Co. Donegal and Co. Mayo until the turn of this century, families bearing these surnames are now found widely scattered throughout the whole country.

HERLIHY

THIS surname derives from the Irish Ó hIarlatha, the name of a family who were erenaghs of St. Gobnet's church in Ballyvourney parish in West Muskerry barony, Co. Cork. The descendants of this family remained mostly in that county but some spread into the adjacent county of Kerry. Because the surname Hurley was common in Co. Cork some Herlihys were recorded as and became known as Hurley although the two names have quite separate origins. Despite the population movements of the present century, Co. Cork and Co. Kerry are still the home of the majority of Herlihy families, a number of whom have assumed the use of the lost prefix O' to become O'Herlihy.

HERNON

FAMILIES bearing the surname Hernon descend from the Ó hIornáin sept. Some of the name still reside in the Aran Islands, an early homeland of the sept, as well as on the mainland of Co. Galway.

HESLIN

THIS surname is borne by descendants of the Ó hEisleanáin sept whose homeland was in the barony of Mohill, Co. Leitrim.

HESSION

FAMILIES of this name were found for the most part in Co. Galway and in lesser numbers in Co. Mayo at the end of the last century and while a few families have since settled in other parts of the country, those two counties remain the home of the majority of Hessions. Their surname derives from the Irish hÓisín.

HEYNE

THIS English surname was adopted in Ireland by descendants of the Ó hEidhin sept who also anglicized it as O'Heyne. The territory of this sept was in the barony of Kiltartan, Co. Galway, where Dungory (Dun-Guaire) Castle near Kinvara was once the stronghold of their chiefs. The Augustinian church at Kilmacdaugh, founded by one of the family, has been known as 'O'Heyne's Church'. As Hynes, descendants of the sept have survived in the largest numbers in Connacht, in Co. Galway, but it is also dispersed now in Munster and other parts of the country.

HICKEY

DESCENDANTS of the ancient family of physicians, Ó hIcidhe, anglicized their surname as Hickey or Hickie. From their early homeland in Co. Clare the family spread into the neighbouring counties of Limerick to the south and Tipperary to the east and from there it was dispersed farther afield.

HIGGINS

THIS English surname may be borne in Ireland by some families descended from English settlers of that name but the majority of Higgins families in Ireland will be descended from the Irish sept Ó hUigín which originated in the Irish midlands but established itself in Connacht in Co. Sligo, mainly in the barony of Tirerril. By the end of the last century Higgins ranked among the hundred commonest surnames in Ireland and at that time one-half of the number bearing the name lived in Connacht, and about one-quarter in Leinster, with the remaining quarter divided between Munster and Connacht. At that time the form O'Higgins was rare but in the present century a few families have resumed the prefix O'.

AMBROSE O'HIGGINS

Belonging to a branch of the Sligo family which was displaced to Co. Meath in the 18th century was Ambrose O'Higgins (1720–1801), who rose from comparatively humble circumstances in the Ireland of the Penal Laws to the exalted position of Viceroy of Peru under the Spanish Crown. His natural son, Bernardo O'Higgins, led the fight for

Chile's independence from Spain and became the first President of the new state in 1818.

HOGAN

THE sept centre of the main Ó hÓgáin sept was at Ardcrony in Lower Ormond barony, Co. Tipperary, whence the family spread into the surrounding counties of Munster and multiplied. Together with those Hogans who may descend from an Ó hÓgáin sept which was located in West Cork the descendants of the Ó hÓgáins bear one of the hundred commonest surnames in Ireland.

HILL

THIS common English surname, which ranks among the twenty-five commonest surnames in England, was brought to Ireland by numerous settlers, especially to the south-east Ulster counties of Down and Antrim and to Dublin. The most prominent of these immigrant families descend from Moyses Hill who came to Ulster in the late 16th century. His descendants, who founded Hillsborough, Co. Down, bear as their coat of arms: Sable, on a fesse, argent, between three leopards, passant guardant, or spotted, of the field, as many escallops, gules.

HOEY

IT appears that most families bearing the surname Hoey, most numerous in Dublin and in Co. Louth, will descend from the south-east Ulster sept, Ó hEochaidh, but it is possible that some may descend from a sept of the same name which was located in Co. Meath.

JOHN HOGAN

A distinguished Irish sculptor belonged to this family. John Hogan (1800–1858) was born at Tallow, Co. Waterford. He started work in his youth as a lawyer's clerk, was then apprenticed to an architect, but soon gained recognition as a sculptor. He studied and worked in Rome for years but returned to his native country for the last ten years of his life. Michael Hogan, the 19th century writer and poet, came from Co. Limerick.

HORAN

FAMILIES named Horan in Connacht will descend from the Ó hOdhráin sept, which was originally located in Co. Galway and spread into Co. Mayo. The name is, however, as common in Munster as it is in Connacht and while some Munster Horans may descend from the Connacht sept, Dr. MacLysaght accounts for the name there as a variant of Haren (in Irish Ó hEaghráin) and also of the name of the south Co. Clare sept Ó hAnracháin or Ó hAnradháin which is usually rendered in English as Hanrahan (q.v.).

HORGAN

UNTIL the beginning of this century the surname Horgan, which derives from the Irish Ó hArragáin (Ó hArgáin), was found exclusively in Munster with the majority of the name in Co. Cork and most of the rest in Co. Kerry. Hourigan, found principally in Co. Limerick and Co. Tipperary, appears to be a variant of Horgan although Father Woulfe opined that it derived from the name of a West Cork sept, Ó hOdragáin. Today the majority of Horgan families still live in Co. Cork. The surname Horrigan found in Co. Cork is a variant of Horgan.

HOULIHAN

THIS surname, and its many recorded variant spellings, Holahan, Holohan, Holoughan, Hoolaghan, Hoolahan, Hoolihan, Hoologhan, Houlaghan, Houlahan, Houlehan, Oolahan, Oulahan, Oulihan, Whoolahan and Whoolehan, derive from the Irish name of two septs of Ó hUallacháin. One of these septs was located in the north of Co. Offaly and the other in Co. Clare. Presumably families named Houlihan and its variants in south-west Munster will descend from the latter sept and those in Co. Kilkenny (where the spelling Holohan has been preferred) will descend from members of the Offaly sept who migrated southwards.

HOURIHAN(E)

THIS Co. Cork surname derives from the name of the sept Ó hAnradhháin which was located in West Cork. There is, however, some confusion with the surname Hanrahan (q.v.) which has been used as the anglicization of Ó hAnradháin as well as Ó hAnracháin.

HOY

THE Ulster surname Hoy derives from a variation in spelling of Hoey (q.v.) and, also, according to Dr. MacLysaght, of Haughey (q.v.).

HOYNE

THIS surname derives from the Irish Ó hEoghain; families of the name have long been concentrated in the neighbourhood of Thomastown, Co. Kilkenny, and until recently Hoynes were found exclusively in that county.

HUGHES

THIS patronymic surname, which is very common in Wales, and ranks among the twenty commonest surnames in England and Wales, was brought to Ireland by numerous settlers over the centuries. It is one of the forty commonest surnames in Ireland, the second commonest surname in Co. Armagh and one of the five commonest surnames in Co. Monaghan. Not all the Hughes families in Ireland will, however, be of settler descent. A very considerable number are of native stock, descendants of one or other of the several Ó hAodha (O'Hugh) septs which were located in Co. Mayo, in Co. Meath, in Co. Donegal, Co. Tyrone and Co. Monaghan, or of the Mac Aodha (Mc Hugh) septs of Co. Galway, their forebears having adopted Hughes as their surname.

HURLEY

IT seems impossible to determine whether families named Hurley, a surname found predominantly in Co. Cork, are descendants of members of the Ó hUirthile sept of Co. Clare, who migrated southwards, or of the Ó Muirthile sept which was located in East Carberry barony in Co. Cork where Ballynacarriga Castle was one of their strongholds. While Hurleys in that area would appear to be of the Ó Muirthile stock this may not be true of all Hurleys in Co. Cork. The Hurley families in Co. Limerick, lying between the early homelands of the two septs, may in consequence descend from one or the other of them.

HUSSEY

THE Norman surname de Houssaye, first corrupted to de Hosé and de Hosey, eventually became Hussey in Ireland where it arrived in the early years of the Anglo-Norman conquest with settlers who established themselves at Galtrim in the barony of Lower Deace, Co. Meath. A branch of the Galtrim Husseys migrated to Co. Kerry where the name still survives. Dr. MacLysaght suggests that Hussey families in Connacht are not of this Norman stock but descend from the sept Ó hEodhusa which was located in Co. Fermanagh.

HYLAND

THIS surname was adopted as an anglicization of their name by persons bearing the Irish surname Ó hAoiléain, itself a variant of Ó Faoláin, a sept which was originally located in Co. Waterford and spread into Co. Kilkenny.

IRWIN

WHILE it is possible that a few families in Ireland bearing the surname Irwin or Irvine might be of native stock, descending from members of the Co. Offaly sept Ó hEireamhóin, who adopted Irwin as an anglicization of their name, it is certain that the majority of Irwins and Irvines descend from Scottish settlers who came to Ulster in the 17th century, particularly to Co. Fermanagh. In fact, Irwin and Irvine are distinct surnames but were frequently confused in Ireland and used interchangeably. Irwin, being the commoner of the two, seems to have absorbed a number of Irvines. Ervine and Ervin are known variants, as is Irving, which is the more usual form in Scotland of Irvine. One prominent settler family named Irvine in Co. Fermanagh made its seat at Castle Irvine in Lurg barony. This family claimed lineal descent from the Irvings of Bonshaw, Dumfriesshire, Scotland, and bore as its coat of arms: Argent, a fess gules between three holly leaves vert.

IVERS

FAMILIES named Ivers of Co. Dublin and Co. Louth descend from Irish ancestors named Mac Iomhair (McIvor) or Ó hIomhair. Quite distinct from them is the family named Ivers or Ievers in Co. Clare which descends from a 17th century English settler and made its seat on the townland of Mountievers in Bunratty Lower barony, Co. Clare.

IVORY

THIS surname was brought to Co. Waterford by an English settler in the 17th century. By the end of the 19th century most families of the name in Ireland were living in and around Dublin where several Ivory families still reside today. The name is not extinct, however, in Co. Waterford, and is thinly scattered in other parts.

JACKSON

THIS surname, one of the twenty-five commonest in England, was brought to Ireland by numerous settlers but principally in the 17th century to Ulster. Over one-half of the Jacksons in Ireland are to be found in that province with the largest part of the remainder in and around the cities of Dublin and Cork.

JAMESON

BOTH Jameson and Jamieson were brought to Ireland by settlers in the 17th century and principally to Ulster. Four out of five Jamesons or Jamiesons in Ireland are living in Ulster and the majority of the remainder in Dublin where one prominent Jameson family traces its descent back to a settler from Clackmannanshire in Scotland and bears as its coat of arms: Azure, a saltire or, cantoned in chief and flanks by Roman galleys ppr., and a bugle horn in base of the second.

JEN(N)INGS

ABOUT half of the Jennings families in Ireland come from Connacht where this English surname was adopted by members of the Mac Sheóinín family, a branch of the Burkes, who also appear in records as Mc Ionyn and Mc Jonine. Lineal descendants of the John Burke, who founded the Mac Sheóinín family, now Jenings, have as their coat of arms: Or, a cross gules, in the first and fourth quarters a dexter hand couped, in the second and third a lion rampant sable. These arms are based on those of Burke. Outside of that province, Jennings families may be descended from English settlers of that name.

JOHNSON

THIS common English and Scottish patronymic surname has been constantly confused with and used interchangeably with the Scottish surname Johnston(e). Johnson is among the ten commonest surnames in England, while Johnston is among the twenty commonest in Scotland. Both names were imported in considerable numbers to Ireland by settlers. Johnson was established in about equal numbers in Ulster, Munster and Leinster but was rare in Connacht. To the Johnsons of settler descent became added some Irish named Mac Seáin who, instead of Mc Shane, took on a translation of their surname as Johnson.

JOHNSTON

AMONG the twenty commonest surnames in Scotland, Johnstons came to Ireland as settlers in such numbers that this surname came to rank among the forty commonest in Ireland. Four-fifths of the Johnston(e) families in Ireland are in Ulster where the majority of settlers from Scotland established themselves. The name has also been confused with Johnson which is less common in Ireland. The variant Johnstone is preferred only by a minority.

JONES

THIS Welsh surname is so common there and in England that it ranks as the second commonest surname in England and Wales, second only but close in numbers to Smith and far ahead of all the other common surnames. It is, therefore, rather surprising that in Ireland it is not even among the hundred commonest surnames. It is, however, found in all the provinces, with the heaviest distribution in Leinster.

JORDAN

HIBERNICIZED descendants of the Anglo-Norman family of d'Exeter, which established itself in Connacht after the Anglo-Norman conquest in the 12th century, took the name Mac Siurtáin (Mc Jordan) from their progenitor Jordan d'Exeter, and became to all intents and purposes an Irish sept. Their particular homeland in Connacht was Gallen barony in Co. Mayo, which was known as Mac Jordans' country. From Connacht the Mc Jordans or Jordans spread into Leinster and in lesser numbers to Ulster and Munster.

JOYCE

THOMAS de Jorse, a 13th century Cambro-Norman settler from Wales who settled in Co. Galway, is reputed to be the progenitor of the Joyce families, always most numerous in Connacht. At the end of the last century about six out of every seven Joyce families were still resident in Connacht, the majority still in Co. Galway and the next largest representation in Co. Mayo. The stronghold of the Joyces was in Ross barony, Co. Galway, commonly known as Joyces' Country.

JOYCE *Joyces River in Connemara, Co. Galway*

JUDGE

THIS mainly Connacht surname is a translation of Mac an Bhreitheamhnaigh, adopted instead of Brehany, Breheny, or Brehon, by many of that family.

KANE

THIS surname derives from Ó Catháin, also rendered in English as Cahan and Keane, the name of a prominent West Ulster sept whose chief, before the Plantation of Ulster, was Lord of Keenaght, now a barony in Co. Derry. The heaviest distribution of Kanes in Ireland is still in Ulster where many families of the name survive in Co. Derry, in the neighbourhood of the ancient territory of their sept.

KAVANAGH

THIS surname began as an eipthet – in Irish, Caomhánach – attributed to one member of the Mac Murrough family of Leinster and perpetuated among his descendants. Kavanaghs are still most numerous in the ancient Mac Murrough lands in Co. Wexford and Co. Carlow and their surname ranks among the sixty commonest in Ireland.

KEAN(E)

SOME Keane families in Ireland bear this name as a variant of Kane or Cahan, being descendants of the Ó Catháin sept of Keenagh in Co. Derry, or of a sept of the same name which was located in Co. Galway and may have been founded by one of the Derry sept. Quite separately, however, the name is known in Munster, in Co. Waterford where it is borne by descendants of a sept from that county, Ó Céin, whose territory was in the eastern part of the barony of Decies without Drum.

KAVANAGH *Ferns Castle, once the seat of the McMurroughs, ancestors of the Kavanaghs*

KEARNEY

THIS surname denotes descent from either one of two Ó Cearnaigh septs, one located in Co. Mayo in Connacht and the other in Co. Clare whence its members moved into Co. Tipperary, or from the Ó Catharnaigh sept, located at Kilcoursey, Co. Offaly, descendants of which also took the surname Fox. These varying origins account for the wide distribution of Kearney families today in all four provinces.

KEARNS

DESCENDANTS of the Ó Ciaráin (Ó Ceirín) sept of north Connacht and of a Cork sept of the same name adopted Kearns as well as Kieran (q.v.) as an anglicized form of their name. Today this surname is commonest in Leinster.

KEATING

THIS surname came to Ireland with Anglo-Norman settlers who established themselves in Co. Wexford at the end of the 12th century. From their first Irish home branches of the family spread through southern Leinster and into Munster so that by the 16th century they were both numerous and influential in Co. Carlow and Co. Leix. There is a townland of Ballykeating as far west as Fermoy Barony in Co. Cork, two Keatingstowns in Co. Kilkenny, one in Crannach barony and one in Knocktopher barony, and there is a Keatingspark in Newcastle barony in Co. Dublin.

KEAVENY

FAMILIES named Keaven(e)y, a name found almost exclusively in Connacht until recently and particularly in Co. Galway and Co. Sligo, descend from the Co. Galway sept Ó Géibheannaigh.

KEEGAN

THE surname Keegan, like the commoner surname Egan, derives from the Irish Mac Aodhagáin. It is found predominantly in Leinster in Co. Dublin and Co. Wicklow and in lesser numbers in Connacht in Co. Roscommon and Co. Leitrim.

KEENAN

THE Ó Cianáin sept of Co. Fermanagh provided the ancestors of the Keenans who migrated from that county into Co. Monaghan and eastwards to the counties of Antrim, Down and Louth.

KELLEHER

THE Kelleher and Kelliher families descend from the Ó Céileachair sept of Co. Clare which migrated southwards to re-establish itself in the 14th century in Co. Cork. The majority of Kellehers and Kellihers has remained in Co. Cork until the present day, the next highest representation being in the adjacent county of Kerry.

KELLY

TOGETHER Kelly and O'Kelly are the second most common surname in Ireland. As may be supposed in the case of such a common name, all the Kelly families do not descend from one ancestor but derive from a number of Ó Ceallaigh septs which were located in various parts of Ireland. The most prominent of these septs held sway in what is now Co. Galway, another belonged to Co. Meath, others were located in Co. Leix, Co. Derry, Co. Antrim, Co. Wicklow and Co. Sligo. Some descendants of Ó Caollaidhe septs in Co. Kilkenny and Co. Clare also took the surname Kelly rather than Queally or Kealy.

KELLY *O'Kelly's Castle, Lough Conn, Co. Mayo*

KENNE(A)LLY

THE earliest known location of this family, in Irish Ó Cinnfhaolaidh, was in the baronies of Upper and Lower Connello, Co. Limerick. It has remained a Munster name but spread eastwards from its county of origin into Co. Tipperary and Co. Waterford and southwards into Co. Cork.

KENNEDY

THE Kennedys and O'Kennedys descend from the Ó Cinnéide sept which was located in Tulla Lower barony in the east of Co. Clare where their name is commemorated in the parish of Killokennedy. From eastern Clare the sept migrated eastwards into Co. Tipperary whence one branch went north and established itself in Co. Antrim. Other members of this populous sept dispersed to neighbouring counties. At the present time Kennedy ranks among the twenty commonest surnames in Ireland. The heaviest distribution is still marginally in Munster with many of the name still in Co. Tipperary but both Leinster and Ulster can claim almost as many Kennedys with a preponderance in Dublin and in Co. Antrim.

KENNY

KENNY families may descend from the Ó Cionnaoith septs, one of which came from Co. Galway and the other from Co. Tyrone, or from the Ó Coinne sept of Co. Down. One landed family of the name in Co. Mayo claims to be of English or French descent and another in Co. Galway traces its lineage to an English settler who came to Co. Wexford from Somerset, named Kenne or Kenney, but these are exceptions among the great majority of the name which is among the eighty commonest in Ireland.

KENNEDY *The Cathedral at Killaloe, Lower Tulla barony, Co. Clare, in the ancestral homeland of the Kennedys and O'Kennedys*

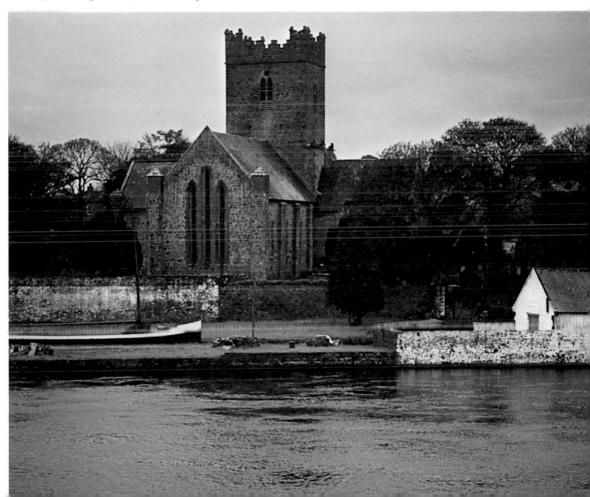

KEOGH

THE surname Keogh, and the frequent but less common variant Kehoe, are borne by descendants of the Mac Eochaidh septs, of which there are three hailing from different parts of Ireland. The Leinster sept was located in south Co. Wicklow and its descendants, many of whom survive in that area and in Co. Wexford, have favoured the spelling Kehoe. The Munster sept was located in Co. Tipperary where their home is commemorated in the name of the townland of Ballymackeogh in the barony of Owney and Arra. The third sept of the name originated in Connacht and Athlone barony, Co. Roscommon, whence branches spread into other parts of the province, as attested by a townland named Ballymackeogh in Clanmorris barony, Co. Mayo. However, at the present time the name is quite rare in Connacht and the great majority of Keoghs and Kehoes are in Leinster.

KEOHAN(E)

THIS surname, which belongs to western Co. Cork, derives from the Irish Mac Eocháin. Keoghan, Keoghane and Cahan have been recorded as variants.

KERIN

THIS Munster surname derives from the same source as Kieran. As it was found mainly in Co. Cork and Co. Kerry until recent years, it would appear that it was the form adopted by descendants of a Cork sept named Ó Céirín or Ó Ciaráin.

KERNAGHAN

THE Ulster surname Kernaghan, and its variant Kernoghan, derives from the Irish Ó Cearnacháin, originally from Co. Donegal but now found mainly in eastern Ulster.

KERR

THIS Scottish surname, which is pronounced Carr, was brought to Ulster in the 17th century by a number of settlers of the name from Scotland where it ranks among the forty commonest surnames. The largest number of these Kerrs settled in Co. Antrim but the name is found in all the nine counties of Ulster.

KERRIGAN

FAMILIES of this name descend from the Connacht sept Ó Ciaragáin whose homeland was in Clanmorris barony, Co. Mayo, where there is a townland named Ballykerrigan. The descendants of this sept have been quite widely dispersed into western Ulster (Co. Donegal) and Leinster.

KEVANE

UNTIL the population movement of the last few decades Kevane families were found for the most part in Co. Kerry not far from the homeland in West Cork of their ancestral sept Ó Ciabháin.

KEY(E)S

THIS English surname was brought to Ireland by settlers but it was also adopted as their name by persons of native Irish stock whose Irish name, Mac Aoidh, was more usually anglicized as McKee and Kee. Most Keys and Keyes families hail from Ulster where their heaviest concentration is in Co. Fermanagh.

KIDD

SETTLERS named Kidd from England and Scotland brought this name to Ireland in the 17th century, mainly to eastern Ulster but also to the Dublin area.

KIELY

THIS surname, which derives from the Irish Ó Cadhla, is found mainly in Munster and in particular in Co. Waterford, Co. Limerick and Co. Cork. It is also found in the variant forms Keily, Keely, Kealy, but these renderings are also known to be used as variants of Queally (q.v.), deriving from Ó Caollaidhe.

KIERNAN

THREE Mac Thighearnáin septs provide the ancestry of the Kiernan and Tiernan families as well, of course, as the Mc Kiernans and Mc Tiernans. The heaviest distribution of Kiernan families is in Co. Cavan and the adjacent counties of Leitrim and Longford, indicating their descent from the Mac Thighearnáin sept of East Breffny, located in Co. Cavan. Another of the septs of the name was also located in Ulster, in Co. Fermanagh, the third was a branch of the O'Conors of Connacht.

KILBANE See McILWANE

KILCOYNE

THIS Connacht surname, found principally in Co. Mayo and in Co. Sligo, derives from the Irish Mac Giolla Chaoine.

KILKELLY

THE surnames Kilkelly and Killikelly, which belong to Co. Galway, derive from the Irish Mac Giolla Cheallaigh.

KILKENNY See McELHINNEY

KILLEEN

THE early homeland of the ancestors of the Killeens, in Irish Ó Cillín, appears to have been in Co. Mayo whence members of the family migrated to Co. Offaly where there are three townlands named Ballykilleen in different parts of the county, and Co. Clare. The name is still found in these three counties, in Co. Galway and scattered farther afield. In Co. Mayo, which can still, however, be identified as the main home of families of this name, there is a townland Ballykilleen in the barony of Costello.

KILMARTIN See GILMARTIN

KILPATRICK

THIS Ulster surname, found principally in Co. Antrim, derives from the Irish Mac Giolla Phádraig.

KILROY See McILROY

KINA(G)HAN

THE lineal ancestors of most Kina(g)han families will be members of the Ó Coinneacháin sept which was located along the Shannon near the present boundaries of Co. Roscommon, Co. Offaly and Co. Westmeath. It appears, however, that the name has also been confused with Cunningham, as the Registrar of Births reported the use of the two names interchangeably in the last century in Ardee Union, Co. Louth, and the use of variant spelling Kinigam and Kinnegan for Cunningham in Castleblayney Union, Co. Monaghan, Markethill Union, Co. Armagh, and Enniskillen Union, Co. Fermanagh.

KIN(N)ANE

THE surname Kin(n)ane survives in Co. Tipperary, where it was long established, deriving like Guinane and Ginnane from the Irish Ó Cuinneáin.

KING

THIS common English surname was brought to Ireland by numerous settlers and now ranks among the hundred commonest surnames in Ireland while its place is among the top forty in England. The most prominent settlers of the name established themselves in Co. Roscommon at the end of the 16th century and have left a numerous progeny. Dr. MacLysaght has pointed out that some Irish families adopted the surname King as a pseudo-translation of such names as Ó Conraoi (more usually anglicized as Conry or Conroy). The Registrar of Births, in the last century, noted the interchangeability of King and Conr(o)y in Ballinrobe Union, Co. Mayo, and reported that in Downpatrick Union, Co. Down, and in Clones and Monaghan Unions in Co. Monaghan, King was used interchangeably with McAree.

KINGSTON

THIS English surname was brought to Ireland by settlers from England and established particularly in West Cork where numerous Kingston families concentrated around Drimoleague, descend from 17th century immigrants of the name. It is interesting to note that a 1980 directory lists twelve Paul Kingstons, ten of them in Co. Cork, one in Co. Kerry and one in Co. Tipperary; of the fourteen Samuel Kingstons in the same directory, all but one has an address in West Cork.

KINSELLA

THIS surname, in Irish Cinnscalach, was originally, like Kavanagh, a name used to distinguish a branch of the McMurroughs of Leinster. Those who formed the Kinsella sept held sway in Gorey barony, in Co. Wexford. The heaviest distribution of the name is still in Leinster and many Kinsellas still reside in the south of Co. Wicklow and the north of Co. Wexford in the neighbourhood of their ancestral homeland.

KIRBY

SOME Kirby families in Ireland will be descendants of settlers from the north of England where this name is fairly common but most, however, are of Irish origin, being lineally descended from forebears named Ó Ciarmhaic (Ó Ciarba) who took Kirby as an anglicized form of their name. That family was located in Co. Limerick whence their descendants spread into Co. Kerry. The surname Kerwick, peculiar to Co. Kilkenny, has the same Irish derivation. The surname Kirby borne by families in Co. Mayo, however, seems to have a different origin, being used there for the Irish Mac Geirbhe.

KIRK

THIS surname was brought to eastern Ulster in the 17th century by settlers from Scotland and the north of England; a number of the name moved southwards into Co. Louth. The Registrar of Births also reported in the last century the use of Kirk in Lismore Union, Co. Waterford, for the local Irish name Ó Cuire, more usually rendered as Quirk(e).

KIRKPATRICK

SETTLERS from Scotland brought this Scottish surname to Ulster and mainly to Co. Antrim in the 17th century.

KIRWAN

REMEMBERED as one of the so-called 'Tribes of Galway', the Kirwans, unlike all but one other of those families, were of native Irish stock, being descendants of the Ó Ciardubháin sept. Strangely now the name is quite rare in Connacht; the majority of Kirwan families are in Leinster, particularly in and around Dublin and in Co. Wexford, far from the ancestral home of the sept.

KISSANE

THIS surname from the south-west of Munster derives from the Irish Ó Cíosáin. It is found principally in Co. Kerry where both Coshman and Gissane have been reported as variants of this name.

KNOX

THIS Scottish surname was brought to Ireland by settlers, principally to Ulster in the 17th century. A number of prominent Knox families who acquired estates in Co. Derry, Co. Mayo,

Co. Tipperary and Co. Dublin trace their lineage to settlers from Ranfurly in Renfrewshire who came to Co. Donegal early in the 17th century.

KYLE

THIS Scottish surname was brought to Ulster by settlers from Scotland in the 17th century. One prominent family of the name in Ulster traces its lineage to settlers from Ayrshire who established themselves in Keenaght barony, Co. Derry.

KYNE

THIS Connacht surname, belonging particularly to Co. Galway, derives from the Irish sept Ó Cadhain whose descendants more frequently anglicized their name as Coyne, q.v.

(de) LAC(E)Y

ANGLO-NORMAN conquistadors brought the name de Lacy to Ireland in the 12th century. It is uncertain, however, whether the de Lacys who flourished in Co. Limerick at a later date were, in fact, descended from the earlier de Lacys or whether, as they appear in medieval records, they were originally de Lees or de Lesse. As de Lacy is rendered as de Léis in Irish the matter is confusing.

LACY

Several de Lacys of the Co. Limerick family of that name distinguished themselves in the Irish diaspora. General Luis de Lacy received the title of Duke of Ultonia (Ulster) from the King of Spain. The most illustrious wild goose of the de Lacy family was, however, Field-Marshal Count Peter de Lacy (1678–1751) who left Ireland as a lad of thirteen after the surrender of Limerick in 1691. He fought in the Irish Brigade for France and then entered the service of Peter the Great. He fought for Russia against the Swedes in Livonia and Finland, against the Danes, and against the Turks, and helped to establish Augustus of Saxony on the throne of Poland. Peter de Lacy, who was appointed Governor of Livonia and Estonia, campaigned in the Russian Imperial service for more than fifty years under the Czarina Anna and the Czarina Elizabeth.

LAIRD

THIS Scottish surname was brought to Ulster* by settlers who came from Scotland following the plantation schemes of the 17th century.

LALLY

FAMILIES named Lally, who are mostly found in Co. Galway and Co. Mayo, descend from the Co. Galway sept Ó Maolalaidh, Lally being a contraction of Mulally.

LALOR See LAWLOR

LAMB(E)

THIS English surname was brought to Ireland by settlers but Dr. MacLysaght has reported that it was also adopted as their surname by some Irish people named Ó Luain.

LAMBERT

THIS English surname was brought to Ireland by settlers. It is found predominantly in Leinster, where some families of the name claim lineal descent from an Anglo-Norman named de Lamporte who came to Co. Wexford in the 12th century, the name later being corrupted from Lamport to Lambert. The prominent Lambert family in Co. Galway, however, descended from a 17th century settler who came to that county from Yorkshire.

LAMONT

THIS Scottish surname was brought to Ulster, and principally to Co. Antrim, by settlers from Scotland since the 17th century.

LANDERS

FAMILIES named Landers resided mainly in Munster but there the name is found as widely apart as Co. Waterford and Co. Kerry. It is of Anglo-Norman origin, deriving from the surname de Londres.

LANE

As well as families descended from English settlers who brought the name over to Ireland, there is evidence that some Lanes in Ireland have this name as a variant of a surname of Irish origin, such as Lehane, Lyne, and Lyons, all names from the province of Munster where most Lane families originate.

LANGAN

THIS surname, formerly found principally in Co. Mayo, derives from the Irish Ó Longáin.

LANIGAN

THIS surname, which belongs to Co. Kilkenny and Co. Tipperary, derives from the Irish Ó Lonagáin.

LAPPIN

THIS surname is borne by descendants of the Co. Donegal sept Ó Lapáin. It is found predominantly in Ulster but now more often in the counties to the east of the homeland of the sept.

LARKIN

FOUR distinct Ó Lorcáin septs, one from Co. Galway in Connacht, one from Co. Monaghan in Ulster, one from Co. Tipperary in Munster and one from Co. Wexford in Leinster, provided the forebears of families named Larkin who are thus found in all four provinces of Ireland.

LAVELLE

FAMILIES named Lavelle who, until recently, resided almost exclusively in Connacht and mostly in Co. Mayo, descend from a North Connacht sept, Ó Maolfhábhail. Dr. MacLysaght has pointed out that descendants of this sept who established themselves in Co. Donegal took the surname Fall.

LAVERTY

THIS surname derives from that of the West Ulster sept Ó Laithbheartaigh which was associated with Co. Tyrone but by the last century the majority of Laverty families lived in Co. Antrim.

LAVERY

AT the end of the last century all the Lavery families in Ireland were living in Ulster, mostly in the east of the province in the counties of Down, Antrim and Armagh, in roughly the same region as the homeland of the sept Ó Labhradha, from which they descend.

LAVIN

THE Co. Roscommon sept Ó Flaithimhín provided the ancestors of families now called Lavin or the variant spelling Lavan. Until the end of the last century these lived almost exclusively in Connacht, 50 per cent of all the families being in Co. Mayo and about another 25 per cent in Co. Roscommon.

LAW

THIS surname was brought by settlers from Scotland and England to Ulster since the 17th century.

LAWLESS

THE name of this family, once counted among the so-called 'Tribes of Kilkenny' but now more numerous in Dublin and in Co. Galway, signifies 'Outlaw'. According to Dr. MacLysaght it came into use as a surname in Ireland after the Anglo-Norman invasion. The Lawless family, a scion of which was created Baron Cloncurry, claimed their descent from an ancestor who had come from Hertfordshire to Co. Dublin and Co. Kilkenny.

LAWLOR

THE surnames Lalor, Lawlor, Lawler, derive from the name of the Co. Leix sept Ó Leathlobhair whose territory lay in what is now East Maryborough barony. Those of the name are found predominantly in Leinster and a number still reside in and around the homeland of the sept in Co. Leix.

LAWRENCE

THIS English surname was brought to Ireland, mainly to Leinster, by settlers since the 17th century.

LEAHY

THIS is a Munster surname belonging originally to the south-western counties of the province. In Irish it is Ó Laochdha.

LEARY See O'LEARY

LEAVY

FAMILIES of this name, found mainly in the Irish midlands in the counties of Longford and Westmeath, and in Co. Monaghan, descend

from the Mac Conshleibhe sept which was located in Co. Longford.

LEE

FAMILIES with the name Lee, quite numerous and widespread in Ireland, are of varied ancestral origin. Some may be descendants of settlers from England where this surname is a common one. The majority of Lee families in Ireland, however, are of native Irish descent from ancestors named O'Laoidhigh (or O'Laidhigh), Mac Laoidhigh, and Mac an Leagha.

LEECH

SOME Leech families in Ireland are of settler lineage descending from immigrants who came to Ireland from Scotland or the north of England. One landed family of the name in Co. Mayo claimed descent from a settler who came there in the 17th century from Cheshire. This family bore as its coat of arms: Ermine, a trefoil vert, on a chief indented gules, three ducal coronets or. The landed Leech family in Co. Wicklow only settled there in the 19th century from Cheshire, their more remote ancestors being from Lancashire. Irish families named Mac an Leagha took the surname Leech as well. the Irish 'liaig', meaning physician, having the same origin as the old name 'leech' applied to a physician in England.

LEHANE

THIS Co. Cork surname derives from the Irish Ó Liathain, more frequently rendered in English as Lyons, q.v.

LENIHAN

THIS surname, most common in Co. Limerick and Co. Cork, derives from that of the Munster sept called Ó Luingeachán or Ó Leannacháin. Lenihan families in Connacht, however, probably descend from the sept named Ó Leannacháin which was located in Co. Roscommon. Many variant spellings of Lenihan are recorded: there are Lenaghan, Lenaghen, Lenahan, Leneghan, Lenehan, Lennehan, Lennihan, Linahan, Linaghan, Linnahan, Linehan, Linnehan and Linighan.

LENNON

THIS surname usually derives from Ó Leannáin which was the name of several septs, one located in Co. Galway, one in Co. Fermanagh, another in Co. Cork, so that Lennon families are now widely dispersed. The Irish names Ó Lonáin and Ó Luinín were also sometimes rendered in English as Lennon.

LEONARD

THIS English surname has been adopted in Ireland by families of Irish origin as a variant of names deriving from Ó Leanáin, Ó Lonáin, and Ó Luinín, otherwise rendered as Lennon, Linnane etc., and also, according to Dr. MacLysaght, used for Mac Alinon (Mac Ghiolla Fhinnéin).

LESLIE

THIS Scottish surname was brought to Ulster by settlers from Scotland early in the 17th century. Prominent Leslie families in Co. Monaghan and the Leslies of Leslie Hill, Ballymoney, Co. Antrim, claim descent from the Leslies, Earls of Rothes and Barons of Balquhair in Scotland through a cadet of that family who came to Ulster in 1614. They bear as their coat of arms: Argent, on a fess azure, three buckles or. The Leslies of Tarbert, Co. Kerry, and the Leslies of Ballyward, Co. Down, are of the same stock in Scotland.

L'ESTRANGE

THIS surname, written Le Strange, L'Estrange and Lestrange, came to Ireland in the latter half of the 16th century with English settlers from Norfolk who acquired lands in Co. Roscommon and Co. Westmeath. The name is now found mostly in Co. Offaly but it may not indicate descent from the settler family because Dr. MacLysaght has reported that members of an Irish family named Mac Conchoigcriche in Co. Westmeath adopted the surname Lestrange.

LEWIS

AMONG the twenty-five commonest surnames in England and Wales and particularly common in Wales, the surname Lewis was brought to Ireland by settlers whose descendants are found in almost equal numbers in Leinster, Ulster and Munster.

LIDDY

THIS surname derives from the name of the Co. Clare sept Ó Lideadha and it is still found in that county.

LIN(N)ANE

THIS surname can be either Ó Linnéain or Lion-náin in Irish. See also Lennon and Leonard.

LINDSAY

THIS Scottish surname came to Ulster with settlers from Scotland in the 17th century who established themselves mostly in the east of the province. The landowning family in Co. Tyrone, who spell their name Lindesay, claim descent from a prominent family in Scotland in Haddingtonshire. Dr. MacLysaght has noted also that members of the Irish family named Ó Loingsigh tended, in Ulster, to anglicize their name as Lindsay.

LITTLE

THIS common English and Scottish surname was brought to Ireland, and particularly to Ulster, where many families of the name are found in Co. Fermanagh.

LIVINGSTON(E)

THIS surname was brought to Ireland, principally to Ulster and to Dublin, by settlers who came from Scotland since the 17th century. It is also not infrequently written Levingston.

LLOYD

THIS common Welsh surname was brought to Ireland by settlers whose descendants are found in all four provinces. Among the incomers in the 17th century were the ancestors of landed families named Lloyd in Co. Roscommon, Co. Limerick, Co. Tipperary, Co. Offaly and Co. Wexford.

LOCKHART

THIS Scottish surname came to Ulster, and particularly to Co. Antrim and Co. Armagh, with settlers from Scotland in the 17th century.

LOFTUS

THE Loftus families in Ireland, of settler descent, trace their lineage to the Loftus family of Swineshead, Yorkshire, members of which came to Ireland in the 17th century, one of whom, Adam Loftus, became the Protestant Primate of Ireland. The surname Loftus is, however, now found mainly in Connacht where it was adopted by descendants of the Ó Lachtnáin sept whose name was more usually rendered as Loughnane (q.v.) in English.

LOGAN

BY far the heaviest distribution of this surname

is in Ulster, particularly in Co. Antrim, where Scottish settlers brought this surname from Scotland in the 17th century. Dr. MacLysaght has stated that in Ireland this surname exists also as a variant of Lohan for the native Irish Ó Leogháin.

LOGUE

THIS surname belonged principally to Co. Derry, whence it spread over into Co. Donegal. It appears there to be an anglicization of Ó Maolmhaodhog (which has also been anglicized as Mulvogue) or of Ó Laoghog.

LONERGAN

THE earliest known territory of the Ó Longargáin sept was in that part of Co. Tipperary to the east of Lough Derg whence they migrated southwards towards Cahir and Cashel. Lonergan is the commonest anglicization of the Irish name of the sept but several variants are on record: Ladrigan, Landregan, Londregan, Londrigan, Lundergan.

LOONEY

THIS Munster family name, found exclusively in that province until the turn of the present century, belonged principally to Co. Clare. It derives from the Irish Ó Luanaigh.

LOUGHLIN See McLOUGHLIN

LOUGHNANE

EASILY confused with the commoner surnames which derive from Mac Lochlainn and Ó Lachlainn, this surname derives from Ó Lachtnáin, the name of several small septs from Connacht.

LOUGHRAN

THIS surname, which derives from the Irish Ó Luchráin, is found principally in Ulster, where in the last century it was most prevalent in the counties of Antrim, Armagh and Tyrone.

LOVE

MOST of the families of this name in Ireland can trace their immediate ancestry to Co. Derry whence their forebears came as settlers from Scotland and England in the 17th century.

LOWE

THIS common English surname was brought by settlers to Ireland where, in almost equal numbers, it was established in Munster and Ulster. It has also been asserted that it was assumed as a surname by descendants of the Irish family Mac Lughadha of Oriel, whose name also became McLoy, Loy and Mc Cloy.

LOWRY

THIS surname came to Ireland, and principally to Ulster, with 17th century settlers from Scotland. It has been confused with Lavery, which derives from the Irish Ó Labhradha. The most prominent Lowry family in Ireland, from which the Earl Belmore descends, claims descent from a settler named Lowry or Laurie who came to Co. Tyrone in the first half of the 17th century from Scotland where he is said to have belonged to the Laurie family of Maxwelton.

LUCAS

THIS English surname was brought to Ireland before the immigration of Elizabethan and Cromwellian settlers in the 16th and 17th centuries. The predominance in Ireland of this surname in Ulster indicates its introduction there also by settlers from England and/or Scotland in the 17th century.

LUCEY

THE surname of this Co. Cork family derives from the Irish Ó Luasaigh.

LUNNEY

THIS Ulster surname, which belongs in particular to Co. Fermanagh and Co. Tyrone, derives from the Irish Ó Luinigh, a sept whose homeland was known in English as Munter-looney.

LYDON

THIS surname, and its variants Leydon, Leyden, Liddane, derive from the Irish Ó Loideáin, the name of a Connacht family, some of whose descendants, once concentrated in Co. Galway and Co. Mayo, have been dispersed southwards into Co. Clare as well as into the other provinces.

LYNAM

THIS south-east Leinster surname, in Irish Ó Laigheanáin, spread from Co. Wexford and Co. Carlow into other parts of the province, mainly Dublin, but it was still predominantly a Leinster surname at the commencement of the 20th century.

LYNCH

THIS surname is one usually associated with Co. Galway – where most of the name in Ireland belonged and where they were among the most influential of the so-called 'Tribes of Galway'. In that place their remoter forebears, named, it seems, de Lench, were of Norman origin. However, the surname Lynch was also adopted as an anglicization of their family name by descendants of the Irish family Ó Loinsigh.

The verb 'to lynch' comes from a member of this family, Colonel Charles Lynch (1736–1796), who settled in North America. He gained a reputation for administering harsh and summary justice. A more colourful but also ruthless member of the family was the courtesan and adventuress Eliza Alicia Lynch, born in Co. Cork in 1835, mistress of the dictator of Paraguay. A more recent prominent member of the family was that determined patriot, General Liam Lynch (1890–1923), the Chief of Staff of the Republican Army during the Civil War, who was killed in an action against the Free State troops (illustrated below).

LYNCH *Coat of Arms of the Lynch family on the 16th century house of a merchant family of the name in Galway city*

LYONS

THE Ó Laighin sept of Co. Galway, where their territory was in the region of Kilconnel, provided the forebears of most of the families who anglicized their surname to Lyon(s) but a considerable number who took this surname descended from the Ó Laighin (Ó Liatháin) family, originally of Barrymore barony, Co. Cork, some of whose descendants opted to be Lyne or Lehane (q.v.).

LYNE *See LYONS and LEHANE*

LYNSKEY

DESPITE its appearance of an Eastern European origin, this surname, which belongs to Connacht and particularly to Co. Galway and Co. Mayo, derives from the Irish Ó Loinsigh which is a variant of Loingsigh which gave us the much commoner Lynch.

LYSAGHT

THIS surname, which, before the 20th century movements of population, was found in Munster, mainly in the counties of Clare and Limerick, derives from the Irish Mac Giolla Iasachta, the name given to one branch of the O'Briens of Thomond. The existence of a few McLysaght families in Ireland today appears to be due to the resumption of the lost prefix.

MACKEN

THREE septs, Ó Macáin of West Cork, O'Macáin of Co. Mayo and Mac Maicín of Oriel, provided the forebears of the Macken and Mackin families found now mainly in the regions of two of their original habitats, in Co. Mayo and in the counties of Louth and Monaghan.

MACKEY

THE majority of Mackey families derive from the Ó Macdha sept of Co. Tipperary where Ballymackey was their sept centre. In that region this surname has survived as well as in the neighbouring county of Cork and in the capital. Mackey families in Ulster, however, are liable to bear the name as a variant of McKea.

MADDEN

THE sept whose name was, in its early form, Ó Madadháin, later Ó Madáin, was a branch of the Ui Maine. The sept held a territory on both sides of the River Shannon, the western part being in Longford Barony in Co. Galway, the eastern part in the barony of Garrycastle, Co. Offaly.

MADIGAN

THE Madigans are of the same stock as the Maddens, their surname being an anglicization of the early name of the sept, Ó Madadháin. The forebears of the Madigans migrated southwards where their descendants are found mostly in the counties of Clare and Limerick.

MAGAURAN See McGOVERN

MAGEE

THIS surname is commoner than McGee, of which it is an elided form. In western Ulster the prefix Mac has more often been retained distinctly so that McGee is found more often in Co. Donegal and Magee in the east Ulster counties of Antrim, Down and Armagh. Some Ulster Magees and McGees are descendants of settlers named McGee who came from Scotland to Ireland in the 17th century but whose remote ancestors were Irish who had gone to Scotland centuries earlier. Other Magees and McGees in Ireland descend from Mag Aodha families who had never left their Ulster homeland. Where the prefix Mac did not become Mag before the vowel in Irish, the name Mag Aodha was Mac Aodha and became McKee (q.v.). See also McHugh.

MAGILL See McGILL

MAGNER

THE origin of this Co. Cork surname seems uncertain but it is found mainly in that county where it appears in records since the 13th century.

MAGUIRE

THIS surname, written Maguire or McGuire, ranks among the forty commonest surnames in Ireland. It is interesting that in Co. Fermanagh, where their ancestors were once the ruling sept, Maguire families have today the commonest name in that county. The stronghold of the MagUidhir chief was at Enniskillen where their castle was built beside Lough Erne. Maguire is the most usual spelling, but in the west of Ireland the distinct prefix has more often been retained so that McGuire is the form favoured in Co. Mayo and Co. Roscommon.

MAGUIRE *Enniskillen Castle, Co. Fermanagh*

Maghan and Maughan are all recorded variants of this surname.

MAHER

THE territory of the Ó Meachair sept, from which Maher and Meagher families are lineally descended, was in the north of the barony of Ikerrin in Co. Tipperary. That county is still the main homeland of these families but they have spread into Co. Kilkenny also in considerable numbers.

MAHON

THIS surname can, of course, be in use as an abbreviation of McMahon (q.v.) but it is also a distinct name when borne by descendants of one or other of the two Connacht septs called Ó Mócháin, one located in the barony of Kiltartan, Co. Galway, the other in Coolavin barony, Co. Sligo. Mohan, Moan, Moghan, Mowen,

MAHONEY *See O'MAHONY*

MALONE

THE Ó Maoileoin sept, whose homeland was at Clonmacnois, Co. Offaly, provided the forebears of families now named Malone, a name found predominantly in Leinster.

MALLEY *See O'MALLEY*

MANAHAN *See MANNIX*

MANGAN

THIS surname is widely distributed in the provinces of Leinster, where it is commonest, Munster and Connacht. There were three Ó

Mongáin septs, one in Connacht, one in the south-west of Munster, and one in Ulster, in Co. Tyrone.

The Irish poet, James Clarence Mangan (1803–1849) has been compared to the French 'poétes maudits'. Baudelaire and Rimbaud indeed shared his tendency to melancholy. Mangan is remembered principally for his English versions of Irish poems such as My Dark Rosaleen. *He died of malnutrition in a Dublin hospital in 1849.*

MANNI(O)N

THE Mannion and Mannin families, and some who have anglicized their name as Manning, trace their descent from the Ó Mainnín sept whose territory was in Tiaquin barony, Co. Galway, with a stronghold at Clogher.

MANNIX

DESCENDANTS of the Ó Mainichín sept, whose homeland was on the shores of Ross Bay in south-western Co. Cork, have taken the surname Mannix and Manahan or Manihan. They are still found mainly in the counties of Cork and Kerry.

MARA *See O'MEARA*

MARKEY

THIS surname, which is found mostly in the counties of Louth and Monaghan and in the capital, is borne by descendants of the Ó Marcaigh sept of Oriel.

MARREN

THE Co. Sligo Marrens and the Co. Monaghan Marrons appear to have a common ancestry in the Ó Mearáin sept whose homeland was in Co. Monaghan.

MARSHALL

THIS occupational surname came to Ireland in considerable numbers with settlers of the name from England. It is now found in all four provinces but predominantly in Ulster. One prominent settler family named Marshall came to Co. Kerry in 1602.

MARTIN

THIS surname, which ranks among the forty commonest in Ireland, is also common in England where it is also among the top forty, and in Scotland where it is among the top fifty. Martin families in Ireland may be of either native or settler descent. Those of native Irish origin may derive their surname from Ó Martain or from Mac Martain, the name of a Co. Tyrone sept; some may also be descended from the Mac Giolla Mhártain sept of Co. Tyrone, more usually anglicized as Gilmartin. The Martins of Galway, one of the Galway 'Tribes', claim to be of ancient settler descent, their forebear having come to Connacht with the de Burgos at the end of the 12th century.

MASTERSON

SOME Masterson families in Ireland are of settler origin, being descendants of an English family of that name which came to Co. Wexford in the 16th century. In the counties of Longford and Cavan, however, the Masterson families are more likely to bear that name as a translation of Mac anMháighistir, the name of a sept from that region sometimes anglicized as McMaster.

MATHEWS

THIS common English surname was brought from England by settlers who established themselves mainly in eastern Leinster, in the counties of Dublin and Louth, and in eastern Ulster, in the counties of Down and Antrim.

MAXWELL

THIS surname was brought to Ulster by settlers from Scotland in the 17th century, most of whom established themselves on lands east of the Bann. One large and prominent Maxwell family in Ulster traces its descent from the

Maxwells of Calderwood, Lanarkshire, Scotland.

MEAGHER *See MAHER*

MEARA *See O'MEARA*

MEEHAN

THE Ó Miadhacháin or Ó Miadhagáin sept originated in West Cork but had established itself in Rosclogher barony, Co. Leitrim, by the 12th century, whence branches migrated into Co. Clare. The descendants of this sept have anglicized their surname as Meighan and Meehan. Of the same stock are the Meegan families, found mainly in Co. Monaghan. The Irish surname Mac Miadhacháin has been anglicized as McMeekin in Co. Antrim and is found with numerous variants as Mc.Machan, Mc.Meechan, Mc.Meichan, Meghan. Descendants of the Ó Maothagáin family of Co. Cork, a name more correctly rendered as Mehegan, have also adopted the surname Meehan.

MELIA *See O'MALLEY*

MELLON

THIS Ulster surname, belonging mainly to Co. Tyrone, derives from the Irish Ó Mealláin, the name of a branch of the Cenél Eoghain long established in that county.

MILLER

THIS surname, common in England and Scotland, was brought to Ireland in large numbers, mostly by settlers in the 17th century. Over three-quarters of the Millers in Ireland are in Ulster, predominantly in Co. Antrim. Many have the form Millar, favoured in Scotland.

MILLIGAN

THE surname Milligan, found predominantly in Ulster, and its variants Miligan, Millican, Milligen, Millikan, Milliken, Millikin, derive from the Irish Ó Maoileagáin. The reports of the Registrar General also indicate that there is liable to be confusion between names of that derivation and the commoner surname Mulligan which is Ó Maolagáin in Irish.

MILLS

THIS common English surname is found in all four Irish provinces but in the greatest numbers in Ulster, having been brought over from England by a number of settlers.

MINIHANE *See MOYNIHAN*

MINOGUE

FAMILIES bearing this surname, found mainly in Co. Clare, descend from the Ó Muineóg sept whose homeland was in the east of that county.

MITCHELL

THIS surname is among the thirty commonest in Scotland and is also common in England. It was brought over to Ireland by numerous settlers and is found throughout the country, although about one-half of the families of the name in Ireland are in Ulster. In the last century the Registrar of Births reported the use of Mitchell interchangeably with Mulvihil in Glennamaddy Union, Co. Galway.

MOCKLER

THIS surname, long found in Co. Tipperary, where the family gave its name to the parish of Grangemockler, came to Ireland in the wake of the Anglo-Norman invasion in its original French form, Mauclerc. Curiously, although the spelling has changed the name is still pronounced in a way which is close to the original French, i.e. Mo-clur, rather than as Mock-ler.

MOFFAT

THIS Scottish surname was brought to Ulster by 17th century settlers from Scotland. Numerous spelling variations are on record.

MOHAN *See MAHON*

MOLLOY

THE Ó Maolmhuaidh sept held sway over a large territory extending over several baronies in what is now Co. Offaly. Their descendants adopted Molloy as the anglicized form of their name as did descendants of a Con-Maoil Aoidh, also anglicized as Millea. Molloy is now found in all four provinces, commonest in Leinster and least common in Munster.

MOLONY

WITH few exceptions, families named Molon(e)y descend from the Ó Maoldhomhnaigh sept whose homeland was in Upper Tulla barony, Co. Clare. Most of the Molony families are still in Munster and many survive in Co. Clare. Dr. MacLysaght has pointed out that some Molony families in northern Co. Tipperary have a different ancestry, being descended not from an Ó Maoldhomhnaigh but from a quite distinct family, that bore the name Ó Maolfhachtna.

MONA(G)HAN

FAMILIES bearing the surname Mona(g)han, now found in all four provinces, descend from a sept named Ó Manacháin, whose territory lay in northern Co. Roscommon along the borders of the baronies of Roscommon and Boyle. Some of the descendants of this sept adopted the surname Monk as a translation of their Irish name.

MOONEY

OVER half of the Mooney families in Ireland were living in Leinster even before the massive migration towards the Dublin area in this century. The name is also fairly common in eastern Ulster. Mooney families will descend from one of the Ó Maonaigh septs, one of which originated in Ulster, another in Co. Offaly and a third in Tireragh barony, Co. Sligo, and a fourth eponymous sept was in Munster.

MONTGOMERY

THIS surname, remotely of French origin, was brought from Scotland to Ulster by settlers in the 17th century, most of whom established themselves on lands east of the Bann. A number of prominent Montgomery families in Ulster trace their descent from settlers who were cadets of the Montgomerys of Braidstane, a younger branch of the Montgomerys of Eaglesham and Eglinton, Renfrewshire, Scotland.

MOORE

THE surname Moore is placed among the twenty commonest in Ireland. Of the several thousand Moore families some will be of settler descent, their forebears being immigrants from England named Moore, who have come to Ireland in considerable numbers over the centuries since the Anglo-Norman invasion. Others will be of Irish descent, descendants of the great O'More sept, in Irish Ó Módha, the principal sept of the seven septs of Leix.

MOORHEAD

THIS surname, a variant of the Scottish Muirhead, was brought to Ireland by settlers who established themselves in eastern Ulster, mainly in Co. Antrim.

MORAN

THE surname Moran ranks among the sixty commonest in Ireland, but over half of the families of this name in Ireland are in Connacht, the province of origin of the two septs from one or the other of which these families will descend. The Ó Mughtáin or Ó Mughráin sept was located in Co. Galway and Co. Roscommon; the Ó Móráin sept was located near Ballina in Co. Mayo.

MORGAN

THIS common Welsh surname, which ranks among the fifty commonest surnames in England and Wales, was brought over to Ireland by settlers who established themselves in all four provinces, with a majority in Ulster.

MOORE *Dunamase Castle in the O'More country, Co. Leix*

MORIARTY

FAMILIES bearing this surname descend from the Ó Muircheartaigh sept, whose territory was in western Co. Kerry in Corkaguiney and Trughanacmy baronies around Castlemain harbour. Until the population movement of the present century 90 per cent of the Moriarty families in Ireland were still living in Co. Kerry and that county still houses the majority of the name in the country.

MORON(E)Y

THIS Munster surname, associated mainly with the counties of Clare and to a lesser extent with Co. Limerick and with Co. Tipperary, derives from the Irish Ó Maolruanaidh, a name that is borne by more than one ancient sept.

MORRIS

THIS surname, which is found scattered throughout Ireland, may derive from one or other of a number of possible origins. Some Morris families will be descendants of settlers of that name who came over from England and Wales where

Kells Priory, Co. Kilkenny, founded by
Geoffrey de Marisco in the 12th century

Morris ranks among the forty commonest surnames. Others are descendants of earlier settlers of the Anglo-Norman invasion period and of Norman origin, whose name de Marreis, or de Marisco in its Latin form, eventually became Morris; the Morris families of Galway city, among the 'Tribes of Galway', are of that stock. Yet others bearing the surname Morris are descendants of the Fitzmaurice family. The Registrar of Births reported the interchangeability of Fitzmaurice and Morris in the last century in Roscommon Union, Co. Roscommon. The surname Morris has also been adopted as an anglicization of the Irish, Ó Muirghis which itself derives from Ó Muirgheasa, the name of a Co. Sligo sept more correctly rendered as Morrissey. In the last century the Registrar of Births reported the use of Morrison interchangeably with Morrissey in Killarney Union and Dingle Union, Co. Kerry.

MORRISON

THIS surname, which ranks among the thirty commonest in Scotland, was brought to Ulster by settlers in and since the 17th century. It is particularly prevalent in the eastern Ulster counties of Antrim and Down. Elsewhere in Ireland some Morrison families may have this name as a literal translation of Fitzmaurice (in Irish Mac Muiris) and as an English surname adopted by forebears named Ó Muirghis and Ó Muirgheasa instead of Morrissey. An instance of the interchangeable use of Morrison and Morrissey was reported in the last century by the Registrar of Births in Lismore Union, Co. Waterford. In Enniskillen Union, Co. Fermanagh, the Registrar reported the use of Morrison interchangeably with Begley and in Inishowen Union, Co. Donegal, with Bryson.

MORRISSEY

THE Ó Muirgheasa sept was located on the southern banks of Sligo Bay in the baronies of Carbury and Tireragh, Co. Sligo. The surname Morrissey, however, which derives from Ó Muirgheasa, has long been rare in Connacht. Three-quarters of the Morrissey families in Ireland at the end of the last century were living in Munster, mainly in the counties of

136

Waterford, Limerick and Cork. It seems probable, therefore, that at least some of those Morrissey families may be descended from hibernicized scions of the de Marreis or de Marisco family of Norman origin who also appeared on record as de Marecy, and whose name in Irish became Mac Muiris, as did the Anglo-Norman patronymic Fitzmaurice.

MORROW

THE homeland of one Mac Muireadhaigh sept was in Co. Leitrim where their descendants have mostly retained the prefix as Mc.Morrow. As Morrow, without the prefix, the families descended from septs named Mac Muireadhaigh, the best-known of which was located in Athlone barony, Co. Roscommon, are now predominantly in Ulster, spread across that province from Co. Donegal to Co. Down.

MOYLAN

THIS surname, in Irish Ó Maoilcáin, belongs to Munster where it is found mainly in the counties of Clare, Cork and Tipperary.

MOYNIHAN

THIS Munster surname, in Irish Ó Muimhneacháin, is found mainly in Co. Kerry, where over half of the Moynihans in Ireland were living at the end of the last century, and in Co. Cork, which was the home territory of almost all the rest.

MULALLY See LALLY

MULCAHY

OVER ninety per cent of the Mulcahy families in Ireland at the end of the last century were living in Munster in the counties of Waterford, Tipperary, Limerick and Cork. They descended from the Ó Maolchathaigh sept long established in the southern part of Co. Tipperary close to the present borders of that county with the counties of Waterford, Cork and Limerick. In the last century the Registrar of Births reported the use of the surname Mulcahy interchangeably with Cahy, Caughy and M'Cahy in Newry Union, Co. Down, a location which suggests that the correct name was McCaughey or McCahey and that it was recorded as Mulcahy quite erroneously due to mishearing.

MULDOON

THREE Ó Maoldúin septs, one in Co. Fermanagh in Ulster, one in Co. Galway in Connacht and one in Co. Clare in Munster, can have provided the forebears of families bearing the surname Muldoon, now found mainly in Co. Fermanagh and Co. Galway.

MULHALL

THIS surname, belonging almost exclusively to Leinster and mainly to the counties of Leix, Carlow and Kilkenny, derives from the Irish Ó Maolchathail.

MULHOLLAND

NINETY per cent of the Mulholland families in Ireland at the end of the last century were living in Ulster which indicates that of the several ancient Ó Maolchalann septs, they would descend from the ones located in Co. Donegal and Co. Derry.

MULLAN(E)

THREE Ó Maoláin septs, one located in Co. Galway, one in the counties of Derry and Tyrone, and a third in Co. Cork, provide the ancestry of the families named Mullan, Mullen, Mullin, Mullane and Mullins. The forms Mullan, Mullen and Mullin, the commonest, combine to place the surname among the seventy commonest in Ireland, even excluding the forms Mullane and Mullins which were favoured by descendants of the Cork sept. Inevitably there has been confusion with the Scottish surname McMullen, which came to Ulster with settlers in the 17th century. While Mullane has been found almost exclusively in Co. Cork and the neighbouring county of Limerick and Mullins mainly in Co. Cork and Co. Clare, the many more families named Mullan, Mullen and Mullin, descended from the northern Ó Maoláin septs, are still found predominantly in Ulster, the home of more than half of them, and in Co. Galway.

MULLIGAN

FAMILIES of this name descend from the Ó Maolagáin sept which held sway in Co. Donegal over a territory in the baronies of Boylagh and Raphoe. Their dispersal at the time of the confiscations and the plantation of Ulster has resulted in their now being found in almost equal numbers in Ulster, Connacht and Leinster with a notable concentration in Co. Monaghan, in Co. Mayo, and in the capital.

MULROONEY

FAMILIES bearing this surname may be descendants of one or other of the Ó Maolruanaidh septs, one of which was located in Co. Fermanagh and another in Co. Galway. See also Morony.

MULROY

MOST of the Mulroy families in Ireland are still

MULLIGAN *Cruit Island, Co. Donegal, in the territory of the Ó Maolagáin sept*

living in Co Mayo, the ancient homeland of their forebears, the Ó Maolruaidh sept.

MULVANY

THIS surname, in Irish Ó Maolmhagna, is found predominantly in Leinster where, outside the capital, it is commonest in Co. Meath. Mulvaney and Mulvanny are known variants and confusion with Mulvenna has been inevitable.

GEORGE FRANCIS MULVANY

Thomas James Mulvany was Keeper of the Royal Hibernian Academy from its foundation in 1823 until his death in 1845. His son George Francis, who succeeded him as Keeper, was a painter of repute, helped to found the National Gallery of Ireland and became its first director in 1862.

MULVENNA

THIS surname, in Irish Ó Maoilmheana, was found exclusively in Co. Antrim at the end of the last century.

MULVEY

THIS surname, in Irish Ó Maoilmhiadhaigh, is still found today mainly in its longtime homeland, Co. Leitrim.

MULVIHIL(L)

Co. Kerry and Co. Limerick became the principal homes of Mulvihill families, whose forebears, the Ó Maoilmhichil sept, belonged to Co. Roscommon whence they migrated across the Shannon into Co. Longford and down through Co. Clare, where some settled, into the south-west of Munster. In the last century the Registrar of Births reported the use of the

English surname Melville for Mulvihil in Kilrush Union, Co. Clare, and of the English Mitchell for Mulvihil in Glennamaddy Union, Co. Roscommon.

MURDOCH

THIS Scottish surname was brought in since the 17th century to Ulster by settlers from Scotland, most of whom established themselves in Co. Antrim.

MURPHY

THIS is the commonest surname in Ireland borne at birth by about one in every seventy-five inhabitants of the country. The name is widely distributed but at the end of the last century the heaviest concentration of Murphys was in Co. Cork, which accounted for over one-third of all the Murphy births in Ireland. Murphy families descend from septs named Ó Murchadha and Mac Murchadha. One of these septs was located in Co. Wexford, where Murphy is still the commonest surname, as it is in the neighbouring county of Carlow, and in Co. Armagh. It is the second commonest surname in Co. Cork and in Co. Kildare and the third commonest in Co. Kilkenny, Co. Wicklow and Co. Louth. The South Leinster Ó Murchada sept was a branch of the McMurroughs.

MURRAY

FAMILIES named Murray bear one of the twenty commonest surnames in Ireland. A considerable number of them, particularly in Ulster, will be descendants of settlers who came over from Scotland where this surname also ranks among the top twenty. However, the name of several Irish septs of Ó Muireadhaigh, the best known of which was located in Athlone Barony, Co. Roscommon, was anglicized as Murray and

Murry as well as Morrow, q.v. McIlmurray, in Irish Mac Giolla Mhuire, has also sometimes become Murray by abbreviation.

McADAM

MOST McAdam families in Ireland at the present time are in Ulster and mainly in Co. Monaghan, in which case their name derives from the Irish Mac Cadáin which was also anglicized as McCadden. There was, however, also a family name, in Irish Mac Adaim, which distinguished a branch of the Barry family in Co. Cork and an Irish family name Mac Adhaimh in Co. Cavan, usually rendered in English as McCaw, which may both, in some cases, account for descendants named McAdam. McAdam is also a Scottish surname and some families of the name in Ireland may descend from settlers also.

McALINDEN

THIS surname was assumed as an anglicization of their name by families of the Oriel sept Mac Giolla Fhiondain. The highest concentration of McAlinden families is still in the region of their ancestral homeland in Co. Armagh.

McALLISTER

THE ancestors of some of the McAllister and McAlister families in Ireland today came from Scotland to Ulster in the 14th century while others arrived in the 17th century as participants in the schemes for the resettlement and plantation of the province. Originally, however, the forebears of these migrants had been Irish who had migrated to Scotland at an earlier date.

McARDLE

FAMILIES with this surname descend from the Oriel sept Mac Ardghail, a branch of the McMahons. Most McArdle families have continued to reside in their ancestral homeland in Co. Monaghan, Co. Antrim and Co. Louth.

McATEER

THIS surname, in Irish Mac antSaoir, is found in eastern Ulster in Co. Antrim where it was first located, and farther west, as the family was dispersed when Ulster was resettled and they migrated to Co. Donegal and on to Co. Sligo in Connacht. Due to the settlement of Scottish McIntyres in eastern Ulster some of the Mac antSaoir families became known by that surname (q.v.), as an anglicization of their Irish name, instead of McAteer.

McAULEY

THE surname McAuley was taken by descendants of both the Mac Amhlaoibh sept, whose territory was Clanawley barony, Co. Fermanagh, a branch of the Maguires, and the Mac Amhalghaidh sept whose sept centre was at Ballyloughloe in Clonlonan barony in Co. Westmeath. Some descendants of this last named sept favoured the form Magawley. Some McAuley families may also descend from the Co. Cork sept Mac Amhlaoibh but usually families of that sept took the surname McAuliffe (q.v.). In Ulster some McAuleys descend from the Scottish Macaulay clan who came over in the 17th century.

McAULIFFE

AT the end of the nineteenth century all the McAuliffe families in Ireland were living in Munster and three-quarters of these were in Co. Cork. They descend from the Mac Amhlaoibh sept, whose sept centre was at Castlemacauliffe in the territory of their parent sept the McCarthys.

McBRIDE

THE families named McBride descend from the Co. Donegal sept Mac Giolla Brighde whose name was also anglicized to McGilbride, whence Kilbride which survived in Connacht but is found now in various parts of Ireland.

McCABE

THE McCabes are of gallowglass descent, with progenitors who came from Scotland in the 14th century as mercenaries in the service of the O'Reillys and O'Rourkes in Breffny. Co. Cavan has remained the principal home of their descendants but they have also established themselves in Co. Monaghan and migrated southwards into Leinster.

McCAFFERTY

THIS surname derives from the Irish Mac Eachmcharcaigh. It is usually in use with its prefix Mac but occasionally without – for example, in Co. Cavan where Cafferty families are found. A variant Cafferky is found in Connacht almost exclusively in Co. Mayo until recent population movements. As McCafferty the name is commonest in Co. Donegal and Co. Derry.

McCAFFREY

BALLYMACAFFRY in the barony of Magherastephana, Co. Fermanagh, was the ancient seat of the ancestors of the McCaffrey and Caffrey families. The vast majority of those who have remained in Co. Fermanagh and in the adjacent county of Tyrone have retained the prefix. The variant spelling McCaffry is also used. The descendants of those who migrated south into Cavan and on into Meath and Dublin abandoned the prefix so that Caffrey and the variant spelling Caffrey is usual in Leinster.

McCALLION

THE McCallions are of gallowglass descent, their progenitors having come to Ulster as mercenaries in the service of the O'Donnells. Today families named McCallion are still found in the ancient territory of the O'Donnells, in Co. Donegal and Co. Derry.

McCANN

FAMILIES bearing this surname are descendants of the Mac Anna (Mac Annadh) sept which anciently held sway on the southern shore of Lough Neagh over a territory in the north of the present county of Armagh. The McCanns are fairly numerous today in that region and have been dispersed to other parts of Ulster, into Connacht, and southwards into Leinster.

McCARRON

FAMILIES who bear this Ulster surname, found mainly in Co. Donegal and Co. Derry, would appear to be descendants of the Mac Cearáin sept which was located in that region.

McCARTAN

THIS surname is borne by descendants of the Mac Artain sept whose territory was the barony of Kinelarty in Co. Down. McCartans are still found mainly in that county and in the neighbouring county of Armagh.

McCARTHY

THIS surname, which is among the twenty commonest in Ireland, ranks as the third commonest in Co. Cork where over half of the McCarthy families in Ireland live. The Mac Carthaigh sept, from which they descend, was a prominent one in Munster anciently known as the Eoghannacht. One eminent branch of the McCarthys was located in the baronies of East and West Muskerry, another in the baronies of East and West Carbery in Co. Cork, and another near Killarney in Co. Kerry.

McCARTNEY

THIS surname, which belongs to a branch of the Scottish clan McIntosh, was brought to Ireland by settlers who came to Co. Antrim in the 17th century. At least half of the McCartney families in Ireland still live in that county.

McCAUSLAND

SCOTTISH settlers brought this surname to Co. Antrim in the 17th century. One prominent family of this name in Ulster traces its descent from the McCausland or McAuslane family of Buchanan in Scotland some of which came to Co. Tyrone in the 17th century.

McCLEAN

THE surnames McClean and McLean were first

McCARTHY *Carrigaphooca Castle, Co. Cork, once a stronghold of the Mc Carthys*

introduced to Ireland by Scottish gallowglass whose descendants are now numerous in Ulster.

McCLELLAND

THE surnames McClelland and McLelland came to Ulster with settlers from Scotland in the 17th century.

McCLINTOCK

THIS surname is found mainly in Ulster where it was introduced by settlers from Scotland in the 17th century. One prominent McClintock family in Ireland traces its descent from a settler who came to Co. Donegal from Argyllshire as early as 1597.

McCLOSKEY

ABOUT half of the McCloskey families in Ireland survive in Co. Derry, the homeland of their ancestral sept, Mac Bhloscaidh, a branch of the O'Cahans. Others have spread to the east of Ulster and to the capital. Mc.Cluskey is a common variant spelling.

McCLURE

THIS surname is usually of Scottish origin, having been introduced to Ulster by 17th century settlers from Scotland, but Dr. MacLysaght has reported that it was also assumed by members of the Oriel sept Mac Giolla Uidhir.

McCOMB

THIS surname, found principally in Ulster, belongs to descendants of members of a branch of the Scottish clan McIntosh who came to Ireland.

McCONNELL

FAMILIES named McConnell are found mainly in Ulster where as many as ninety per cent of them were living at the end of the last century. They are not of the same stock as the southern O'Connells as their name is used for the Irish Mac Dhomhnaill.

McCONVILLE

DESCENDANTS of the Oriel sept, Mac Conmhaoil, bearing the surname McConville, are found still mainly in the region of their ancestral homeland in Co. Armagh and also in Co. Antrim.

McCORMACK

THE patronymic surnames McCormick and McCormack are found in all four provinces of Ireland where they are borne as anglicized forms of the Irish Mac Cormaic.

McCOURT

FAMILIES bearing the surname McCourt are found mainly in Co. Louth and Co. Armagh not far from the homeland of their ancestral Oriel sept, Mac Cuarta.

McCOY *See McHUGH*

McCRORY

THIS patronymic surname is a variant form of McRory, which it has supplanted numerically. It originated as an anglicization of the name of the Co. Derry family, Mac Ruaidhri. At the end of the last century half of the McCrory families were in Co. Tyrone adjacent to their ancient homeland.

McCULLOUGH

FAMILIES bearing the surnames McCullough and McCullagh, which are found principally in Ulster, may be of native Irish descent when their name was taken as an anglicization of the Irish Mac Cú Uladh or Mac Con Uladh, or they can be of Scottish origin, in which case they are descendants of settlers from Scotland named McCulloch.

McDAID *See DEVITT*

McDERMOT

THE Mac Diarmada septs sprang from a branch of the royal O'Connors of Connacht. The most prominent of these held a vast territory covering much of the modern county of Roscommon, with its sept centre at Coolavin, another held sway in the north of that county in the barony of Boyle. The surname McDermot has survived in such numbers in its homeland that it ranks as the second commonest surname in Co. Roscommon. Due to the dispersal of the descendants of the Mac Diarmada septs, however, less than half of the McDermots in Ireland today are still in the province of Connacht. The second heaviest distribution is in Ulster and the next heaviest in Leinster.

McDONAGH

THE surname McDonagh, and its variants McDonogh, McDonough, and Donaghy (which was confined to western Ulster), are borne by descendants of septs called Mac Donnchadha. The majority appear to be of the stock of the Connacht sept which was a branch of the McDermots located in Co. Sligo. The other Mac Donnchadha sept, a branch of the McCarthys, held sway in the barony of Duhallow, Co. Cork, with their stronghold at Kanturk.

McDONALD

THIS is properly the name of the Scottish clan McDonald and as such is borne in Ireland as a surname by descendants of members of that clan who settled in Ulster in the 17th century. However, many McDonalds in Ireland must also bear the name as a variant of McDonnell (q.v.), being either of gallowglass lineage or descendants of one of the Irish Mac Domhnall septs.

McDONNELL

THIS surname is one of the hundred most common in Ireland. Families of the name do not all share the same ancestry but will mainly derive from either the McDonnells, who came from Argyllshire in Scotland in the 13th century to Ulster where they carved out a territory for themselves in Co. Antrim, or from the MacDomhnaill sept of Co. Fermanagh, or from the Mac Domhnaill sept in Co. Clare. In addition, a few who now bear the name McDonnell may descend from Scottish settlers of the clan MacDonald, the two cognate names having, inevitably, been confused. Inversely some McDonnells became McDonald. The gallowglass McDonnells displaced the McQuillans in northern Antrim and, having seized their stronghold, Dunseverick,

improved and fortified it and then entrenched themselves in the Glens of Antrim. The Co. Clare sept appear to be still well represented by a sizeable distribution of McDonnell families in southern Co. Clare and in Co. Limerick.

McDOWELL

THIS surname, found mainly in eastern Ulster, belongs to families descended from Scottish gallowglasses who came to Ireland as mercenaries several centuries before the great Scottish immigration of the 17th century. In Scotland the same name is rendered MacDugall.

McELHINN(E)Y

DESCENDANTS of the West Ulster sept Mac Giolla Chainnigh, who remained in the region of their ancestral homeland in Co. Donegal, Co. Derry and Co. Tyrone, have usually taken either McElhinn(e)y or McIlhenn(e)y as their surname. These surnames have also been rendered as Macklehenny following the way they are pronounced. Some descendants of the same sept who migrated to Connacht adopted Kilkenny as their surname.

McELLIGOTT

Until the end of the last century the surname McElligott, in Irish Mag Uileagóid, was found almost exclusively in Co. Kerry.

McELWEE See McKELVEY

McEVOY

EVEN before the massive population movement towards the capital in the present century, over half of the McEvoys in Ireland were living in Leinster, in Co. Louth, in Co. Leix, and in the capital. Their ancestors belonged to the Mac Fhiodhbhuidhe sept, once one of the most prominent in Co. Leix.

McFADDEN

THIS surname, found predominantly in Ulster, is borne by families of ancient Irish descent (Mac Phaidín) and also by others of Scottish settler descent.

McFARLAN

THIS Scottish surname, now more often written McFarland in Ulster, came to Ireland with settlers from Scotland during the 17th century schemes for the re-settlement of the province. Inevitably it has been confused with the surname

McPartlan (q.v.) and its variants McPartland and McPartlin which all derive from the Irish Mac Parthaláin from Co. Armagh.

McGARRY

FAMILIES of this name, in Irish Mag Fhearadhaigh, are found in almost equal numbers in Ulster, Connacht and Leinster and it is not clear whether they share any common origin, although within each of those provinces they are clustered in a given area – the Leinster McGarrys live mainly in the capital, the Ulster McGarrys live mainly in Co. Antrim and the Connacht McGarrys are mostly in Co. Leitrim and Co. Roscommon.

McGEE *See MAGEE*

McGILL

THIS surname, found mostly in Ulster, can derive either from the Irish Mac an Ghaill or, as an abbreviation, from one of the names which begin in Irish Mac Giolla. The form Magill was favoured in eastern Ulster while McGill was preferred in western Ulster. Gill, which is scattered in various parts of Ireland, may derive from the same Irish names or, in a feE cases, from Scottish or English settlers named Gill.

Mac GILLYCUDDY

THE MacGillycuddy families (whose surname is pronounced Macklecuddy) are, in fact, lineally descended from the O'Sullivans, a branch of whom in Magunihy and Dunkerrin baronies Co. Kerry were distinguished as O'Sullivan alias Mac Gillycuddy (Mac Giolla Chuda) and eventually by that last name only for the last three or four hundred years. Co. Kerry is still the home of most who bear the name, including the chief, the MacGillycuddy of the Reeks, whose seat is near Beaufort in that county.

McGINLEY

THIS surname, in Irish, Mag Fhionnghaile, belongs to Co. Donegal. Some of the name have become McKinley (q.v.) due to the phonic similarity of the two surnames.

McGILLYCUDDY *The Reeks in Co. Kerry, the county where most of this name live*

McGINN

THE surname McGinn, found dispersed throughout Ulster, and its Connacht variant, McGing favoured in Co. Leitrim and farther west in Co. Mayo, are anglicizations of the Irish name Mag Fhinn.

McGINTY

McGINTY families survive in Co. Donegal, the homeland of their ancestral sept, Mag Fhinneachta. Branches which moved into Connacht generally lost the prefix to become Ginty, a surname found almost exclusively in that province until families of the name were scattered in the course of 20th century population movements.

McGLINCH(E)Y

THIS Ulster surname, in Irish, Mag Loingsigh, belongs to Co. Donegal whence families of the name have spread into the neighbouring counties of Derry and Tyrone.

McGLYNN

FAMILIES with the surname McGlynn are found in Ulster, Connacht and Leinster. They are the widely dispersed descendants of the Mag Fhloinn sept whose homeland was in the neighbourhood of Athlone on the Co. Westmeath-Co. Roscommond borders.

McGOLDRICK

THIS surname is borne by descendants of the Mag Ualghairg sept, a branch of the O'Rourkes, who were rulers of Breffny. This sept was located on the Leitrim-Fermanagh borders. The descendants of the sept were scattered so that the surname McGoldrick now is found mainly in Co. Tyrone and Co. Sligo as well as Co. Fermanagh. McGolrick, McGoulrick and McGorlick are variant spellings on record while the English surname Goulding has been reported by the Registrar of Births as used interchangeably with McGoldrick in Downpatrick Union, Co. Down.

McGONIGLE

THIS surname is borne by descendants of the Co. Donegal sept Mac Congail. Its modern homeand is still in that county and in the neighbouring county of Derry. Several variant spellings the name are recorded, McGonagle, McGonegal, McGonigal etc.

McGOVERN

THE surnames McGovern, and the now less common Magauran, belong to families descended from the Co. Cavan sept Mag Shamhradháin whose sept centre was at Ballymagauran in Tullyhaw barony. Magauran is a spelling retained mainly in Co. Cavan. McGoverns are found principally in that county and in the neighbouring counties of Leitrim and Fermanagh.

McGOWAN

FAMILIES who bear this surname descend from the Mac an Ghabhain sept which was located in Co. Cavan near to its border with Co. Leitrim. Many descendants of that sept, however, along with descendants of the Ó Ghabhahn sept of Co. Down, bear the English occupational surname Smith, their forebears having thus called themselves, smith being the Irish translation of ghabhain. McGowan was retained and survived mainly in Co. Donegal, Co. Sligo, Co. Leitrim and Co. Cavan.

McGRATH

THE families of McGrath or Magrath inherit their surname from septs named Mag Raith. One of these had its sept centre at Termon McGrath near the River Termon which, flowing into Lough Erne, divides Lurg Barony in Co. Fermanagh from Tirhugh barony, Co. Donegal. The other MagRaith sept had its home in Co. Clare, where it was associated with the ruling O'Briens and whence its descendants spread across the Shannon to settle in Co. Tipperary and eastwards through Munster into Co. Waterford. The descendants of the Munster sept are much more numerous than those of the Ulster sept to judge by the present distribution of the name, which ranks among the sixty commonest surnames in Ireland.

McGUIGAN

THE Irish Mag Uiginn has been anglicized as McGuigan, Maguigan, McGuckin, found mostly in Co. Derry, McGuckian, found mostly in Co. Leitrim, McGookin, found mostly in Co. Antrim, McQuiggan, McWiggin and Wigan or Wiggin. The Registrar of Births reported in the last century the use of Pidgeon and Fidgeon interchangeably with McGuigan in Carrick-macross Union, Co. Monaghan.

McGUINNESS

 THIS surname is usually in use in Ireland with its prefix Mac but is certainly better known throughout the world as Guinness, the name of the brewery founded by one of the family in the 18th century who had abandoned the prefix. The Mag Aonghusa sept, from which they descend, was a prominent one in Ulster, holding a territory in the baronies of Lower and Upper Iveagh in Western Co. Down. The surname is found not infrequently with the prefix elided as Maguinness and Magennis. In the last century the Registrar of Births reported that McCreech was used interchangeably with McGuinness in Newry Union, Co. Down, and Magreece in Irvinestown Union, Co. Fermanagh. There are also many variant spellings of Guinness on record, with one or two n's, one or two s's, without the u, and with an i instead of an e for the last vowel.

McGUIRE See MAGUIRE

McGURK

FAMILIES bearing the surname McGurk, and its variant McGuirk, descend from the Mag Oirc sept which was located in Co. Tyrone.

McHALE

THE Mac Céile sept, whose descendants bear the anglicized form of their name, McHale, belonged to Co. Mayo where they were erenaghs at Killala. McHale families were found exclusively in Co. Mayo until fairly recently. Dr. Mac-Lysaght has noted that an immigrant Welsh family named Howell, which settled in Tirawley barony, Co. Mayo, the homeland of the Irish

McHales, adopted the name of the neighbours as their own in lieu of Howell. The McHales who are descended from the *ci-devant* Howells cannot now be distinguished from the Mac Céile sept.

McHUGH

Two Mac Aodha septs, both located in Co. Galway, were the forebears of the numerous McHugh families which have resided mainly in the counties of Galway, Mayo and Leitrim in Connacht and in western Ulster in Co. Donegal and Co. Fermanagh. McCue is the commonest variant spelling of McHugh, but other variants are recorded such as McCoy, McKew, and McKee, which is phonically close to the Irish Mac Aodha. The Scottish surname McKay has also been confused with Mac Aodha in Ireland. In the last century the Registrar of Births, in two separate Unions, Tuam, Co. Galway, and Enniskillen, Co. Fermanagh, reported the use of the English surname Hewson interchangeably with McHugh as a literal translation of the Irish.

McILHENN(E)Y See McELHINN(E)Y

McILROY

THE surnames McIlroy and McElroy, found predominantly in Ulster, and Gilroy and Kilroy, found mostly in Connacht, all derive from the Irish Mac Giolla Rua. Early places of settlement of families of the name are pinpointed by the names of three Ulster townlands, Ballymacilroy in Upper Toome barony, Co. Antrim, Ballymackilroy in Clogher barony, Co. Tyrone, and Ballymackilroy in Magherastephana barony, Co. Fermanagh.

McILVEEN

THIS surname, in Irish, Mac Giolla Mhin, is found mainly in Co. Down, its earliest home, and in the adjacent county of Antrim. McElvaine, McElveen and McKilveen are known variants and there is evidence of interchangeability due to confusion with McIlwaine (q.v.) and with the immigrant Scottish surname McIlvaine.

McILWAINE

DESCENDANTS of the Mac Giolla Bháin sept, which was located in Co. Sligo, took as the anglicized form of their name the surname Kilbane, which survives mainly in that county, and McIlwaine, sometimes written Mackelwaine, McElwaine and McElweane. These latter names, of which the spelling McIlwaine is the commonest, are now found mainly in Ulster where they may be in use as a corruption of the Scottish name McIlvaine which was brought over by settlers, or by confusion with the Co. Down name McIlveen (q.v.).

McINERNEY

THIS surname is commonest in the counties of Limerick and Clare, indicating that, for the most part, McInerney families will be descendants of the Mac an Airchinnigh sept which was located in Lower Bunratty barony, Co. Clare, with its sept centre at Ballycally. There were, however, other erenaghs whose descendants became known as Mac an Airchinnigh and some present-day McInerneys may be descended from these. The descendants of one such erenagh family, custodians of St. Patrick's Elphin, Co. Roscommon, still survive in Co. Roscommon where their name has been corrupted to Nerney. There are a number of spelling variants of McInerney on record, MacAnerney, McEnerney, McInnerney, and also the variants Keverny and McKeniry in Co. Clare.

McINTYRE

MEMBERS of the clan McIntyre in Scotland settled in Ulster in the 17th century and their descendants are still living in the province, mainly in Co. Antrim. Some families bearing the surname McIntyre, however, are of native Irish descent, their forebears living in the same areas where McIntyre settlers established themselves, having assumed this Scottish surname as an anglicization of their Irish name, Mac an tSoir, rather than McAteer (q.v.).

McIVOR See McKEEVER

McKAY

Members of the Scottish clan McKay crossed to Ulster at the time of the re-settlement of that province under the 17th century plantation schemes and their descendants are found mainly in Co. Antrim. There is evidence also that the surname McKay was taken by some descendants of the Irish Mac Aodha septs (see McHugh).

McKEE

THIS surname is found predominantly in Ulster where in the majority it is a variant of the Scottish settler surname McKay, but it is known to have been assumed also by descendants of the Irish sept MacAodha as a variant of the more usual McHugh (q.v.) and McCue.

McKEEVER

BOTH McKeever, which is found mainly in Co. Antrim and Co. Derry, and McIvor, which is found mainly in Co. Tyrone and Co. Derry, are anglicized forms of the Irish, Mac Iomhair.

McKELVEY

FAMILIES bearing this surname descend from the Mac Giolla Bhuidhe sept which was located in Co. Donegal whence they moved eastwards into Co. Derry and central Ulster. There are many variant renderings of this Irish surname on record: McCalvey, McElvee, McElvie, McElwee, McGilvie, McKilvie. McElwee has survived in the same regions as McKelvey.

McKENNA

THE McKennas descend from the Mac Cionaoith sept whose territory was in the barony of Trough in Co. Monaghan. Their progeny was prolific so that McKenna ranks among the hundred commonest surnames in Ireland but it is still predominantly an Ulster name and most heavily distributed in the counties of Monaghan, Tyrone, Armagh and Antrim.

McKEOWN

THE surname McKeown, and its variant McKeon (occasionally both found also without the prefix Mac), belong in Ireland both to descendants of early Scots settlers who had established themselves in the Glens of Antrim in the 13th century and who took the Irish name Mac Eoin in lieu of their own surname Bissett, and of Irish septs named Mac Eoghain (Mac Eoin).

McKINLY

THIS surname was brought to Ulster by settlers from Scotland and that will be the origin of most McKinley families in Co. Antrim. McKinley was taken by families of Irish origin whose name would be more correctly McGinley (q.v.), in Irish Mag Fhionnghaile.

McKINNEY

At the end of the last century this surname was found in Ireland exclusively in Ulster. The majority of McKinney families will be of settler lineage, descendants of 17th century immigrants from Scotland where the McKinneys are a sept of the clan McKinnon. There is evidence, however, that some McKenna families of native Irish origin also became known as McKinney.

McKNIGHT

The present location in Ireland of the majority of McKnight families in the eastern seaboard counties of Ulster suggests that they are of Scottish origin, their name being a form of the Scottish Mac Neachtain.

McLOUGHLIN

Descendants of the Ó Maoilsheachlainn sept of the stock of Maoilsheachlainn, the 10th century High King of Ireland whose homeland was in Meath, became known as McLoughlin and McLaughlin rather than O'Melaghlin, the earlier anglicized form of their name which after losing the prefix, was transformed into a Mac prefixed name because of its sound. Other McLoughlins and McLaughlins, however, descend from the Ulster Mac Lochlainn sept whose territory was Inishowen barony, Co. Donegal. The families descended from that sept will be found mostly still in Co. Donegal and Co. Derry.

There was also an Ó Lochlainn sept which provided the forebears of O'Loughlin and Loughlin families and some who favour the spelling O'Loghlen. This sept was located in the barony of Burren in Co. Clare and the families of this stock are found there and in the neighbouring counties of Munster as well as in the capital.

McMAHON *15th century tomb of the Mc Mahon family in Ennis Friary, Co. Clare*

McMAHON

This surname ranks among the seventy commonest in Ireland and is the commonest surname in Co. Clare, which was the homeland of one of the two septs called Mac Mathghamha, a branch of the ruling O'Briens established in western Co. Clare and known since the 12th century by the patronymic of their ancestor Mathghamha a son of Murcheartaigh Mor O'Brien, High King of Ireland. The other sept of the same name belonged to Ulster and was located in Oriel, in Co. Monaghan, in which county McMahon ranks as the third commonest surname at the present time. Mahon (q.v.), is not usually an abbreviation of McMahon.

McMANUS

This surname is the second commonest in Co. Fermanagh, the ancient homeland of the Mac Maghnuis sept, a branch of the ruling Maguires. In Connacht some Mac Manus families may not be of this stock but of that of a Mac Maghnuis sept located in the barony of Boyle,

149

Co. Roscommon, a branch of the ruling O'Connors, distinguished by the patronymic of their particular progenitor since the 12th century.

McMASTER

FAMILIES bearing this surname, which is commonest in the eastern seaboard counties of Ulster, will, for the most part, be of settler descent, their ancestors having come over from Scotland in the 17th century. Some McMaster families, however, may be of native Irish extraction, descendants of a Breffny sept, Mac an Mhaighistir, which was located in the north of Co. Longford. The more usual anglicization assumed by the descendants of that sept was Masterson, q.v.

McMENAMIN

THIS surname, in Irish, Mac Meanman, belongs almost exclusively to western Co. Tyrone and eastern Co. Donegal, with noticeable concentration around Letterkenny and Ballybofey. Various spelling variations have been recorded, McMenamen, McMenemen, McMenimin and in Omagh Union, Co. Tyrone, McMenim as an abbreviated form.

McMILLAN

THIS name was brought to Ulster in the 17th century by settlers belonging to the Scottish clan McMillan. It is now less common in Ulster than its synonym McMullan, q.v.

McMULLAN

THIS Scottish surname is a synonym of McMillan, particularly favoured in Ireland where it was brought to Ulster by settlers from Scotland in the 17th century who established themselves mainly on lands east of the Bann. See also Mullan.

McMURROUGH

THE Mac Murchadha sept, whose chief was the ruler of Leinster, became divided into branches which were known not by the name of the sept but by the distinguishing name of the branch so that the name McMurrough itself was extinguished. The descendants of the sept now bear the names

of the branches, Kavanagh, Kinsella, Davis (from Mac David or Mac Davie More) and Murphy (from the Irish Ó Murchadha) which came into usage in place of O'Morchoe.

McNALLY

THE surname McNally, and its variant McAnally, are found mainly in Ulster, the home of more than half of the families of the name in Ireland; it has long been associated with Oriel and survives in the counties of Armagh and Monaghan. Dr. MacLysaght has noted that in Ulster this name was used as an English synonym of the Irish Mac Con Uladh, although the usual Irish form of McNally is Mac an Fhailghigh.

McNAMARA

TODAY McNamara is the second commonest name in its ancient homeland, Co. Clare, where the Mac Conmara sept was next in importance only to the ruling O'Briens to whom they were marshals. A Mac Conmara also officiated at the inauguration of the O'Brien chief who ruled over Thomond. One branch of the sept held sway in Bunratty barony with its stronghold at Bunratty castle and the other in Upper and Lower Tulla baronies.

McNAMEE

THE principal homeland of McNamee families is in Co. Derry, although they are found today in other counties of Ulster and farther south in the province of Leinster. They descend from hereditary poets to the Ulster O'Neills in Co. Tyrone whose name in Irish was Mac Conmidhe.

McNAMARA *Bunratty Castle, Co. Clare. A stronghold of the Mc Namaras before it passed to the O'Briens*

McNEILL

THIS Ulster surname is borne by a family of gallowglass descent whose ancestors came to Co. Antrim and Co. Derry as mercenaries. The surname is still found predominantly in those counties.

McNICHOLAS

THIS surname, which belongs exclusively to Co. Mayo, came into being with a branch of the de Burgo famile (see Burke) which was distinguished by this patronymic.

McNULTY

FAMILIES bearing this surname descend from the Mac an Ultaigh sept which was located in Co. Donegal. That county and Co. Mayo are the principal home counties of McNulty families today.

McPARLAND

THIS spelling is the commonest anglicized form of the Irish Mac Parthaláin. Other variant spellings in use are Mac Partlan, McPartland, McPartlin. The earliest home of the family appears to have been in Co. Armagh where descendants survive. Inevitably in Ulster there has been confusion between this surname and the Scottish surname McFarland or McFarlane which is found in about the same numbers.

McQUAID

McQuaid and McQuade families, whose name in Irish was Mac Uaid, are found principally in Ulster in the counties of Monaghan, Fermanagh and Antrim.

McQUILLAN

FAMILIES of this name descend from settlers who established themselves in the extreme north of Co. Antrim soon after the Anglo-Norman invasion and held sway over a territory known as The Route and had their stronghold in the castle of Dunluce. It appears that the first of the family to come to Co. Antrim were of Norman origin and that the name McQuillan (in Irish Mac Iughilin or Mac Uidhilin) comes from the

forename, Hugelin, of their progenitor Hugelin de Mandeville.

McSHANE

THIS surname, in Irish Mac Seáin, is found mainly in Ulster where the family traces its descent from a branch of the O'Neills which came to be known by this patronymic distinction.

McSHARRY

FAMILIES bearing this surname, found mainly in Co. Leitrim and in the neighbouring counties of Sligo and Donegal, descend from the Co. Leitrim sept Mac Searraigh.

McSWEENEY

THE McSweeney and McSwiney families are descendants of the gallowglass warriors who settled in Co. Donegal, where they had come as mercenaries. By the 15th century they had formed three septs named Mac Suichne. The surname Mac-Sweeney is now mainly found in Munster, particularly in Co. Cork where a branch of the family migrated from Ulster, established itself, flourished and multiplied.

McTEAGUE See TIGHE

McVEIGH

THIS East Ulster surname, in Irish, Mac An Bheatha, has a number of variants, McVeagh, McVey, McBay, McVea, etc.

McWILLIAM(S)

THIS surname, found in Ireland mainly in Ulster, is of Scottish origin, McWilliam(s) having been adopted as their surname by a branch of the McFarlane clan. Also in the last century the Registrar of Births reported the interchangeable use of McWilliams with the Irish surname McQuillan in Newry Union, Co. Down, and that McWilliams appeared as McQuilliams in Magherafelt Union, Co. Derry.

McVEIGH *The Kilnasaggart Stone in Co. Armagh, in the region where this name originated*

NAGLE

THIS Munster surname, found mostly in Co. Cork, derives from the Norman surname de Angulo. Descendants of that family in Connacht became Nangle but Nagle was the form which developed in Co. Cork, where the family gave its name to Nagles Mountains in the south of Fermoy barony.

NAUGHTON

THE best-known Ó Neachtain sept was first located near Loughrea in Co. Galway whence it migrated to Athlone barony, Co. Roscommon, in the eake of the Anglo-Norman penetration of Connacht. Another Ó Neachtain sept was located in Inchiquin barony, Co. Clare, not far distant from Loughrea but was of different stock. Naughton families are found predominantly in Connacht in the counties of Galway, Mayo and Roscommon, denoting their descent from the first-named sept and in Munster in Co. Clare, denoting descent from the latter-named sept. The English surname Norton has occasionally been substituted for Naughton. The Registrar of Births cited such cases in the last century in

Mullingar Union, Co. Westmeath, Mountbellew Union, Co. Galway, and Lisnaskea Union, Co. Fermanagh, and also reported that in Listowel Union, Co. Kerry, Behane was used interchangeably with Naughton. McNaghton is a distinct Scottish surname which is often written McNaughton and McNaughten in Ulster and could have given rise to some Naughtons descended from Scottish settlers of that name who abandoned the prefix.

NEARY

THIS surname, in Irish Ó Naradhaigh, is found mostly in the Connacht counties of Mayo and Roscommon, in Co. Louth, and in the capital; it appears to have originated in Connacht. The variant spelling Nary has been noted at Strokestown, Co. Roscommon.

NEILAN

THIS surname, most usually written Neilan, Neylan, or Nilan, is also found in records transformed into the English surname Neyland and even as Kneeland. It is, however, of Irish origin, being the name used by descendants of the Ó Nialláin sept of Co. Clare where the Neilan families were fairly numerous, although the name is now found more frequently farther north in Connacht.

NEILL See O'NEILL

NELSON

THIS surname came to Ireland as Neilson or Nelson with settlers, mostly from Scotland, and also as Nelson with settlers from England. Consequently it is commonest by far in Ulster where it was established by settlers of the 17th century plantation schemes in that province.

NERNEY See McINERNEY

NEVILLE

WHILE some Neville families in Ireland may trace their lineage back to an English settler, such as the Richard Neville who acquired an estate in Co. Kildare in the 17th century, the frequency of the name in Munster, where it is found mainly in Co. Cork and Co. Limerick, is due to it having been assumed, according to Dr. MacLysaght, by descendants of the Ó Niagh family instead of the more usual Nee.

NEWELL

THE prevalence of this surname in Ireland in the eastern seaboard counties of Ulster suggests that most of the name there will be of settler descent, their forebears having come to the province when it was re-settled with immigrants from England and Scotland. There was, however, a small Irish sept in the north of Co. Kildare called Ó Tnuthghaill whose descendants assumed Newell and Knowles as anglicized forms of their Irish name.

NEWMAN

THIS English surname has been brought to Ireland from England by settlers over the centuries, so that it became well established in Co. Cork, which accounted for almost half of the Newman families in the country, and also in the Pale counties of Dublin and Meath. Many of the Cork Newmans will be descendants of Richard Newman from Wincanton, Somerset, who acquired property in Cork city and county in the 17th century.

NICHOLL

As distinct from Nicholson and McNicholas, the surname Nicholl is found mostly in Ulster as the anglicization of the Irish Mac Niocaill but independently it was brought to Ulster from Scotland also by Scottish settlers with the surname Nicoll, a spelling which has also survived in Ireland.

NICHOLSON

BEARERS of this surname are usually of English or Scottish settler descent. There were several prominent settler Nicholson families whose forebears came from Westmorland and Cumberland to Ulster in the 17th century. In Connacht, where it is found mainly in Co. Sligo, Nicholson was also assumed as a translation of their name by McNicholas families (q.v.) and possibly also by some named McNicholl.

NIXON

THIS English surname is found mainly in Ulster where it was brought by settlers in the 17th century who established themselves principally in Co. Fermanagh and Co. Cavan.

NOBLE

THIS English surname was brought to Ireland by 17th century settlers and is now found mainly in Co. Antrim and in the capital. One prominent family of the name traces its lineage to a settler from Cornwall who acquired lands in Co. Fermanagh.

NOLAN

FAMILIES named Nolan are descendants of the Ó Nualláin sept whose territory was in the barony of Forth in Co. Carlow. Nolan ranks among the fifty commonest surnames in Ireland but nevertheless almost all of the name are of the same stock, the exceptions being some who may descend from a small Ó Nualláin sept which was located in West Cork. About two-thirds of all the Nolan families in Ireland still live in their ancient home province of Leinster but there is a fair representation of the name in Connacht where some of the Leinster sept migrated in the 16th century.

NOONAN

ABOUT three-quarters of the families in Ireland bearing the surname Noonan, in Irish Ó Nuanáin, live in Munster, the province where that name seems to have originated in Co. Cork.

NOONE

FAMILIES bearing the surname Noone, found mostly in Connacht, descend from the Ó Nuadháin sept which was located in Co. Sligo. Today Noones are found mainly in the counties of Mayo, Roscommon and Galway.

NUGENT

THE ancestors of the Nugents came to Ireland at the period of the Anglo-Norman invasion at the end of the 12th century at which time they were called de Nogent, from their place of origin in France. In Ireland they established themselves in the counties of Meath and Westmeath with their principal stronghold in the barony of Delvin, Co. Westmeath. From their earliest places of settlement they spread northwards into Ulster and southwards into Munster where one branch made its home near Carrigaline in Co. Cork, so that today the name is widespread.

O'BRIEN

THIS surname ranks among the ten commonest in Ireland with over half of the O'Brien families in the province of Munster. The sept from which these families descend took its name from Brian Boru (Boroimhe) High King of Ireland in the 10th century. Subsequently the great Ó Briain sept divided into several branches in Co. Clare, Co. Limerick, Co. Tipperary and Co. Waterford. Those families who had lost their prefix O' have, in this century, for the most part, reassumed it so that Briens without the prefix are now very much in the minority.

O'BRIEN *Ballynalacken Castle, Co. Clare*

O'CALLAGHAN

ALTHOUGH at the end of the last century there were four times as many births registered in Ireland as Callaghan than O'Callaghan, today the surname is much more frequently in use with its prefix O' than without. The ancient territory of the sept was in the barony of Kinlea in the south of Co. Cork whence they moved northwards in the 13th century and re-settled in the neighbourhood of Mallow in the same county. Their descendants are still largely to be found in Co. Cork; they have become so numerous that their surname is now one of the fifty commonest in Ireland. It is also found among families indigenous to the southern Ulster counties of Monaghan and Armagh, and to county Louth, descendants of a quite distinct sept, Ó Ceileachain, whereas

O'BRIEN *Effigy of Conor O'Brien, in Corcomroe Abbey, Co. Clare*

descendants of this Oriel sept who settled in Co. Westmeath have preferred to spell their name Kellaghan or Kelleghan.

O'CONNELL

IN the present century a great number of families descended from the Co. Kerry sept Ó Conaill have reassumed the prefix O' which about three-quarters of them had lost, so that today the great majority bear the surname O'Connell and only a minority still uses Connell. The home of the sept was the barony of Magunihy, Co. Kerry, where many of the name still live but the progeny of the sept is very numerous and while the heaviest distribution of O'Connells and Connells is still in Munster, the name is also widely distributed throughout the rest of the country.

O'CONNELL

Of the Kerry family was the hero of Roman Catholic emancipation in Ireland, Daniel O'Connell, M.P. (1775–1847), known as 'The Liberator'. He was born near Cahirciveen, Co. Kerry, educated in France, where his uncle Count Daniel O'Connell enjoyed a prominent position, was called to the Irish Bar in 1798, and practised as a lawyer with great success for many years. He

gave up his career to devote himself to politics in the cause of the oppressed majority of the population. Two of his sons also entered parliament, Morgan (1804–1885) and John (1810–1858).

O'CONNOR

THE name of the family, which once ruled Connacht and provided Ireland with her last two High-Kings, is now one of the ten commonest surnames in the country, in use both with and without its prefix O'. The great Ó Conchobhair sept of Connacht was not the only sept to bear this name, however.

The Munster Ó Conchobhair sept held sway in the northern part of Co. Kerry, with the stronghold of their chief at Carrigafoyle Castle in the barony of Iraghticonor. The Ó Conchobhair sept of Co. Offaly once held a large territory stretching from the borders of Co. Kildare to the Shannon. Yet another sept of the name was seated in the north-west of Co. Clare in the barony of Coromroe.

Today families named Connor or O'Connor are most heavily distributed in Munster where a descent from the Kerry O'Connors and the Corcomroe O'Connors may be presumed, but they are numerous also in the other provinces.

The family of the O'Conor Don, which is seated at Belanagare in

Co. Roscommon, can demonstrate its lineal descent from the royal family of Connacht which had retained its last medieval stronghold, Ballintober Castle, Co. Roscommon, until the sequestrations of the 17th century.

O'DEA

THE descendants of the sept of Ó Deághaidh, whose territory was in the barony of Inchiquin in Co. Clare, mostly retained the prefix O' and the minority who did lose the prefix appear to have reassumed it for, while there were some Dea families in Ireland at the beginning of this century, there appear now to be none. A number of O'Dea families have settled in the capital but the name is still firmly established in Munster, having spread from Co. Clare into the adjacent counties of Limerick and Tipperary and down into Co. Cork.

ODELL

ALTHOUGH members of this family made their name look Irish by writing it O'Dell, they are, in fact, of settler descent, their common ancestor having come to Limerick from England in the Elizabethan plantation of Munster in the 16th century. In England, where the name was pronounced Odle, it derived from Wodell and Wodehull and belonged to the Northampton-shire-Bedfordshire region. The family bore as its coat of arms: Argent, three crescents Gules.

O'DONNELL

THE O'Donnell families share one of the fifty commonest surnames in Ireland. By no means all will descend from the famous sept Ó Domhnaill which was originally located in Kilmacrenan barony in northern Co. Donegal. The ancient inauguration place of the O'Donnell chiefs of this sept was the Rock of Doon. This was the sept, of course, to which belonged the

adventurous Earls of Tyrconnell. The massive north tower of Donegal castle remains of their stronghold and residence there. There were, however, other Ó Domhnaill septs from which O'Donnells descend. One of these was located in West Clare and another in Co. Galway. This accounts for the present distribution of the name O'Donnell which is heaviest in Ulster, about three-quarters of that number in Munster, and in Connacht about one-half the number found

O'DONNELL *Donegal Castle, originally a stronghold of the O'Donnells, later the seat of settlers called Brooke*

157

in Munster. Until the recent heavy migration of families to the capital, the name was comparatively sparsely represented in Leinster.

Maxen 20/11 1759.

COUNT JOHN O'DONNELL

Since the daring Red Hugh O'Donnell, chief of the O'Donnells of Tir Conaill, went to Spain in 1602 after the battle of Kinsale, followed in 1607 by his brother Rory, Earl of Tyrconnell, who died in Rome in 1608, members of the O'Donnell family have gained fame and fortune outside Ireland. Field-Marshall Con O'Donnell from Larkfield, Co. Leitrim, became Governor of Transylvania; his brother, Count John O'Donnell, was also a Field-Marshal in the Austrian Imperial service. A branch of the family in Spain was honoured with the title of Duke of Tetuan in the person of Leopold O'Donnell, 1809–1867, Minister of War

in the Spanish government and Governor of Cuba.

O'DONOGHUE

FAMILIES who descend from the Ó Donnchada septs have widely reassumed the prefix O' to their surname which is now found as O'Donoghue, O'Donohoe and O' Donohue in much greater numbers than Donoghue, Donohoe and Donohue which were in the majority at the end of the last century, when only about one family in six used the prefix. The distribution of the form Donohoe, which was then more numerous, has diminished which indicates that some families of that name, when resuming the prefix also reverted to the more correct spelling, O'Donoghue. One Ó Donnchadha sept was located in south Co. Kilkenny, another in Co. Galway and another in Co. Cavan and another, the best known, in West Cork whence they migrated to Co. Kerry, forming two branches, one with its stronghold at Ross Castle on Lough Leine near Killarney, and the other with its sept centre in the eastern part of the same barony (Magunihy) in the glens near Glenflesk. Many families of the name still reside in the neighbourhood of Killarney.

O'DONOVAN

THE families descended from the Ó Donnabháin sept are among those Irish families which have widely reassumed the prefix O' in the present century so that now the great majority is O'Donovan whereas one hundred years ago in Ireland there were twenty Donovans for every one O'Donovan. The original location of the sept was in the neighbourhood of Bruree, along the banks of the River Maigue in the south of Co. Limerick but they migrated to West Cork where the sept re-established itself in the south of the baronies of East and West Carbery at about the end of the 12th century. Co. Cork is still the principal home of families of this name and many still live in the neighbourhood of settlement of their ancestors. Branches have also migrated and established themselves in Co. Kilkenny, Co. Waterford and Co. Wexford.

O'DOWD

AT the beginning of this century there were about five persons named Dowd in Ireland for every one O'Dowd, although a number of families, mostly in Co. Sligo, had retained the prefix O'. Today, due to a widespread reassumption of the prefix by Dowd families, there are many more O'Dowds in Ireland than Dowds. The name of the sept from which they descend was Ó Dubhda, it once held sway over a wide territory which stretched across northern Co. Mayo into Co. Sligo, comprising Erris and Tirawley baronies in Co. Mayo and Tireragh barony in the north-west of Co. Sligo. The surname Doody found in Munster appears to be a synonym of Dowd but there is no evidence of connection with the Connacht sept. There was another known Ó Dubhda sept but it was located in western Ulster where its descendants, most of whom are found in Co. Derry, use the form Duddy as their surname.

O'DRISCOLL

THE majority of the families descended from the West Cork sept O'Driscoil (Ó hEidersceoil) had lost their prefix O' and at the end of the last century nine out of ten were called Driscoll. Widespread reassumption of the prefix in this century has resulted in a complete reversal of the proportions, those still called Driscoll being a very small minority and the O'Driscolls forming the majority. They are all still found predominantly in Co. Cork.

O'DWYER

THE territory of the Ó Duibhir sept, from which the Dwyers and O'Dwyers descend, was located in the baronies of Kilnamanagh Upper and Lower in western Co. Tipperary. At the end of the last century Dwyer without the prefix O' was six times as prevalent as O'Dwyer, but this is one of the surnames where the majority bearing it has reassumed the prefix so that now the O'Dwyers outnumber the Dwyers. They are still to be found in numbers in Co. Tipperary and have dispersed mainly to Co. Limerick, Co. Cork and Co. Kilkenny.

O'FLAHERTY

At one time the O'Flaherty sept commanded a wide area in southern Co. Galway, right along the north coast of Galway Bay and including the Aran Islands, although the earlier home of the sept, prior to Anglo-Norman settlement in Connacht, had been on the east side of Lough Corrib. Aughnanure Castle on the banks of the Lough was a stronghold of the O'Flaherty chieftains until the 17th century.

O'GARA

ONE Gadhra, a member of the Ó hEaghra sept which held as its territory Leyny barony in Co. Sligo, established a separate chieftainry in the southern part of the barony. This man was the forebar of the Ó Gadhra families, anglicized as O'Gara and Gara, while from the senior branch in northern Leyny descend the families whose name was anglicized as O'Hara. From southern Leyny the

O'Garas extended their influence in the late middle ages into the adjacent county of Mayo. By the 16th century their sept centre had moved to the region of Lough Gara in Coolavin barony, Co. Sligo. By the end of the last century the majority of descendants of the sept had lost the use of the prefix O'; Garas outnumbered O'Garas by more than three to one, but a general resumption of the prefix has reversed this situation and this surname is now rarely found without the prefix.

O'GRADY

THE Ó Grádaigh sept originated in Co. Clare, although the O'Gradys are often thought of as a Limerick family because for several hundred years their stronghold and the seat of the head of the family was at Kilballyowen in Co. Limerick. Although the descendants of the Ó Grádaigh were among those families who did not all abandon the use of their prefix O', nevertheless at the end of the last century there were more Grady families in Ireland than O'Gradys. The fact that there were, however, still many families who had retained the prefix, together with the renown of the 19th century scholar Standish Hayes O'Grady and the survival of the chieftainship in the O'Gradys of Kilballyowen contributed to the widespread resumption of the prefix so that today the Gradys are very much in the minority, very few compared with the O'Gradys.

O'HAGAN

THE O'Hagans and Hagans descend from the Ó hAodhagáin sept which had its seat at Tullaghoge in Dungannon Upper barony, Co. Tyrone, the inaugural place of the O'Neills as sovereigns of Ulster. Some descendants of the sept retained the prefix O' to their name during the centuries of anglicization but at the end of the last century the Hagans outnumbered the O'Hagans by two to one. In the present century those Hagans who had lost the prefix have widely resumed it so that O'Hagans are now more numerous than Hagans.

O'HALLORAN

Two Ó hAllmhuráin septs, one from the region of Lough Corrib in Co. Galway and the other from Ogonnelloe in Tulla Lower barony on the shore of Lough Derg in Co. Clare, provided the forebears of the O'Halloran and Halloran families. Due to the widespread resumption of their prefix O', the O'Hallorans now by far outnumber the Hallorans.

O'HANLON

THE O'Hanlons and Hanlons descend from the Ulster sept of Ó hAnluain, chiefs of Orior, now Upper and Lower Orior baronies in Co. Armagh. Descendants of the sept have, however, been widely dispersed so that the name became as common in Munster as in Ulster and twice as common in Leinster. Hanlons without the prefix O' outnumbered O'Hanlons by four to one at the end of the last century, the majority of those who had retained the prefix being in their ancient homeland in Co. Armagh. Since then many Hanlons have resumed the prefix.

O'HARA

THE O'Haras are one of the relatively few old Irish families which did not, for the most part, ever lose the prefix O' to the surname. Even prior to the Gaelic Revival and the consequent reassumption of the prefix by many other families in the present century, the vast majority of O'Haras were using the prefix; in fact, in the 1890's the O'Haras outnumbered the Haras by slightly more than twenty to one. They descend from the Ó hEaghra sept which held sway in the barony of Leyny, Co. Sligo, and which formed two main branches in the 14th century, the respective chiefs being the O'Hara Boy and the O'Hara Reagh. Another branch migrated northwards and settled in the north of Co. Antrim.

O'HARE

FAMILIES of this name are found mainly in the region of Oriel, for the most part in Co. Armagh and in Co. Louth and Co. Down. Oriel was the homeland of their ancestral sept, Ó hEir. Hare may be in use as an anglicization of Ó hEir, at least one settler family was named Hare and brought that English surname to Ireland.

O'HEA

THE common Irish surname Ó hAodha was anglicized as Hayes, Hughes and O'Hea. There were about a dozen Ó hAodha septs with their homelands as far apart as the south-west of Co. Cork, and Co. Clare in Munster, Co. Tyrone, Co. Monaghan and Co. Donegal in Ulster, Co. Meath and Co. Wexford in Leinster, Co. Mayo, Co. Galway and Co. Sligo in Connacht.

O'KEEFFE

THE O'Keeffes were one of the few families where many members retained the prefix O' through the years of Gaelic submergence. At the end of the last century there were about four O'Keeffes to every five Keefes. Widespread resumption of the prefix by those who had lost it now places the Keefes in a very small minority. The Ó Caoimh sept, from which the O'Keeffes descend, were located in north-eastern Co. Cork whence they were displaced and migrated westwards into the barony of Duhallow in the same county. Co. Cork is still the home of the majority of O'Keeffe families; many of the remainder live in the adjacent counties of Munster.

O'LEARY

TOGETHER the families named O'Leary and Leary rank among those bearing one of the seventy commonest surnames in Ireland. At the end of the last century the families named Leary, without the prefix O', outnumbered the O'Learys by about three to one. However, as almost all those families who had lost the prefix resumed it in this century, those who are still Leary are a very small minority of the descendants of the sept O' Laoghaire. The earliest known homeland of the sept was in south-west Cork but it migrated northwards to settle in West Muskerry barony near Inchigeelagh. Co. Cork remains the home of most O'Leary families today.

O'LOUGHLIN *See Mc LOUGHLIN*

O'MAHONY

At the end of the last century there were more than ten times the number of Mahonys than there were O'Mahonys in Ireland, the great majority of both being in Co. Cork and most of the remainder in Co. Kerry. The ancient territory of their ancestors, the Ó Mathghamhna sept, was in the barony of Kinalmeaky, Co. Cork. Due to a widespread resumption of the prefix O' in the present century the O'Mahonys now outnumber the Mahonys.

O'MALLEY

FAMILIES of this name are the descendants of the Co. Mayo sept, Ó Máille, famed for its maritime exploits on the Atlantic coast. The surname Melia is a variant. At the end of the last century at least half of the O'Malley families in Ireland were still living in Co. Mayo and many still reside in the baronies of Murrisk and Burrishoole, the territory of their ancestral sept.

O'MEARA

THIS surname, with its variant spelling O' Mara, is one of those where most of those of the name, having lost the prefix O', have re-assumed it in the present century so that Meara and Mara without the prefix are now rare whereas at the end of the last century they were more numerous than O'Mearas. The sept from which they descend, Ó Meadhra, was located in the north of Co. Tipperary where they gave their name to Toomyvara (in Irish Tuaim ui Mheadhra) in Upper Ormond barony.

O'NEILL

THE famous Ó Néill sept of Ulster was not the only sept of the name in Ireland. A distinct Ó Néill sept held a territory in Munster, in the barony of Bunratty, Co. Clare, and some of its de-scendants survive in that county. Another Ó Néill sept was located in the barony of Rathvilly, Co. Carlow, and descendants of that sept are found in that region. Yet another Ó Néill sept was located in the barony of Decies, Co. Waterford, whence their descendants have scattered through that county and the neighbour-ing counties of Tipperary and Cork. The Ulster sept which furnished kings and high-kings of Ireland belonged to a territory covering Co. Tyrone, most of Co. Derry and part of Co. Donegal, called Tir Eoghan, from which Co. Tyrone takes its name; the inauguration place of their chiefs was at Tullaghoge in Upper Dun-gannon barony in that county. Branches of the O'Neill sept migrated southwards into Co. Meath and eastwards into Co. Antrim. Today O'Neills are found in every one of Ireland's thirty-two counties, but there is still a heavy

concentration of the name in the Ulster counties of Tyrone and Antrim.

Sir Neill O'Neill of Killeleagh, died 1690 in the Battle of the Boyne

O'REGAN

THE surnames Regan and O'Regan rank to-gether among the seventy commonest surnames in Ireland. Most of the descen-dants of the Ó Riagáin septs lost the prefix O' during the period of Gaelic suppression but the majority has re-assumed the prefix in the present century. One sept of the name was one of the Four Tribes of Tara. On being displaced from its homeland in Co. Meath, this sept settled in what is now Co. Leix. Another Ó Riagáin sept, of the same stock as the O'Briens, was located in the north of Co. Limerick. At the present time most families of the name are in Munster and would appear to descend from the Co. Limerick sept which spread into Co. Cork, Co. Tipperary and Co. Waterford.

The ancestors of Ronald Reagan, President of the U.S.A., came from Co. Tipperary

O'REILLY

THE Ó Raghailligh sept held sway over the east of Breffny extending its influence beyond Co. Cavan into Co. Westmeath and Co. Meath. The descendants of the sept are very numerous; together Reilly and O' Reilly rank among the twenty commonest surnames in Ireland. At the end of the last century the Reillys outnumbered the O'Reillys by almost ten to one but they are another instance of widespread resumption of the prefix, and the O'Reillys are now the more numerous. Over half of these families are now in Leinster but a fair number still reside in the neighbourhood of the ancient ancestral lands of the sept in Co. Cavan also, particularly in Clon-mahon and Castlerahan baronies.

O'RIORDAN

THE O'Riordans are another family to have resumed the use of the prefix O', thus reversing the situation at the end of the last century when Riordans outnumbered O'Riordans. They are still found mainly in Munster where the Ó Riordáin sept was located in Co. Tipperary. The townland of Ballyreardon in Barrymore barony Co. Cork commemorates the home of a branch of the sept which established itself there.

O'ROURKE

THE descendants of the Ó Ruairc sept of Breffny were widely scattered after the confiscation of their ancestral lands in Co. Leitrim, although some are still living in that county in the region of the ancient seat of the chiefs of the sept at Dromahire in the barony of the same name. Most of the descendants of the sept lost the prefix O' but reassumed it in the present century. O'Rorke is a variant spelling.

It was Dearbhforgaill (Dervorguila), wife of Tiernan O'Rourke, the ruler of Breffny, whose elopement with, or abduction by, Dermot, King of

Leinster, caused a power struggle which resulted in the involvement of Anglo-Norman knights in Ireland and, eventually, the takeover of the country by the English Crown. A romantic figure of the old Gaelic order was Sir Brian-na-Murtha O'Rourke, chief of the sept, knighted in 1578. He was frequently in rebellion against the Crown and fell foul of the authorities by sheltering a large number of shipwrecked survivors of the Spanish Armada on his lands in Co. Leitrim. He refused to bow to Queen Elizabeth I when he was apprehended and taken to London where he was executed as a traitor at Tyburn in 1591. After the Jacobite defeat several O'Rourkes emigrated to the continent to escape the degradation of a penurious existence in Ireland. Owen O'Rourke, created Viscount and Baron of Breffny, was in the service of the Duke of Lorraine and Ambassador of the exiled Stuarts to the Emperor at Vienna where he died in 1742. His cousin, Count Tiernan O'Rourke, was killed at the battle of Luzzara in 1702. Another cousin Count John O'Rourke was created a peer of France by Louis XV; his brother Cornelius, who settled in Russia, was the father of General Count Joseph Kornilievitch O'Rourke, one of the Russian generals who defeated Napoleon (illus. p. 163).

ORR

THIS Scottish surname was brought to Ireland from Scotland by settlers who came in the 17th century to Ulster at the time of the re-settlement of that province; their descendants are now quite numerous in the counties of Antrim, Down, Derry and Tyrone.

O'SHAUGHNESSY

THE barony of Kiltartan, Co. Galway, was the territorial homeland of the Ó Seachnasaigh sept, the forebears of the O'Shaughnessy and Shaughnessy families. Those of the name who left Co. Galway generally tended to migrate southwards through Co. Clare to C. Limerick.

A distinguished member of this family was Sir William Brooke O'Shaughnessy (1890–1889). He was born in Limerick but belonged to the Co.

Clare-Co. Galway family of the name and was a grand nephew of the Roman Catholic Biship of Killaloe. He went to India as a surgeon but was knighted in 1856 for his services there in laying down the electric telegraph service connecting Calcutta, Agra, Bombay, Peshawar and Madras, extending over four thousand miles. He also published works on chemistry.

O'SHEA

THE surnames Shee and Shea together with O'Shea rank among the fifty commonest surnames in Ireland. Families of these names are descended from the Ó Séaghada sept which originated in the far west of Kerry in the Ivcragh barony.

Shea and O'Shea are still, together, the third commonest surname in Co. Kerry. Branches of this sept migrated eastwards into Co. Tipperary and eventually some established themselves in Co. Kilkenny where they became prominent in the county town and are remembered also by the name of one of their ancestral seats, the townland of Sheastown in Shillelogher barony in that county.

The painter Sir Martin Archer Shee belonged to the Shee family of Kilkenny

164

O'SULLIVAN

TOGETHER with Sullivan, O'Sullivan is the third commonest surname in Ireland and it is the commonest surname in both Co. Cork and Co. Kerry. And these two counties account for about eighty out of every hundred families of the name living in Ireland. The two branches of the Ó Súileabháin sept from which the Sullivans and O'Sullivans descend were known as O'Sullivan Mor and O'Sullivan Beare. The stronghold of the former was in the barony of Dunkerron South in Co. Kerry, while the latter held sway on the other side of the estuary of the Kenmare River in West Cork in the baronies of Bear and Bantry overlooking Bantry Bay and on Bear Island. Sullivans and O'Sullivans are still thick on the ground in those regions.

O'TOOLE

THE great Ó Tuathail sept originated in Co. Kildare but migrated to Co. Wicklow where they held a territory which was co-extensive with the Diocese of Glendalough. Although their homeland was so close to Dublin and the English Pale the O'Tooles were not anglicized and maintained their independence for several centuries after the Anglo-Norman invasion. Today most O'Toole families are still living in Co. Wicklow or in the nearby capital. Toole without the prefix is now rare but at the

O'SULLIVAN *Kenmare River, Co. Kerry*

end of the last century the Tooles far outnumbered the O'Tooles. A smaller sept, also called Ó Tuathail, was located in Co. Monaghan. The descendants of that sept took the surname Toal rather than O'Toole and as such are found in Co. Antrim, Co. Armagh and Co. Monaghan.

O'TOOLE *St. Kevin's at Glendalough; the site is associated with St. Laurence O'Toole*

OWEN(S)

THIS Welsh surname is found in most counties of Ireland. Presumably some Owen(s) families will descend from settlers who came to Ireland from Wales. It appears, however, that the surname Owen(s) was taken instead of McKeown by Irish families of that name. Owens was certainly substituted for the Irish surname Hynes (q.v.), a fact reported by the Registrar of Births in the last century when instances were cited in Banbridge Union, and Downpatrick Union in Co. Down, Castlederg Union, Co. Tyrone, and Bawnboy Union, Co. Cavan.

PALMER

THIS surname was brought to Ireland from England at various times by unrelated settlers and thus established in various parts of the country. One prominent settler family of the name came to Co. Kerry in the reign of Elizabeth I in the 16th century, others came to Co. Meath, Co. Leix, Co. Offaly, and Co. Mayo as well as to Co. Antrim with the 17th century re-settlement.

PARKER

THIS English surname, like the preceeding one, was brought to Ireland at various dates by unrelated settlers who established themselves in various parts of the country. In Ireland, Parker families are most numerous in Ulster where their forebears came mainly in the 17th century. A Parker family claiming to have come from Devonshire was in Co. Limerick by the 17th century. The descendants of that family acquired estates in that county and in Co. Tipperary. Another Parker family was prominent in Co. Cork.

PAT(T)ERSON

THIS Scottish surname which ranks among the twenty commonest in Scotland, is now widely distributed in Ulster where it arrived in the 17th century with immigrants from Scotland who participated in the schemes for the plantation of that province. In the last century the Registrar of Births reported the use, also, of Patterson interchangeably with Cussane (in Irish Ó Casáin) in two districts of Glennamaddy Union, Co. Galway.

PATTON

FAMILIES bearing this surname and the variant spelling Patten are found for the most part in Ulster where most will be of settler lineage, their forebears having come to the province from Scotland. Dr. MacLysaght has reported, however, that Patten and Patton were also used, as well as Peyton, as anglicizations of an Irish name from Co. Donegal, Ó Peatáin.

PEOPLES *See DEENEY*

PHELAN

TOGETHER Whelan and Phelan, which are both anglicized forms of the Irish Ó Faoláin, rank among the fifty commonest surnames in Ireland. Of the two forms Whelan is the commoner, outnumbering Phelan by a little more than two to one. The form Phelan is favoured by families belonging to Co. Waterford and Co. Kilkenny while Whelan was the form adopted more frequently in Co. Wexford and Co. Carlow. The Ó Faoláin sept from which they descend originated in the baronies of Decies in Co. Waterford whence a branch went into Iverk barony in Co. Kilkenny.

PHILLIPS

THIS patronymic surname is very common in Wales and ranks among the fifty commonest surnames in England and Wales. It was brought to Ireland by settlers and is found now in all provinces of Ireland with the greatest number in Leinster. One prominent settler family of the name acquired an estate in Co. Kilkenny in the 17th century.

PLUNKET(T)

THIS surname, remotely of French origin, came with the Anglo-Normans at the end of the 12th century to Ireland where the family established itself in Co. Meath. Their descendants are still found in that county and in the adjacent counties of Louth and Dublin.

Saint Oliver Plunket (1625–1681), a native of Co. Meath, in his lifetime Roman Catholic Archbishop of Armagh and Primate of Ireland, was hanged, drawn and quartered at Tyburn in 1681 for

high treason for his alleged complicity in the Titus Oates plot. Long revered as a martyr he was beatified in 1920 and canonized in 1975, the first Irishman to be made a saint since St. Laurence O'Toole was canonized in 1226. The crozier of St. Oliver Plunket is preserved by the Plunket family at Dunsany Castle, Co. Meath, now represented by Randal, 19th Baron Dunsany, whose father, Edward, the 18th Baron, is remembered as a successful poet, author and playwright.

POLLOCK

THIS Scottish surname is found in Ireland mainly in Ulster where it came with settlers from Scotland mostly in the 17th century.

PORTER

THIS common English surname was brought to Ireland sporadically and to various places by settlers from England over the last six centuries, but as over eighty per cent of the Porter families in Ireland now are in Ulster it would appear that they are descended from settlers who came to that province from England and Scotland in the 17th century plantation immigration.

POWER

THIS surname which is now so numerous that it ranks among the top sixty in Ireland is not of native Irish origin having arrived in Ireland, as Le Poer, with the Anglo-Normans at the end of the 12th century. The family settled first in Co. Waterford where, today, Power is the commonest surname in the county. The original spelling Poer did not entirely vanish, surviving in the title of Baron Le Poer, and in the last century one family which had long since become Power assumed instead the surname de la Poer. In Callan Union, Co. Kilkenny, the Registrar of Births reported in the last century the use of Poor as a variant of Power.

PRENDERGAST

THE ancestor of the Prendergast families in Ireland was an Anglo-Norman, or more accurately a Cambro-Norman, magnate who came in the 12th century invasion and acquired considerable estates in Ireland. One branch of his descendants remained in the south-east where they are still found in Co. Waterford while another settled in Connacht where Prendergast families are found mainly in Co. Mayo. A number of variant spellings of this surname appear in records, such as Prendergast and Pendergrass. Not infrequently the name was shortened to Pender a form which has survived particularly in Co. Wexford. Other variants reported by the Registrar of Births in the last century were Pendy, in Tullamore Union, Co. Offaly, Pinders, in Parsonstown Union, Co. Offaly, Pindy, in Dingle Union, Co. Kerry and Prender in several districts. In Tralee Union, Co. Kerry the Registrar reported that Shearhoon was used as an Irish form of Prendergast.

PRICE

THIS Welsh patronymic surname which is a contraction of Ap Rice (ap Rhys) ranks among the fifty commonest surnames in England and Wales. Due to the arrival of settlers of the name over the last six centuries it is now found in all four provinces of Ireland but mostly in Leinster.

PRUNTY

BETTER known to the world as Brontë, the form adopted by the Rev. Patrick Brunty from Co. Down, father of Charlotte, Anne and Emily

Brontë, the surname Prunty and its variants Pronty and Brunty derive from the Irish Ó Proinntigh in eastern Ulster.

PURCELL

THE Purcells descend from early settlers from England who were themselves of Norman-French descent. By the 14th century they were well established in Co. Tipperary where their stronghold was Loughmoe Castle in the barony of Eliogarty. Their descendants are most numerous in Co. Tipperary and Co. Kilkenny, and in the capital. Purcill, Pursell, and Purtill have been reported as variants of the normal spelling.

QUAID See McQUAID

QUEALLY

THIS anglicized form of Ó Caollaidhe, the name of a sept from Co. Kilkenny and one from Co. Clare, is now rare, members of the family having favoured Kealy or Keel(e)y in its stead. See also Kiely and Kelly.

QUIGLEY

THE original homeland of the Ó Coigligh sept, a branch of the powerful northern Ui Fiachra, was in the beautiful barony of Carra in County Mayo. Now Quigley families are found in all four provinces although more frequently in the counties of Donegal and Derry in Ulster, and in the counties of Sligo and Galway in Connacht. When the sept was scattered during the upheavals of the 17th century some of its members settled also in the east of Ireland in Co. Louth. Coghley, Kegley and Twigley have been reported as variants of Quigley.

QUILLIGAN

FAMILIES named Quilligan, in Irish Ó Cuileagáin, are now found mostly in Co. Limerick where their forebears migrated from Co. Clare. Culligan, a variant anglicization of Ó Cuileagáin has survived in Co. Clare.

The Brontë sisters, Charlotte, Anne and Emily: portrait by their brother Patrick Bramwell Brontë

QUINLAN

THE Ó Caoindealbháin sept, a branch of the southern Uí Néill, orignated in northern Meath but migrated to Munster where the family was concentrated in Co. Tipperary by the latter half of the 17th century. The surname is still fairly common in that county and also scattered through the counties of Cork and Limerick and as far west as Kerry. Kindelan, a variant of this name, is now rare in Ireland but survives in Spain where members of the sept emigrated in the 17th century from Co. Meath and rose to prominence. The form Kindlon is still found in Co. Louth.

QUINLIVAN

THIS surname is found mainly in northern Limerick and southern Co. Clare; it is an early variant of Quinlan, see above.

QUINN

As this surname, in Irish, Ó Cuinn, derives from the popular given name Conn it is not surprising that it is among the twenty commonest surnames in Ireland and found in every county in the country although more frequently in Ulster where, curiously, Protestant families of the name tend to distinguish themselves by the spelling Quin with one 'n' from the Roman Catholic Quinns who use two. However, this is, of course, not a hard and fast rule. There were five septs of the name with origins as widespread as the Glens of Antrim in the north, County Longford in the midlands and the barony of Inchiquin in Co. Clare in the west of the island.

QUIRK(E)

THIS surname, in Irish, Ó Cuirc, is found mainly in south-eastern Tipperary in the region where that county marches with Kilkenny and Waterford counties, but also in the south-west of Ireland in Co. Kerry, where it occurs mainly in the neighbourhood of Cahirciveen.

RABBIT

THIS surname found mainly in Connacht in Co. Galway and also in Leinster is in fact a translation of cunneen, the Irish for rabbit. The families who have inherited the name in fact originated as Mac Coinin, Mac Cunneen and Cunneen or Cunnane in Co. Mayo in Connacht and as Ó Coinin in Co. Offaly in Leinster. Rabbitte is a variant spelling.

RAFFERTY

FAMILIES bearing this surname are found scattered throughout the country but predominantly in Ulster. They descend from one or other of the two Ó Raithbheartaigh septs of Co. Donegal and Co. Sligo. The variant Roarty survives in Donegal where that family were hereditary coarbs of St. Columcille, Tory Island.

RAFTER

THE small Ó Reachtabhair sept which was located in Co. Kilkenny provided the forebears of families named Rafter, found mainly in Leinster and most frequently in Co. Leix.

RAFTERY

A CONNACHT family descended from the Ó Reachtaire sept in Co. Galway where the name is still found as well as in the neighbouring counties of Roscommon and Sligo.

RAINEY

THIS surname is found mainly in eastern Ulster, in Co. Antrim and Co. Down, where it may denote descent from an Irish family, Ó Raighne, or may be of settler origin. There is evidence also that in Co. Down it was interchangeable with the Scottish surname Rennie. Reaney, an anglicization of Ó Raighne, is found in Connacht.

RAMSAY

THIS Scottish surname and its variant spelling Ramseye came to Ireland in the 17th century with immigrants from Scotland who settled in Ulster where most families of the name in Ireland are still found.

RANKIN

THIS Scottish surname, like the preceeding one, came from Scotland to Ulster in the 17th century with the plantation of that province, where it is commonest in Co. Derry and Co. Donegal.

REDDY

FAMILIES bearing this Leinster surname, in Irish, Ó Reidigh, are found mainly in Co. Kilkenny and in the capital.

REDMOND

THIS surname, a form of Raymond which developed in Ireland, is of Norman origin having come to Ireland at the end of the 12th century as Raymond, with the Anglo-Norman invaders. About half of the Redmond families are found in Co. Wexford and Co. Wicklow and most of the rest in the capital. Co. Wexford was where their ancestors settled, in particular the barony of Forth.

REGAN See O'REGAN

REID

THE presence in Ireland of the Scottish and Northern English surname Reid and the English Read(e) is due mainly to 17th century immigration to Ulster of settlers of the name.

REIDY

FAMILIES of this name, most numerous in Co. Kerry and Co. Clare, descend from the Ó Riada sept whose homeland was in Co. Tipperary.

REILLY See O'REILLY

REYNOLDS

REYNOLDS families are found in all four provinces of Ireland but this surname is commonest in Connacht where it is usually an anglicization of Mac Raghnaill, the name of a south Co. Leitrim sept which in the past has also appeared in English as McRannall and McGrannell. Elsewhere in Ireland persons named Reynolds may be of the same stock or may be descended from settlers who brought the common English surname Reynolds from England.

RICE

THIS Welsh surname (Rhys) was brought to Ireland by settlers. The family of the name in Co. Kerry was established in Dingle as early as the reign of Henry VIII. Today the Rices are most numerous in Ulster and are also numerous on the eastern seaboard of Leinster in Co. Louth and Co. Dublin across the channel from their ancestral Wales, unless some of them are, as Dr. MacLysaght has claimed for Rice families in Co. Armagh and Co. Louth, of native Irish origin, their ancestral name Ó Maolchraoibhe having been changed from Mulcreevy to Rice.

RICHARDSON

THE ancestors of Richardson families in Ireland came from England or Scotland. One prominent family of the name in Ulster trace their lineage to an immigrant from Worcestershire who settled in Co. Armagh in the 17th century; another which had estates in Co. Monaghan, Co. Tyrone and Co. Cavan claimed descent from an immigrant from Norfolk who came to Ireland in the 16th century.

RIORDAN See O'RIORDAN

ROBINSON

WELL over half of the Robinson families in Ireland are in Ulster where Robinsons arrived from Scotland and England with the 17th century settlement of the province. Settlers of the name also came in lesser numbers to other parts of Ireland from England where Robinson is one of the twenty commonest surnames.

ROCHE

THE Roche families in Ireland are of Norman stock, their ancestors having come over at the time of the Anglo-Norman invasion. They are now found scattered throughout Ireland but about one half are in Co. Cork, the county with which Roches have been associated for centuries and where they gave their name to the town of Castletown-roche in the barony of Fermoy, to two townlands named Rochestown, one in the barony of Cork and one in East Carbery. There is also a Roches-town on the Dublin-Kildare border, two Rochestowns in Co. Kilkenny, one in Co. Limerick, one in Co. Meath, one in Co. Tipperary, one in Co. Westmeath, and six in Co. Wexford where the first settlers of the name established themselves when they came to Ireland.

ROGERS

OVER half of the Rogers family in Ireland are in Ulster. The surname is a common one in England and many of the name in Ireland will be descendants of immigrant ancestors. There is evidence, however, that Rogers was taken as an anglicization of their name by families of native Irish origin whose Irish name Mac Ruaidhri was otherwise anglicized as McRory and McCrory. Instances of the interchangeability of McCrory, McGrory, McRory, and Rogers were reported by the Registrar of Births in the last century in Armagh Union, Co. Armagh, Cavan Union, Co. Cavan, Dungannon Union, and Strabane Union, Co. Tyrone, Enniskillen Union, Co. Fermanagh.

RONAYNE

THIS surname, which is also found as Ronan, belongs to families descended from Ó Rónáin septs, the best-known of which was located in eastern Co. Cork. About half the Ronayne and Ronan families in Ireland today still live in Co. Cork.

ROONEY

FAMILIES of this name are found in about equal numbers in Ulster, Connacht and Leinster. The homeland of their ancestral sept, Ó Ruanaidh, was in Lower Iveagh barony, Co. Down.

ROSS

ULSTER is the province in which the surname Ross is found most frequently in Ireland due to the immigration of settlers during the plantation schemes in the 17th century; one of the name was Commissioner of Ulster in the reign of James I.

ROSSITER

UNTIL recently the surname Rossiter was found exclusively in Co. Wexford, and was mostly concentrated in the barony of Forth where their ancestors, English settlers of the name, established themselves in the 13th or 14th century.

ROULSTON

THIS surname, also found now as Rolston, Rowlston and Rollstone, is borne by families living mainly in Ulster. They descend from an English settler family named Rolleston from Rolleston, Staffordshire, which settled in the Manor of Teemore in the barony of West Oneilland, Co. Armagh, early in the 17th century.

ROURKE See O'ROURKE

RUANE

Ruane families descend from the Ó Ruadhain sept which was located in the barony of Clonmacnowen, Co. Galway. Today Ruane is commoner in Co. Mayo than Co. Galway.

RUSSELL

THIS English surname which is remotely of Norman origin (Roussel) was brought to Ireland by various settlers of the name over the centuries since the Anglo-Norman invasion, so that their descendants are now numerous in Ireland, present in every province, but with over half living in Ulster.

RYAN

RYAN is among the ten commonest surnames in Ireland and is the commonest surname in two counties, Limerick and Tipperary. Most families named Ryan descend from the Ó Maoilriain sept which was established since the 14th century in Owneybeg barony, Co. Limerick and the adjacent barony of Owney and Arra in Co. Tipperary. There was, however, also a small Leinster sept, Ó Riain, and there is evidence that some Ruanes have become Ryan also.

SARSFIELD

THIS surname was brought from England to Ireland by the 13th century by settlers who followed the first wave of Anglo-Norman adventurers and acquired lands in Co. Cork.

SAUNDERS(ON)

THIS Scottish and Northern English patronymic surname which, like Sanders, Saunderson and Sanderson, derives from Alexander and is found in all provinces of Ireland although scarce in Connacht. It came to Ireland with various unrelated immigrants who settled there. One family of the name established itself in Co. Kerry, another descends from the Cromwellian Governor of Kinsale who obtained an estate in The Deeps, Co. Wexford. The townlands of Saunderscourt in East Shelmaliere Barony, Co. Wexford and Saundersgrove in Upper Talbotstown barony, Co. Wicklow, were named for that family. The most prominent Saunderson family descends from a Scottish settler who served as High Sheriff of Co. Tyrone and acquired an estate in the barony of Upper Dungannon which was erected into the Manor of Sanderson in 1630. Castlesaunderson townland in Tullygarvey Barony, Co. Cavan, was named for that family.

SAVAGE

FAMILIES named Savage are still found predominantly in Ulster where their ancestors came from England and settled in the barony of Ards Co. Down in the latter quarter of the 12th century. Their descendants became hibernicized and the name acquired an Irish form, Mac an tSábhaisigh. In the last century the Registrar of Births reported the use of the surname Sage interchangeably with Savage in Belturbet District, Co. Cavan, Carrick-on-Shannon Union, Co. Leitrim, and Nenagh Union, Co. Tipperary. Dr. MacLysaght has stated also that the surname Savage was assumed as well as Savin by the small south Munster sept called Ó Sabháin.

SCANLAN

FAMILIES named Scanlan and the variant spelling Scanlon are found mostly in southwest Munster in the counties of Kerry, Limerick and Cork. These will be descendants of the Munster sept Ó Scannláin. The name also occurs, however, in some numbers in Connacht, mainly in Co. Sligo where they may descend from an Ó Scannlain sept but it appears that in that area descendants of the Connacht Ó Scannail sept became Scanlan instead of Scannell. At the same time it appears that the Scannell families now found almost exclusively in Co. Kerry and Co. Cork should really be Scanlan being

descendants of the Munster Ó Scannláin sept. There was also a Mac Scannláin sept of Oriel whose sept centre was Ballymascanlan, in the barony of lower Dundalk, Co. Louth. However the rarity of the name Scanlan now in that area indicates that this sept either became extinct or was absorbed.

Cornelius Scanlan of Maine and Ballinaha, Co. Limerick, died 1761

Mary (née O'Connell) wife of Cornelius Scanlan of Maine and Ballinaha

SCOTT

About three-quarters of the Scott families in Ireland are in Ulster where this surname, the tenth commonest surname in Scotland, came with numerous immigrants at the time of the plantation of Ulster in the 17th century. Others settled sporadically in other parts of Ireland including one family which acquired lands in Co. Leix at the end of the 17th century.

SCULLY

The Ó Scolaidhe sept was once located in Co. Westmeath but being displaced as the Anglo-Normans extended their power through the Midlands this sept migrated to Co. Tipperary where a branch re-established itself in the barony of Lower Ormond in the north of the county and

another in Clanwilliam and Middlethird baronies in the south of the county. Long associated with Co. Tipperary the Scullys are now more widely dispersed and the name is now commoner in Leinster than Munster although rare in the other two provinces.

SEXTON

The Sexton families in Ireland are not, as would appear from their English surname, of immigrant descent. Usually the name Sexton has been assumed in Ireland by families of the Irish name Ó Seasnáin. Most of the Sexton families in Ireland are to be found in Munster where the name has long been prominent in Limerick. In the last century the Registrar of Births reported the use of the surname Tackney interchangeably with Sexton in Cootehill Union, Co. Cavan;

both Tackney and Sexton survive as surnames in Co. Cavan albeit in small numbers.

SHANAHAN

THIS Munster surname is borne by families descended from the Ó Seanacháin sept which was located in the barony of Tulla Upper, Co. Clare.

SHANLEY

Families of this name, most frequent in Connacht, descend from the Co. Leitrim sept Mac Seanlaoich whose territory was in the south of that county in the south of Mohill Barony.

SHANNON

SOME Shannon families descend from the Ó Seanacháin sept of Co. Clare, Shannon in that case being a contracted form of the more usual anglicized form, Shanahan (q.v.). Shannon was also assumed as an anglicized form of Ó Seanáin and of Mac Giolla tSeanáin, which was also anglicized to Giltenan and Gilsenan. In the last century the Registrar of Births reported that Shannon was still used interchangeably with Giltenane and Giltinane in Killadysert and Kilrush Unions, in Co. Clare. Shannons are still numerous in Co. Clare but this surname is now commonest in Ulster where Ó Seanáin (O'Seanan) was listed as one of the principal Irish surnames in the mid-17th century in the neighbourhood of Enniskillen, Co. Fermanagh.

SHARKEY

SHARKEYS are most numerous in Ulster where the name is found mostly in the west of the province in the counties of Derry, Tyrone and Donegal but it is also found in Connacht, mainly in Co. Roscommon, and in Leinster. Co. Tyrone was the homeland of their ancestors whose Irish name was Ó Searcaigh.

SHAUGHNESSY See O'SHAUGHNESSY

SHAW

THIS Scottish and Northern English surname is now found in all four Irish provinces but predom-

inantly in Ulster, now the home of more than half of the Shaw families in Ireland due to the immigration of settlers from Scotland and England of the name to that province when it was re-settled in the 17th century. A number of Shaw families in Munster and Leinster (including that of the famous dramatist) trace their lineage to a 17th century settler who was born in Hampshire but was of Scottish descent; he died in Co. Kilkenny and his numerous descendants resided mostly in that county as well as in Co. Cork and Co. Tipperary and in the capital.

George Bernard Shaw the celebrated dramatist was born in Dublin of a Kilkenny branch of the settler family of the name.

SHEA *See O'SHEA*

SHEE *See O'SHEA*

SHEEHAN

This surname with its variant spelling Sheahan ranks among the eighty commonest surnames in Ireland. It is concentrated predominantly, however, in Munster; at the end of the last century about ninety per cent of all the Sheehans in the country lived in that province and about one half of these were in Co. Cork. The homeland of their ancestral sept, Ó Siodhacháin, was in the barony of Lower Connello in Co. Limerick.

SHEEHY

THIS surname, formerly Mac Shechy, in Irish Mac Síthigh, belongs to Munster which at the end of the last century was the home of about ninety percent of the Sheehy families in Ireland. Within that province the name is commonest in Co. Kerry followed by Co. Limerick. The ancestors of the Sheehys were not, however, a native Munster sept or even a native Irish one, but gallowglass fighters from Scotland who came over to Ireland as mercenaries and were established near Rathkeale, Co. Limerick, by the early 15th century where they were in the service of the FitzGerald Earls of Desmond.

SHERIDAN

THE surname Sheridan, the anglicized form of the Irish Ó Sirideáin, is found scattered throughout Ireland, now commonest in Leinster and least common in Munster. The early home of the Ó Sirideáin families was, however, in the barony of Granard in Co. Longford, whence they spread into Co. Cavan, a county with which they have now long been mainly associated and where Sheridan ranks now among the ten commonest surnames.

SHIEL(D)S

SHIELS, Sheils, Shields and Sheilds are variant anglicized forms of the Irish name Ó Siadhail. From the Registrar General's returns at the end of the 19th century it can be seen that of about every hundred births of children of Ó Siadhail descent about sixty were registered as Shiels or Sheils in almost equal numbers, and about forty as Shields and Sheilds with about twice as many of the former spelling than the latter. The greater proportion of all births of this surname group occurred in Ulster. The early home of the Ó Siadhail sept of physicians was in Co. Donegal.

SHERLOCK

EARLY settlers in the Pale, the progenitors of the Sherlock families in Ireland, came over from England and had established themselves in Co. Kildare by the 14th century. The parish of Sherlockstown and the townland of the same name in the barony of North Naas, Co. Kildare mark their principal place of settlement where their seat was Sherlockstown Castle. The surname Sherlock is now found principally in the capital but also in Co. Meath and scattered in other counties.

SHINE

THIS Munster surname, in Irish Ó Seighin, is found predominantly in the west of the province being most numerous in Co. Cork and then in Co. Kerry.

SHORT(T)

THIS surname came to Ireland with immigrants from Scotland and England whose descendants are now found in about equal numbers in Leinster and Ulster.

SHORTALL

THE progenitors of the Irish Shortalls came to Ireland from England in the 13th century since when they have been principally associated with Co. Kilkenny. The townlands of Shortallstown in the barony of Kells, Co. Kilkenny and Shortalstown in the barony of Forth, Co. Wexford, commemorate two early places of settlement of the family. Shortall families are found today mainly in Co. Kilkenny and in the capital.

SIMPSON

THIS patronymic surname deriving from Sim (Simon) ranks among the fifty commonest surnames in Scotland. It was brought from Scotland and also from England to Ireland by settlers the majority of whom were 17th century immigrants to Ulster where about three-quarters of the Simpson families in Ireland are living.

SLATTERY

ABOUT two thirds of the Slattery families in Ireland are in Munster dispersed through the counties of Clare, Limerick, Kerry, Cork and Tipperary. Their forebears whose Irish name was Ó Slatraigh or Ó Slatara came from Co. Clare where the townland of Ballyslattery in the barony of Tulla Upper was their early home.

SLOAN

OVER half of the Sloans in Ireland belong to Co. Antrim which with Co. Down has long been the home of the descendants of the East Ulster Ó Sluagháin family who thus anglicized their name.

SMITH

THE commonest surname in England and Wales is Smith. It is also the commonest surname in Scotland. The fact that it ranks as the fifth commonest surname in Ireland is not, however, entirely due to the immigration of Smiths from England and Scotland. Smith was assumed as their surname instead of Mac Gowan by descendants of the Mac Gabhann sept of Co. Cavan and instead of Gowan or O'Gowan by the descendants of the Ó Gabhan sept also. This accounts for the particularly high concentration of Smiths in Co. Cavan. Over half of the Smith families in Ireland are in Ulster while they are more sparsely scattered in Munster and Connacht and thin on the ground in the western counties such as Co. Kerry. The spelling Smyth has been favoured by almost one family in three in Ireland.

SOMERVILLE

THIS surname is readily associated in Ireland with Co. Cork because of the distinguished family in that county descended from a settler who came from Scotland in the 17th century. Families of this surname are, however, much more numerous in Ireland in the province of

Ulster where other Somervilles from Scotland settled in the 17th century. In the last century the Registrar of Births reported that in Oughterard Union, Co. Galway, Somerville was used interchangeably with Summerly which with Somers and Summers was an anglicized surname assumed by descendants of the Ó Somacháin family in Connacht.

SPELLISSEY See SPILLANE

SPELMAN See SPILLANE

SPENCE

THIS Scottish surname belonging to a branch of the clan MacDuff was brought to Ulster by settlers from Scotland most of whom established themselves in the east of the province. Over half of the Spence families in Ireland now are in Co. Antrim.

SPILLANE

FAMILIES bearing the surname Spillane may descend either from the Mac Spealáin sept or the Ó Spealáin sept. Over ninety percent of the Spillanes in Ireland at the end of the last century were living in Munster; one half were in Co. Cork and one half of the remainder were in Co. Kerry. Spallane and Spellane are recorded variant spellings of Spillane. Descendants of a branch of the Ó Spealáin sept in Connacht, however, assumed the surname Spelman as the anglicized form of their name. In Castlegregory District and Anascaul District, both in Dingle Union, Co. Kerry, the surname Spillane was used interchangeably with Spelessy and Spillessy according to reports of the Registrar of Births in the last century. Spellissey is, however, known as a distinct surname also, in Irish, Ó Spealghusa, and found today in Co. Clare. Spollen, a surname found today in the neighbourhood of Tullamore, Co. Offaly and in Athlone, is generally believed to be yet another variant of Spillane.

STACK

THIS surname was found in Ireland exclusively in Munster until recent years and within that province over half of those of the name were in Co. Kerry and most of the remainder in about equal numbers in Co. Cork and Co. Limerick. Their ancestors were settlers from England who came to western Munster as long ago as the 13th century.

STA(U)NTON

STANTON and Staunton families belong mostly to Connacht. Two thirds of those of the name in Ireland at the end of the last century were in that province, most of them in Co. Mayo. Their progenitors came to Connacht from England soon after the Anglo-Norman invasion. Families bearing the surname McEvilly share the same ancestry, being descendants of a branch of the Stauntons distinguished by the patronymic Mac an Mhílidh, meaning son of the soldier (or knight) which was anglicized as McEvilly. There were also later immigrants named Staunton who came to Ireland from England and left descendants. One of these, from Buckinghamshire, settled in Co. Galway in the 17th century.

STEELE

THIS surname is found mainly in Ulster with over one half of the Steele families in Ireland living in Co. Antrim. The name came to Ireland from England and Scotland in and since the 17th century.

STEVENSON

SETTLERS from England and Scotland, most of whom came to Ulster in the 17th century, but some to other parts of Ireland, were the ancestors of families in Ireland named Stevenson and Stephenson. It is possible also that Stephenson was assumed as an anglicization of their own name by some Irish families named Mac Giolla Stiofáin and hibernicized families of Anglo-Norman origin named McStephen and Fitz-Stephen (in Irish Mac Stiofáin).

STEWART

THIS Scottish surname, less often written Stuart, ranks among the ten commonest surnames in Scotland and due to the settlement in Ireland of immigrants of the name, the majority of whom came to Ulster in the 17th century, Stewart is now among the sixty commonest surnames in Ireland. About eighty per cent of the Stewart families now in Ireland are in Ulster.

SULLIVAN See O'SULLIVAN

SWEENEY See McSWEENEY

SYNNOTT

FAMILIES with the surname Synott or Sinott are found mainly in Co. Wexford and in and around the capital. The progenitors of these families came to Ireland from England in the 13th century and established themselves in Co. Wexford in the baronies of Forth and Bargy. The townland of Sinnottstown in the barony of Forth was an early place of their settlement. The coat of arms of the family is: Argent, three swans close in pale sable, ducally gorged or.

TAAFFE

THE forebears of the Taaffes in Ireland came to Ireland from Wales soon after the Anglo-Norman invasion at the end of the 12th century and established themselves first in Co. Louth. Early in the 14th century the Taaffes held estates in the barony of Ardee, one of which, Smarmore, still belongs to some of their descendants.

Nicholas Taaffe, 6th Viscount, (1677–1769) a native of Co. Sligo, entered the Austrian Imperial service in which he distinguished himself as an officer. He acquired estates in Silesia where he introduced the potato from Ireland, and in Bohemia where he died.

TAGGART

TAGGART and McTaggart are anglicized forms of the Irish Mac an tSagairt, others being Teggart, Mc Enteg(g)art, McEntag(g)art, Mc.Integ(g)art, Mc Intag(g)art. All these surnames are found principally in Ulster where they are commonest in Co. Antrim.

TAYLOR

THIS occupational name is the fourth most common name in England and ranks among the top thirty in Scotland. Settlers of the name have come to Ireland since the 14th century but the bulk of them came in the 17th century. Like most English and Scottish surnames in Ireland it is commonest in Ulster and is found in lesser numbers in the other provinces.

THOM(P)SON

THIS patronymic is the fourth commonest surname in Scotland where the more usual spelling is without the 'p' and ranks among the twenty commonest surnames in England and Wales. Having come to Ireland with numerous Scottish and English settlers it now figures among the fifty commonest surnames in Ireland. In Ireland, the Thom(p)sons are most heavily concentrated in Ulster which is now the home province of three-quarters of all those of the name in the country. A very few families may also be of native Irish descent their progenitors having assumed Thom(p)son as an anglicized form of their Irish name as reported by the Registrar of Births in the last century in Ballymoney Union, Co. Antrim where Thom(p)son was used interchangeably with McCavish and McTavish. These names are anglicizations of a rare Co. Cavan name, in Irish, Mac Thámhais, a name which is close to the translation of Thom(p)son as son of Thomas, which would be Mac Thomáis or Mac Thómais in Irish.

THORNTON

THIS English surname is found in about equal numbers in Connacht and Leinster and less frequently in the other two provinces. Some families of the name in Ireland will be of settler lineage, descended from English immigrants. One such Thornton family from Sussex but with early connections in Yorkshire came to Co. Derry late in the 17th or early 18th century. Another settler family named Thornton came to Co. Limerick in the 16th century with the Elizabethan plantation of Munster. Many Thornton families in Ireland, however, are of native Irish stock, their progenitors having assumed this English surname in lieu of their Irish name. Thus the presence of Thorntons in Connacht can be accounted for by families of the Ó Draighneán sept whose name was otherwise anglicized to Drennan, having assumed the surname Thornton because the English translation of draighneán is blackthorn. Instances of this were cited in the last century by the Registrar of Births in Ballinrobe Union, Co. Mayo and in Tuam and Oughterard Unions, Co. Galway. Similarly, because the English translation of sceach is briar, while some of the Oriel sept Mac Sceacháin took the surname Skehan, others became Thornton. This interchangeable usage was cited by the Registrar of Births in Monaghan Union, Co. Monaghan. The use of Thornton for Meenagh, because the Irish for thorns is muineach, was reported in Ballinrobe Union, Co. Mayo. In Co. Cork in Kanturk and Millstreet Unions the Registrar reported the interchangeable use of Thornton and Tarrant, a name used as an anglicization of Ó Toráin.

TIERNAN See KIERNAN

TIERNEY

FAMILIES of this name, which is found in all four provinces of Ireland but more frequently in Leinster and Munster, are descendants of one of the Ó Tighearnaigh septs unless they bear the surname as a variant of Tiernan (in Irish Ó Tighearnáin) for which see Kiernan. The most prominent Ó Tighearnaigh sept held sway in the barony of Carra, Co. Mayo. Other septs of the name were located in Co. Donegal and Co. Westmeath. The Munster Tierneys seem to have originated in Co. Tipperary but may have been a branch of one of the three known Ó Tighearaigh septs.

TIGHE

THIS Connacht surname derives from the Irish forename Taidhg which became the name of four distinct Ó Taidhg septs. The Registrar of Births reported in the last century that in Cootehill Union, Co. Cavan, the surname Kangley was used interchangeably with Tighe. This must be for the curious reason that ceangal is the Irish translation of the English word tie which has the same pronunciation as Tighe. The surname McTigue which is found principally in Co. Mayo and its variants McTeague, McTague,

McTeigue, McTeige, in Connacht and Ulster and McKeag in Ulster, also derive from the forename Taidhg. There was a Mac Taidhg sept in Co. Galway. It appears that Tighe was used interchangeably with McTeague and McTeigue in Bawnboy Union, Co. Cavan.

TOAL *See O'TOOLE*

TOBIN

THIS surname is found principally in Munster where it is widely dispersed in Co. Waterford, Co. Cork, Co. Limerick and Co. Tipperary. It is found less frequently in Leinster but mainly there in Co. Kilkenny and in the capital. Tobin is rare in Connacht and Ulster. It is not a native Irish name being a corruption of St. Aubin or St. Aubyn, a name which came to Ireland with the Anglo-Normans at the end of the 12th century as de Saint Aubyn. The earliest Irish home of the family was in Co. Tipperary and Co. Kilkenny. The townland of Ballytobin (now Ballaghtobin) in the barony of Kells, Co. Kilkenny, which commemorates their name was an early seat.

TODD

THIS Scottish and English surname, borne today in Ireland mostly by families in eastern Ulster east of the Bann, was brought by settlers, most of whom arrived in the 17th century.

TONER

THIS surname Toner, in Irish, Ó Tomhrair, originated on the west bank of the Foyle in Co. Donegal but the family moved eastwards into Co. Derry where the name is found today as well as farther east in Co. Armagh and Co. Antrim.

TOOLE *See O'TOOLE*

TRAC(E)Y *See TREACY*

TRAVERS

FAMILIES in Ireland bearing this English surname may be of settler stock, several immigrants of the name having come to Ireland in the 16th and 17th centuries. One large settler family of the name descends from a Travers family from Lancashire which was established in Cork at the end of the 16th century. In Co. Leitrim, however, some native Irish families named Ó Treabhair assumed the surname Travers as an anglicization of their name: Travers familes from that area are likely to be of that origin.

TRAYNOR

OVER half of the Traynor, Trainor and Treanor families in Ireland are in Ulster in the Co. Tyrone – Co. Monaghan – Co. Armagh region and Co. Antrim. Almost all the rest are in the capital. Their ancestors, whose name in Irish was Mac Thréinfhir, belonged to Oriel, the main area of residence of their progeny.

TREACY

THIS is the most popular spelling of the surname which is otherwise written Tracey or Tracy. These are anglicized forms of the Irish Ó Treasaigh, a name borne by septs once located in Co. Galway, Co. Cork and Co. Leix. Today these surnames are widely scattered in Ireland but are more numerous in Munster and Leinster than in the other two provinces.

TROY

THIS surname found in equal numbers in Leinster and Munster but rarely, if at all, in the other two provinces, is borne by families descended from the Ó Troighthigh sept which appears to have originated in Co. Clare but was long established in Co. Tipperary where their homeland is commemorated by the name of the townland of Ballytrehy in the barony of Iffa and Offa West in the extreme south of the county. From that area some dispersed southwards into Co. Waterford, but branches moved north so that subsequently Troys were most numerous in the Co. Tipperary baronies of Ikerrin and Eliogarty, adjacent to Co. Leix and Co. Offaly.

TULL(E)Y

THIS surname is found in all four provinces of Ireland but is most numerous in Connacht. The families who bear this name descend from the ancient Irish families of physicians called Mac an Tuile or Ó Maoltuile whose home was in the Co. Cavan–

Co. Longford region where their one-time presence is commemorated in the name of the townland of Tullystown in the barony of Fore, Co. Westmeath close to the Co. Longford and Co. Cavan borders. Tally is a recorded variant of Tully but the English surname Flood was assumed by some of the Tullys because the Irish translation of flood is tuile.

TUOHY

THIS surname which is borne by descendants of the Ó Tuathaigh sept has many variant spellings ranging from Tooey and Toohy to Twohy and Twoohy. Tuohig and Twohig are variants favoured in Co. Cork where all the families in Ireland of those names were living at the end of the last century. The ancestral sept was first located in the south of Co. Galway where families of the name survive as well as in the neighbouring county of Clare and scattered farther south in Munster.

TURLEY See CURLEY

TURNER

THIS common English and Scottish occupational surname, among the thirty most common surnames in England and Wales, was brought by immigrant settlers to various parts of Ireland. Today it is most prevalent in Ulster but is found in all the provinces.

TWOMEY

THREE quarters of the families in Ireland with the surname Twomey, in Irish, Ó Tuama, belong to Co. Cork. Most of the remainder are from the neighbouring counties of Kerry and Limerick or in the capital. Toomey is a variant spelling favoured in Co. Limerick. Tuomy is another variant which has survived.

TYNAN

THE Ó Teimhneáin sept whose homeland was in Co. Leix provided the forebears of families named Tynan. This surname is still found in that county and the neighbouring counties of Leinster.

TYR(R)ELL

THIS surname came to Ireland with Anglo-Norman settlers at the end of the 12th century, where they settled in the Pale and on its western marches. The family gave its name to Tyrellspass and Tyrellstown in the barony of Fartullagh, Co. Westmeath, to Tyrellstown in Narragh and Reban West barony, Co. Kildare, to Tyrellstown in the barony of Castleknock, Co. Dublin and to Big Tyrellstown and Little Tyrelstown in the barony of Balrothery East, Co. Dublin. From

TWOMEY *Croom, Co. Limerick, the home of the 18th century poet Sean O Tuama (O'Twomey the Gay). His wife kept a drinking house there*

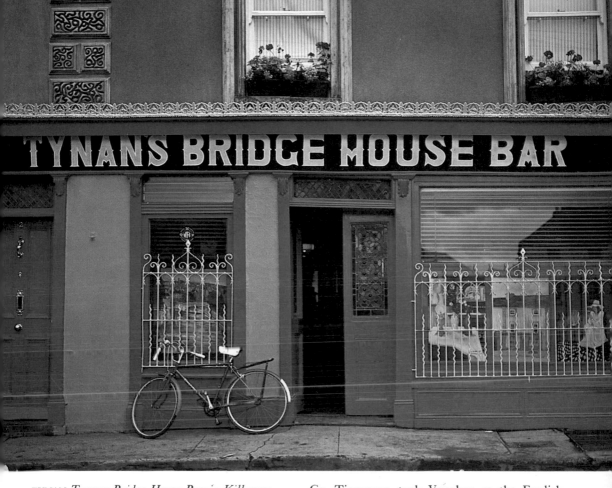

TYNAN *Tynans Bridge House Bar in Kilkenny*

Co. Dublin and Co. Kildare the family spread southwards into Co. Wicklow where a number of their descendants are found today in the neighbourhood of Arklow.

VAUGHAN

THIS Welsh surname is found in all four provinces of Ireland but was commonest in Munster. There certainly were a number of immigrants of the name who settled in Ireland like the Vaughans from Pembrokeshire who established themselves in Co. Offaly but while some Vaughans in Ireland will be of such settler stock others are descendants of Irish families who assumed this surname. The Ó Beacháin family from Co. Clare who gave their name to the townlands named Ballyvaughan in Owney and Arra barony and in Iffa and Offa East barony,

Co. Tipperary, took Vaughan as the English form of their name. The Registrar of Births reported, moreover, in the last century that in two districts in Callan Union, Co. Kilkenny, Vaughan was interchangeable with Moghan and Moughan, names which may have derived from Ó Mócháin.

WADDING

THIS surname, long associated with Co. Waterford, is of Anglo-Norman origin. Of the several notable ecclesiastics of the name the most famous was the 17th century Franciscan theologian, Luke Wadding, founder of the Irish Franciscan College in Rome and of a college in Rome for Irish secular priests. His portrait by Maratta is illustrated overleaf (p. 182).

WADE

OVER half of the Wade families in Ireland are in the capital. Most will descend from English immigrants who brought this English surname

LUKE WADDING

to Ireland. However, the Registrar of Births in the last century reported the interchangeable use of Wade and McQuade in Longford Union, Co. Longford and this may well not have been an isolated instance of a McQuade or McQuaid (q.v.) family becoming Wade.

WALDRON

THIS surname in Connacht is usually the anglicized form of Mac Bhaildrin, the name of a branch of the Costello family of Co. Mayo. However, Waldron is an English surname as well and was brought also to Connacht as such by a family of that name from Leicestershire who first acquired lands in Co. Cavan and later in Co. Leitrim and Co. Roscommon.

WALKER

IT is surprising that this common English and Scottish surname which ranks among the twenty commonest surnames in England and Wales and among the thirty commonest surnames in Scotland, is not more numerous than it is in Ireland. Nevertheless there are more than five thousand persons of the name in Ireland, well

over half of them being in Ulster. Settlers from Scotland or England brought the surname Walker mostly to that province in the 17th century and also to the Dublin area and to Co. Wexford, Co. Louth and Co. Leix.

WALL

THIS surname found in Munster and Leinster, was introduced to Ireland soon after the Anglo-Norman invasion. Two of the name witnessed charters in Dublin between 1177 and 1186, spelling their name de Valle, presumably a corruption of the French du Val. The first place of settlement of the family in Ireland was in Co. Carlow, at Ardristan in the barony of Rathvilly, and at Rathtoe in the barony of Forth and Co. Kilkenny at Inchyolaghan (Castleinch) and Tulachany in the barony of Shillelogher. From that region branches of the family spread to the south into Co. Waterford and west into Co. Limerick and into Co. Cork where they settled at what is now Wallstown in the barony of Fermo in the 13th century.

WALLACE

THIS Scottish surname is found in all four Irish provinces but over half of the families are in Ulster where settlers of that name established themselves in the 17th century. Wallis is a variant spelling. As the Registrar of Births cited the use of Wallace and Walsh interchangeably in the last century in Galway Union, Co. Galway it is possible that some Wallace families could be of Walsh descent.

WALSH

THE fourth commonest surname in Ireland, Walsh ranks as the commonest surname in Co. Mayo and the second commonest surname in two other counties, Kilkenny and Waterford. It is otherwise widely distributed although most thinly dispersed in Ulster. The commonness of the

WALSH *Ruins of a stronghold on the Nore in Co.
Kilkenny, an area settled by many of this name*

name is due to the fact that, meaning Welsh, i.e.
from Wales, it was given independently to
numerous Welshmen who arrived in Ireland
from Wales with the Anglo-Norman and Cambro-Norman conquerors. Families thus distinguished gave their name to the Walsh Mountains
in Co. Kilkenny an early settlement area of some
of this surname. Walshe and Welsh are variant
spellings and Walsh has been used interchangeably with Brannagh, a phonetic rendering of
Breathnach, the Irish for Welshman.

WARD

THE surname Ward, commonest in Ireland in
the province of Ulster, but also widely distributed in considerable numbers in the other three

provinces, is borne both by descendants of immigrant English settlers of the name which
ranks among the thirty commonest surnames in
England and Wales, and by descendants of
native families whose name in Irish was Mac an
Bháird, the name of families of hereditary bards
in Ulster and Connacht. Ward families of Irish
descent are still well represented in Co. Donegal
where their forebears were bards to the O'Donnells and in Co. Galway where their forebears
were bards to the O'Kellys.

WARREN

THIS surname was brought from England to
Ireland by settlers over the past centuries. One
family which settled first in Co. Monaghan and
acquired estates in Co. Wicklow claimed to have
come from Cheshire. The descendants of a 17th
century settler who established himself in East

Carbery barony, Co. Cork, became numerous in that county, one branch giving its name to Warren's Court, formerly Kilbarry, in that barony.

WATERS

THIS is an English surname found in Ireland in about equal numbers in each of the four provinces. Not all Waters families in Ireland will necessarily be of settler descent, however. In the last century the Registrar of Births reported the interchangeable use of Waters with Toorish, Tourisk and Turish in Stranorlar Union, Co. Donegal and in Oughterard Union, Co. Galway and the interchangeable use of Waters and Uiske in Ballinrobe Union, Co. Mayo because *uisce* is the Irish for water. There is also evidence of confusion of the surname Waters in Ireland with Walters and McWalters, surnames found in eastern Ulster.

WATSON

THIS common English and Scottish patronymic surname, meaning son of Wat, a diminutive of Walter, ranks among the thirty commonest surnames in Scotland and among the fifty commonest in England and Wales. Watson families are numerous in Ireland in Ulster, especially in the east of that province, due to the immigration of settlers of the name, mostly from Scotland, in the 17th century.

WEBB

THIS common English surname is found in Ireland in about equal numbers in and around the capital and in Ulster in Co. Antrim having come to Ireland since the 17th century with immigrant settlers. One settler family of the name in Munster claimed to have come from Gloucestershire to Co. Limerick whence one branch of the family moved into Co. Tipperary.

WEIR

SOME families bearing the name Weir will be of Scottish descent, their forebears having come from Scotland to Ulster at the time of the 17th century schemes for the resettlement of that province. Others will descend from a native family in Ulster whose Irish name Mac an Mhaior was anglicized both as McWeir and Weir and as McMoyer. Dr. MacLysaght has stated also that Mac Giolla Uidhir was anglicized McGillaweer and thus also became corrupted to Weer and Weir. It appears also that Weir has been assumed, due to mistranslation, by descendants of an Irish family named Ó Corra.

WHELAN *See PHELAN*

WHITE

THIS surname, which ranks among the fifty commonest in Ireland, is found in every county in the country. It is in fact a very common English surname, among the twenty-five commonest in England and Wales and common also in Scotland where it is among the top fifty. In Ireland it is distributed in about equal numbers in Ulster, Leinster and Munster, being a little more numerous in Ulster than in the other two provinces; it is also found in Connacht but in far lesser numbers than in the other provinces. Having come to Ireland with settlers since the 14th century it is not surprising that some of their hibernicized descendants were, in the 19th century, as reported by the Registrar of Births, using an Irish translation of the name, White being used interchangeably with Bann, Bawn, and Banane in such widely scattered places as Banbridge Union, Co. Down, Castlebar Union, Co. Mayo, Lismore Union, Co. Waterford and Tobercurry Union, Co. Sligo. Because of the Irish *geal* meaning white, the surname Galligan in Co. Cavan has also been used interchangeably with White as reported by the Registrar of Births in Cavan Union.

WILKINSON

LIKE a number of other common English surnames which were brought to Ireland, Wilkinson was adopted by some persons of native Irish descent as their surname in lieu of their own name or a close anglicization of their own name. In this case, due to the similar sound of the names, it was the Irish name Mac Uilcin, usually rendered in English as McQuilkin, which was transformed by some into Wilkinson, as reported by the Registrar of Births in the last century who cited the occurrence of this in Ballycastle Union, Co. Donegal. Mac Uilcin was a Connacht name but in Ulster its derivative, McQuilkin, seems also to have been confused with the Scottish surname Mc Kellican. Wilkie has also been used interchangeably with Wilkinson in Ireland while Wilkison and Wilkisson have appeared as variants.

WILLIAMS

THIS patronymic surname, the third most common surname in England and Wales, is less common in Ireland than might be expected considering its prevalence across the channel. Families of the name are fairly widely scattered in Ireland where it came with immigrant settlers, but they are most prevalent in Leinster, especially in the capital.

WILLIAMSON

NEARLY all the families bearing this patronymic surname in Ireland are to be found in Ulster whence their forebears came from Scotland mostly in the 17th century, to settle in the areas where land was re-allocated under the schemes for the plantation of the province with loyal Protestant settlers.

WILLIS

THIS English surname is found in Ireland mainly in Ulster but also, in lesser numbers, in Munster and Leinster. The ancestors of the families of the name in Ireland will have been immigrant settlers.

WILSON

THIS patronymic surname was brought to Ireland in such numbers and has proliferated there to such an extent that it now rates among the thirty commonest names in the country. Many of the settlers of the name came to Ireland from Scotland where it ranks among the ten commonest surnames, others from England where it is among the top fifteen. In Ireland, Wilson is far commoner in Ulster than elsewhere, four fifths of all those of the name in the country being in that province.

WOOD(S)

FAMILIES named Woods outnumber those named Wood in Ireland by about ten to one. Understandably the two surnames are easily confused and so have, on accasion, been used interchangeably. While the English surname Wood, which is among the fifteen commonest surnames in England and Wales, is usually borne by families of settler descent, the surname Woods is borne both by families whose ancestors came to Ireland from England like a Woods family in Co. Meath, Co. Kildare and Co. Dublin whose progenitor came over from Yorkshire in the 17th century, and by descendants of a number of Irish families who took the surname Woods in

place of their Irish name. Because the Irish for wood is *coill*, a number of Irish surnames with a component part sounding similar to *coill*, were anglicized as Woods. In the last century the Registrar of Births cited the use of Woods interchangeably with Coyle in Longford Union; the same with McElhill, in Irish Mac Giolla Choille, a surname also anglicized as McIlhoyle and Woodman. In Ballymoney Union, Co. Antrim and in Armagh Union, Woods was used interchangeably with McIlhone. Other variants reported were Elwood, in Lurgan Union, Co. Armagh and Smallwoods in Newtownlimavady Union, Co. Derry.

WO(U)LFE

THIS surname was brought to Ireland in the wake of the Anglo-Norman invasion at the end of the 12th century by settlers who estabblished themselves in Co. Kildare and subsequently in Co. Limerick. The name is now most prevalent in Munster and particularly still in Co. Cork but a few descendants of the Co. Kildare Wolfes have survived in that county.

WRIGHT

A NUMBER of settlers of this name came to Ireland, mostly to Ulster. About three quarters of the Wright families in Ireland live in that province and the majority of the remainder in Dublin. This occupational surname is very common in England where it ranks among the fifteen commonest surnames in England and Wales.

WYLIE

WELL over ninety per cent of the Wylie families in Ireland are in Ulster, mostly in Co. Antrim. They descend from 17th century settlers who came over from Scotland and England. Wiley, Wilie, and Wily are known variant spellings of this surname.

WYNNE

THIS Weosh surname, which has the same derivation as Gwynn, is found in Ireland in almost equal numbers in Connacht and Leinster and far less frequently in the other two provinces.

The Connacht Wynnes claim descent from a settler who came to Co. Sligo from Denbighshire in the 17th century. Instances were reported in the last century by the Registrar of Births of the use of the surname Wynne instead of Guiheen and Guihen in Carrick-on-Shannon Union, and Manorhamilton Union, Leitrim, and Boyle Union, Co. Roscommon. Seemingly this would be due to the similarity in sound of Wynne with wind, the English translation of gaoth from which Guiheen, in Irish Ó Gaoithin, is derived. McGee was also used interchangeably with Wynne as reported in Bawnboy Union, Co. Cavan.

YEATES

THIS locational surname from the north of England, of the same derivation as Gates, was brought to various parts of Ireland by immigrant English settlers; a number of these chose to establish themselves in Ulster in which province about half of the families of the name in Ireland are now found. The forebears of the famous Irish man of letters of the name settled, however, in Co. Sligo in the 17th century. Yates and Yeats are variant spellings.

YOUNG

THIS surname is among the twenty commonest in Scotland. It was brought to Ireland from Scotland and England by immigrant settlers the majority of whom came with the wave of settlers from Scotland who established themselves in Ulster in the 17th century. About two thirds of the families of the name in Ireland are in the province of Ulster. The Youngs of Culdaff, Co. Donegal claimed descent from a settler from Devonshire; a settler family of the name in Co. Roscommon claim descent from a settler from Yorkshire.

WILLIAM BUTLER YEATS

YEATES *The ancient High Cross in the churchyard at Drumcliffe, Co. Sligo, where the poet and dramatist W. B. Yeats is buried*

INDEX OF ADDITIONAL NAMES MENTIONED IN THE
ALPHABETICAL TEXT

AHEARN   See HEARN
AHERNE   See HEARN
BAWN   See WHITE
BEHANE   See NAUGHTON
BERRIGAN   See BERGIN
BIRD   See HENEHAN
BISSETT   See McKEOWN
BRANNAGH   See WALSH
BREHON   See JUDGE
BROTHERS   See BRODER
CADELL   See BLAKE
CAHAN   See KANE, KEANE
                  and KEOHAN
CAHY   See MULCAHY
and variants
CLUSBY   See GILLESPIE
CLUVANE   See CLIFFORD
COMASKEY   See CUMISKEY
CONAGHAN   See CUNNINGHAM
CONDREN   See CONDRON
CONEGAN   See CUNNINGHAM
CONRAHY   See CONROY and
                  CONRY
CONNELLAN   See CONLON
COPPINGER   See GOULD
COSHMAN   See KISSANE
COUMEY   See COONEY
COURTNEY   See COURNANE
COUSINS   See CUSSEN
CRAMPSY   See BONAR
CRIMMINS   See CREMIN
CUNNEEN   See RABBIT
CUSSANE   See PATTERSON
DALGETTY   See GETTY
DARGAN   See DORGAN
DAVERNE   See DAVOREN
DAWNEY   See DOHENY
DELANTY   See DELAHUNTY
DENNY   See DENNEHY
DERMOTT   See DARMODY

DEVER   See DIVER
DEVERELL   See DEVEREUX
DEVEY   See DEERY
DEVILLY   See DEELY
DEVOY   See DEERY
DIGNAM   See DUIGNAN
DIGNAN   See DUIGNAN
DONAGHY   See McDONAGH
DORCEY   See DARCY
DOWNING   See DINNEEN
DRENNAN   See THORNTON
DRUMMOND   See DRUMM
DRUMMY   See DRUMM
DUANE   See DEVANE
DULANTY   See DELAHUNTY
DUNICAN   See DONEGAN
FALL   See LAVELLE
FALLOON   See FALLON
FARICY   See FARRISSEY
FARLEY   See FARRELLY
FARSHIN   See FORTUNE
FEEHARRY   See FITZHARRIS
FEEHELY   See FEELY
FEEHILLY   See FEELY
FEIGHAN   See FAGAN, FEGAN
                  and FEEHAN
FENAGHTY   See FENTON and
                  FINNERTY
FERRALL   See FARRELL
FINAGHTY   See FENTON and
                  FINNERTY
FINNEY   See FEENEY
FITCH   See FITZPATRICK
FITZHENRY   See FITZHARRIS
FITZWALTER   See BUTLER
FLAVIN   See FLAHAVAN
FLOOD   See TULLY
FRIZELL   See FRASER
GALVIN   See GALLIVAN
GARVAN   See GARVEY

GAUGHNEY	See GAFFNEY	KINIGAM	See KINAHAN
GAVAGHAN	See GAUGHAN	KINUCANE	See FINUCANE
GEAVENEY	See GAFFNEY	KNEAFSEY	See CRAMPSY
GILDOWNEY	See DOWNEY	KNOWLES	See NEWELL
GILL	See McGILL	LADRIGAN	See LONERGAN
GILLESBY	See GILLESPIE	*and variants*	
GILLIGAN	See GALLIGAN	LA POER	See POWER
GILSENAN	See SHANNON	LEHANE	See LANE
and variants		LEVINGSTON	See LIVINGSTON
GINTY	See McGINTY	LIDDANE	See LYDON
GISSANE	See KISSANE	*and variants*	
GLASHBY	See GILLESPIE	LOHAN	See LOGAN
GOULDING	See McGOLDRICK	LONIGHAN	See LENIHAN
GREEVE	See GREER	*and variants*	
GREVES	See GREER	LYNN	See FLYNN
GRIEVES	See GREER	MACKLEHENNY	See McELHINNY
GRIMES	See GORMLEY	*and variants*	
GUINANE	See KINANE	MAGAURAN	See McGOVERN
HALFPENNY	See HALPIN	MAGAWLEY	See McAULEY
HALPENY	See HALPIN	MANNING	See MANNION
HANAHAN	See HANNON	MEENAGH	See THORNTON
HAREN	See HORAN	MEIGHAN	See MEEHAN
HARGADEN	See HARE	*and variants*	
HARNETT	See HARTNETT	MELVILLE	See MULVIHIL
HARVISON	See HARBISON	MILLEA	See MOLLOY
HAVERN	See HEFFRON	MILLIKAN	See MILLIGAN
HAVERON	See HEFFRON	*and variants*	
HAVRON	See HEFFRON	MUIRHEAD	See MOORHEAD
HEFFERAN	See HEFFRON	MOGHAN	See VAUGHAN
HELY	See HEALY	*and variants*	
HENDRY	See HENRY	MONK	See MONAGHAN
HENEKAN	See HENEHAN	MOWEN	See MAHON
HERBERT	See HARBISON	*and variants*	
HERBISON	See HARBISON	MULCREEVY	See RICE
HEWSON	See McHUGH	MULDOWNEY	See DOWNEY
HIGERTY	See HEGARTY	MULVOGUE	See LOGUE
and variants		McALESHER	See GREEN(E)
HOLOHAN	See HOULIHAN	McAREE	See KING
and variants		McATILLA	See FLOOD
HONEEN	See GREEN(E)	McBAY	See McVEIGH
HORRIGAN	See HORGAN	*and variants*	
HOUGHEGAN	See GEOGHEGAN	McCADDEN	See McADAM
HOUNEEN	See GREEN(E)	McCARRON	See GAFFNEY
HOWELL	See McHALE	McCAW	See McADAM
HYNES	See HEYNE	McCUE	See McHUGH
IRVINE	See IRWIN	McCREECH	See McGUINNESS
IRVING	See IRWIN	*and variants*	
KEALY	See KELLY and	MacDUGALL	See McDOWELL
	QUEALLY	McELVAINE	See McILVEEN and
KEGLEY	See QUIGLEY	*and variants*	McILWAINE
KEHELLY	See COAKLEY	McENTAGGART	See TAGGART
KEHILLY	See COAKLEY	*and variants*	
KEHOE	See KEOGH	McEVILLY	See STANTON
KELLAGHAN	See O'CALLAGHAN	McGLASHAN	See GREEN(E)
KERWICK	See KIRBY	MacHUGO	See COOK
KEVERNY	See McINERNEY	McILLESHER	See GREEN(E)
and variants		McILMURRAY	See MURRAY
KILBRIDE	See McBRIDE	McJONINE	See JEN(N)INGS
KINDLON	See QUINLAN	*and variants*	
and variants			

McKEA	See MACKEY	PATRICK	See FITZPATRICK
McLEAN	McLEAN	PENDY	See PRENDERGAST
McLOY	See LOWE	*and variants*	
and variants		PEYTON	See PATTON
McMEEKIN	See MEEHAN	POOR	See POWER
and variants		PURTILL	See PURCELL
McMOYER	See WEIR	QUEENAN	See CUNNANE
and variants		QUIDDIHY	See CUDDIHY
McNICHOLL	See NICHOLSON	QUILLINAN	See CULLINAN
McPARTLIN	See McFARLAN *and*	RENNIE	See RAINEY
	McPARLAND	ROARTY	See RAFFERTY
McQUILKIN	See WILKINSON	ROLLESTON	See ROULSTON
and variants		*and variants*	
McRANNELL	See REYNOLDS	SAGE	See SAVAGE
and variant		SAVIN	See SAVAGE
McRORY	See ROGERS	SCANNELL	See SCANLON
and variants		SHANNAGHY	See FOX
McSTEPHEN	See STEVENSON	SKEHAN	See THORNTON
and variants		SPILLESSY	See SPILLANE
McTAVISH	See THOMPSON	*and variants*	
and variants		SUMMERLY	See SOMERVILLE
NANGLE	See COSTELLO *and*	*and variants*	
	NAGLE	TACKNEY	See SEXTON
NARY	See NEARY	TARRANT	See THORNTON
NEE	See NEVILLE	TOORISH	See WATERS
NORTON	See NAUGHTON	*and variants*	
O'BOLAN	See BOLAND	TWIGLEY	See QUIGLEY
O'BRAOIN	See BREEN	TWOHIG	See TUOHY
OOLAHAN	See HOULIHAN	*and variants*	
and variants		WALTERS	See WATERS
PARAGON	See FITZPATRICK	WHOOLAHAN	See HOULIHAN
PARRICAN	See FITZPATRICK	*and variants*	
PATCHY	See FITZPATRICK	WIGAN	See McQUIGAN
		and variants	

GLOSSARY OF TERMS

BARONY   division of land within a county containing a number of parishes

BREHON   judge (judicial)

COARB   heir (successor) to an ecclesiastical office

ERENAGH   hereditary custodian

GALLOWGLASS   mercenary foot soldier

MAC OR MAG   son of (Mc and M' are abbreviations of Mac)

O'   descendant of

SEPT   a clan or branch of a family (probably a corruption of sect)

TOWNLAND   division of land within a parish

FURTHER READING

1. de BREFFNY, Brian, *Bibliography of Irish Family History*, Cork and Dublin, 1974

2. GREHAN, Ida, *Irish Family Names*, London, 1973

3. MAC LYSAGHT, Edward, *The Surnames of Ireland*, 3rd edition, Dublin, 1978

4. MAC LYSAGHT, Edward, *Irish Families, Their Names, Arms and Origins*, 3rd edition, Dublin, 1972

5. MATHESON, Robert E., *Special Report on Surnames in Ireland*, Dublin, 1894

6. MATHESON, Robert E., *Varieties and Synonyms of Surnames and Christian Names in Ireland*, Dublin, 1890

7. WOLFE, Rev. P., *Sloinnte Gaedhal is Gall*, Dublin, 1923

8. WOLFE, Rev. P., *Irish Names & Surnames*, Dublin

9. *The Irish Genealogist* (annual journal), official Organ of the Irish Genealogical Research Society

10. *The Irish Ancestor* (bi-annual journal), by subscription from the editor, Pirton House, Sydenham Villas, Dublin 14

ACKNOWLEDGMENTS

Black and white illustrations are reproduced by courtesy of the following:
Page
74 Henry Clarke, Duc de Feltre *(Musees Nationaux de France)*
78 Rt. Hon. Wm. Connolly, MP *(The National Gallery of Ireland)*
84 Brigid Scanlan (née Finucane) *(Miss M. P. Ringwood)*
90 Michael Davitt *(The National Gallery of Ireland)*
115 Ambrose O'Higgins *(University of Chile)*
115 John Hogan *(The National Gallery of Ireland)*
124 General Liam Lynch *(The National Gallery of Ireland)*
132 James Clarence Mangan *(The National Gallery of Ireland)*
139 George R. Mulvany *(The National Gallery of Ireland)*
155 Daniel O'Connell *(BBC Hulton Picture Library)*
158 Johann O'Donell *(Bildarchiv National Library of Austria)*
167 Sir Neill O'Neill *(The Courtauld Institute of Art, London)*
163 Count Joseph O'Rorke *(Hermitage, Leningrad)*
163 President Ronald Reagan *(Syndication International, London)*
164 Sir Martin Archer Shee *(The National Gallery of Ireland)*
167 Archbishop Oliver Plunket *(The National Gallery of Ireland)*
168 The Brontë Sisters *(The National Portrait Gallery, London)*
173 Cornelius Scanlan *(The Irish Ancestor)*
173 Mary Scanlan *(The Irish Ancestor)*
174 George Bernard Shaw *(The National Portrait Gallery, London)*
177 Viscount Taaffe *(The National Gallery of Ireland)*
182 Luke Wadding *(Father Guardian OFM, St Isidore's, Rome)*
186 William Butler Yeats *(The National Portrait Gallery, London)*
All colour photographs have been taken by George Mott, with the exception of page 22 *(Colour Library International)*